RAI

WELCOME TO NEW JAPAN

MATT KINDT | CLAYTON CRAIN

CONTENTS

Collection Cover Art: Clayton Crain

Writer: Matt Kindt
Artist: Clayton Crain
Letterer: Dave Lanphear
Cover Artist: Clayton Crain

David Aja
Raúl Allén
Kalman Andrasofszky
David Baron
CAFU
Clayton Crain
Khari Evans
Romulo Fajardo
Sina Grace
Trevor Hairsine
Bryan Hitch
Rian Hughes
JG Jones
Matt Kindt
Paul Mounts
John Rauch
Brian Reber
Paolo Rivera
Riley Rossmo
Bart Sears
Stephen Segovia
Mico Suayan

Associate Editor: Alejandro Arbona
Editor: Warren Simons

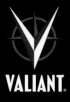

Peter Cuneo
Chairman

Dinesh Shamdasani
CEO & Chief Creative Officer

Gavin Cuneo
Chief Operating Officer & CFO

Fred Pierce
Publisher

Warren Simons
VP Editor-in-Chief

Walter Black
VP Operations

Hunter Gorinson
Director of Marketing, Communications & Digital Media

Atom! Freeman
Matthew Klein
Andy Liegl
Sales Managers

Josh Johns
Digital Sales & Special Projects Manager

Travis Escarfullery
Jeff Walker
Production & Design Managers

Alejandro Arbona
Editor

Tom Brennan
Kyle Andrukiewicz
Associate Editors

Peter Stern
Publishing & Operations Manager

Chris Daniels
Marketing Coordinator

Ivan Cohen
Collection Editor

Steve Blackwell
Collection Designer

Rian Hughes/Device
Trade Dress & Book Design

Russell Brown
President, Consumer Products, Promotions and Ad Sales

Jason Kothari
Vice Chairman

Rai®: Welcome to New Japan. Published by Valiant Entertainment LLC. Office of Publication: 424 West 33rd Street, New York, NY 10001. Printed in the U.S.A. Second Printing.
ISBN: 9781939346414.

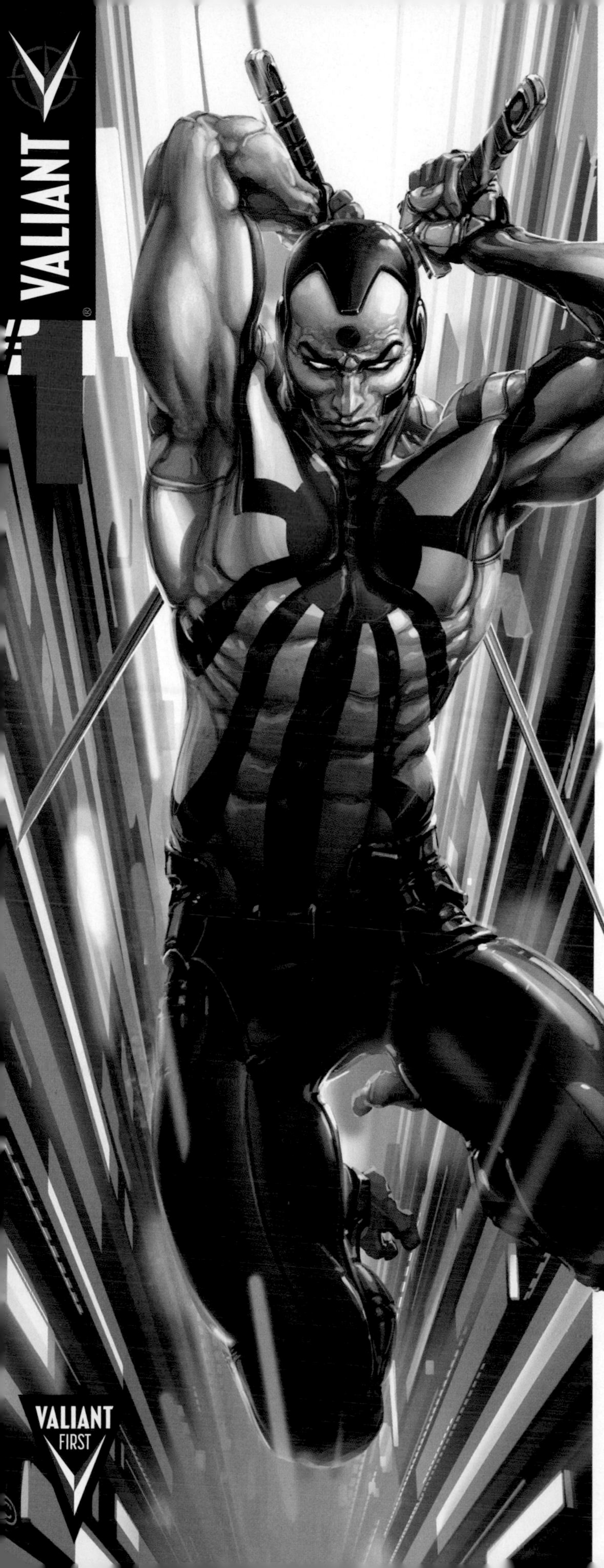
VALIANT
#1
VALIANT FIRST

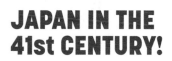

RAI

JAPAN IN THE 41st CENTURY!

MATT KINDT
CLAYTON CRAIN

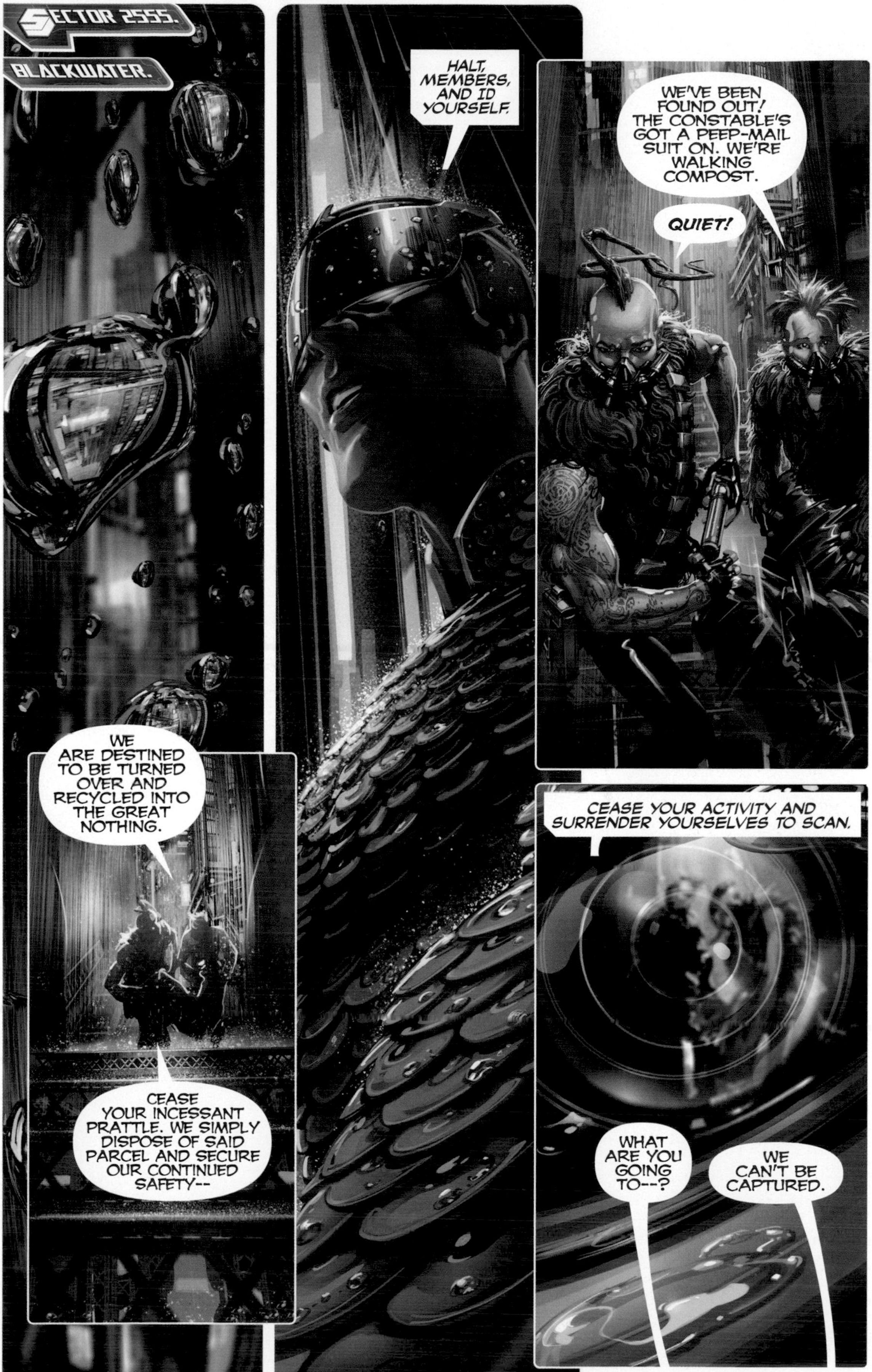
SECTOR 2555.
BLACKWATER.
HALT, MEMBERS, AND ID YOURSELF.
WE'VE BEEN FOUND OUT! THE CONSTABLE'S GOT A PEEP-MAIL SUIT ON. WE'RE WALKING COMPOST.
QUIET!
WE ARE DESTINED TO BE TURNED OVER AND RECYCLED INTO THE GREAT NOTHING.
CEASE YOUR INCESSANT PRATTLE. WE SIMPLY DISPOSE OF SAID PARCEL AND SECURE OUR CONTINUED SAFETY--
CEASE YOUR ACTIVITY AND SURRENDER YOURSELVES TO SCAN.
WHAT ARE YOU GOING TO--?
WE CAN'T BE CAPTURED.

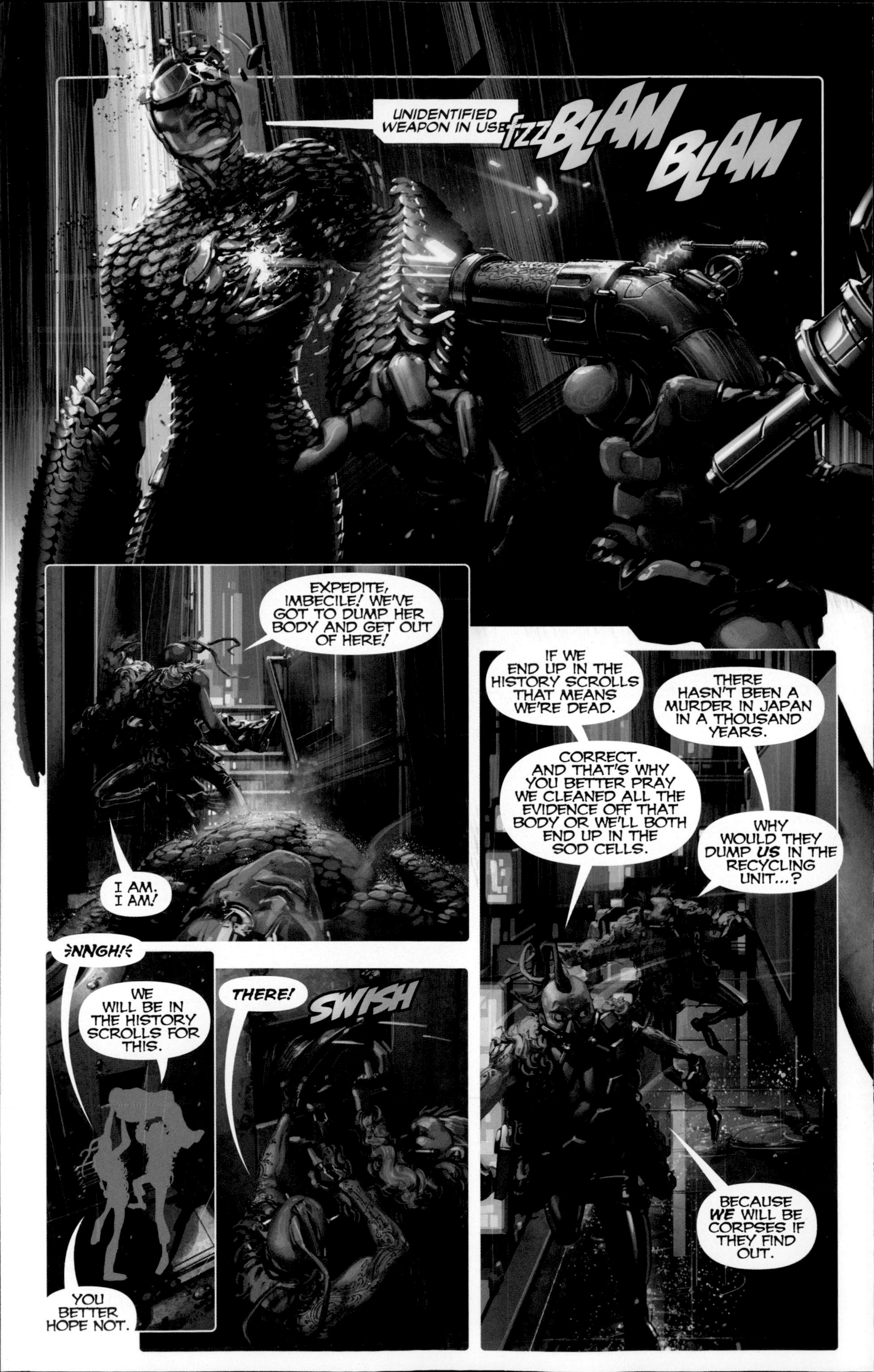
UNIDENTIFIED WEAPON IN USE
fzzBLAM BLAM
EXPEDITE, IMBECILE! WE'VE GOT TO DUMP HER BODY AND GET OUT OF HERE!
I AM. I AM!
NNGH!
WE WILL BE IN THE HISTORY SCROLLS FOR THIS.
YOU BETTER HOPE NOT.
THERE!
SWISH
IF WE END UP IN THE HISTORY SCROLLS THAT MEANS WE'RE DEAD.
CORRECT. AND THAT'S WHY YOU BETTER PRAY WE CLEANED ALL THE EVIDENCE OFF THAT BODY OR WE'LL BOTH END UP IN THE SOD CELLS.
THERE HASN'T BEEN A MURDER IN JAPAN IN A THOUSAND YEARS.
WHY WOULD THEY DUMP US IN THE RECYCLING UNIT...?
BECAUSE WE WILL BE CORPSES IF THEY FIND OUT.

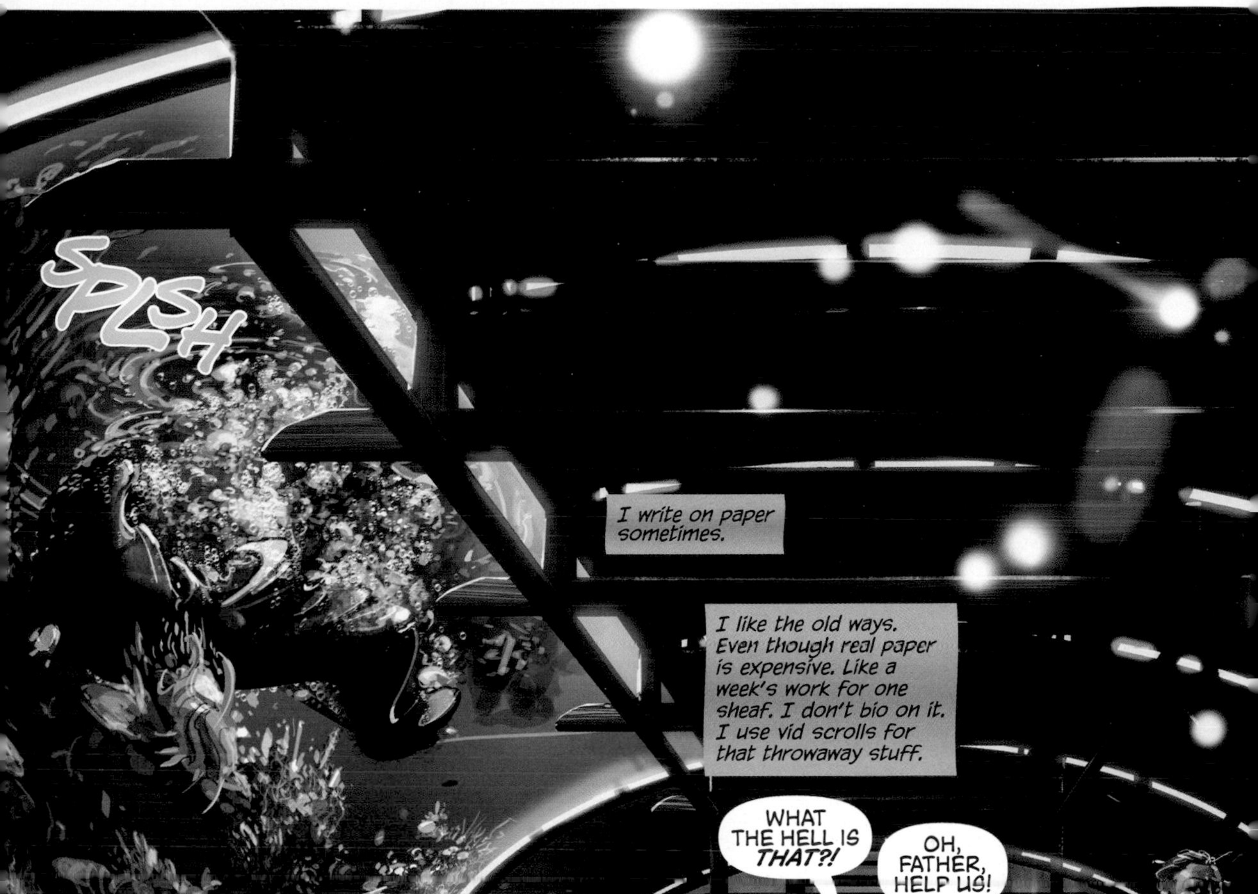
SPLSH
I write on paper sometimes.
I like the old ways. Even though real paper is expensive. Like a week's work for one sheaf. I don't bio on it. I use vid scrolls for that throwaway stuff.
WHAT THE HELL IS *THAT?!*
OH, FATHER, HELP US!

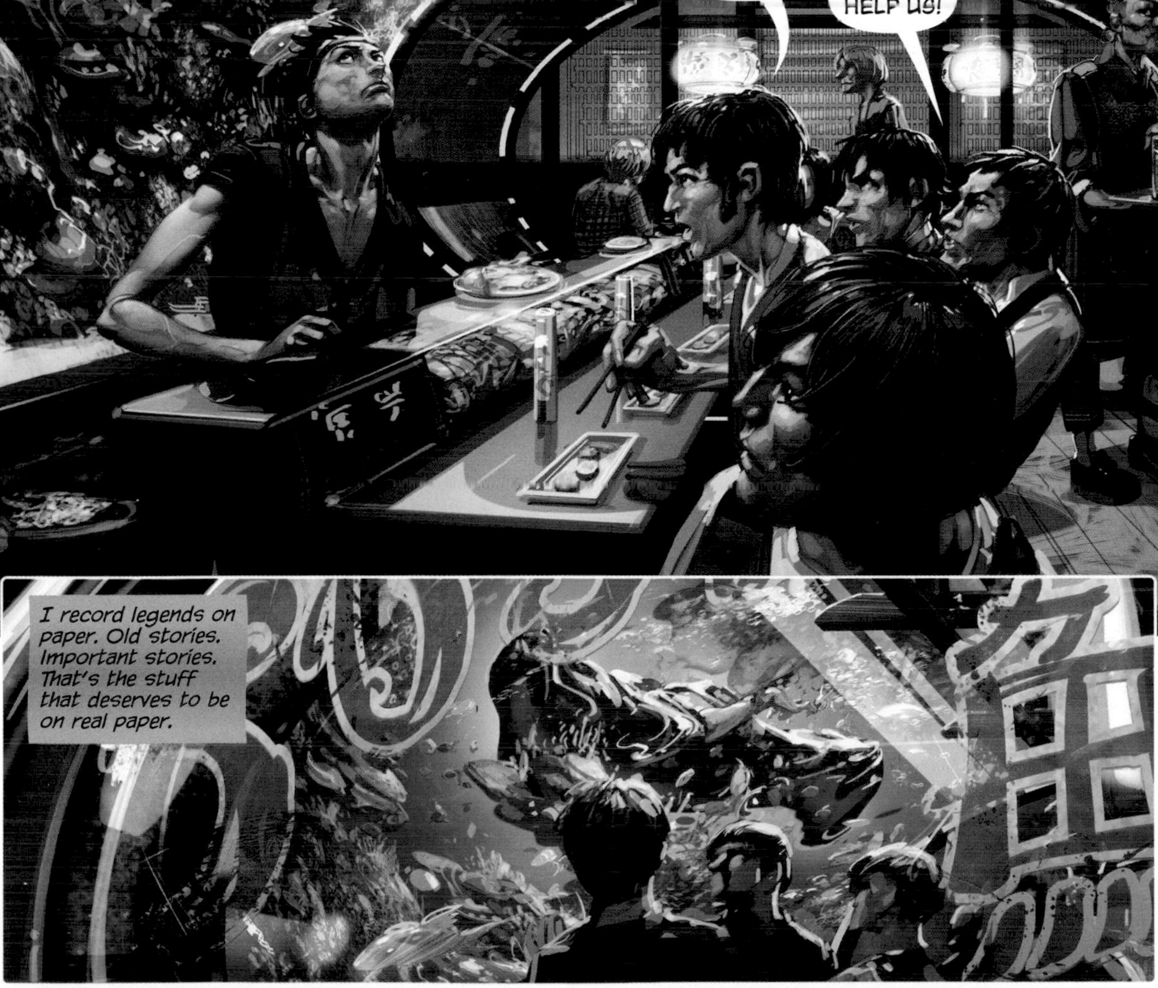
I record legends on paper. Old stories. Important stories. That's the stuff that deserves to be on real paper.

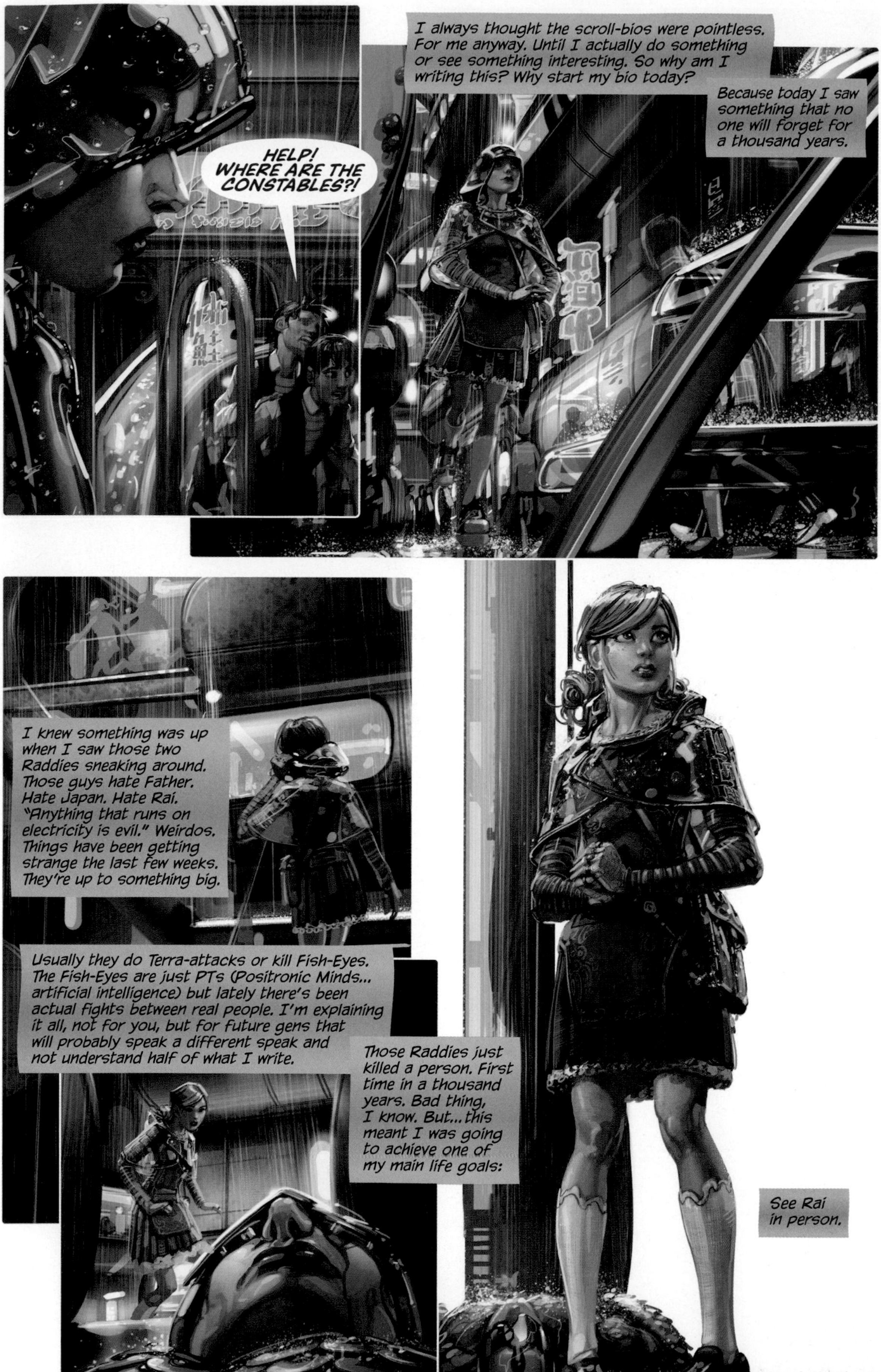
HELP! WHERE ARE THE CONSTABLES?!
I always thought the scroll-bios were pointless. For me anyway. Until I actually do something or see something interesting. So why am I writing this? Why start my bio today?
Because today I saw something that no one will forget for a thousand years.
I knew something was up when I saw those two Raddies sneaking around. Those guys hate Father. Hate Japan. Hate Rai. "Anything that runs on electricity is evil." Weirdos. Things have been getting strange the last few weeks. They're up to something big.
Usually they do Terra-attacks or kill Fish-Eyes. The Fish-Eyes are just PTs (Positronic Minds... artificial intelligence) but lately there's been actual fights between real people. I'm explaining it all, not for you, but for future gens that will probably speak a different speak and not understand half of what I write.
Those Raddies just killed a person. First time in a thousand years. Bad thing, I know. But... this meant I was going to achieve one of my main life goals:
See Rai in person.

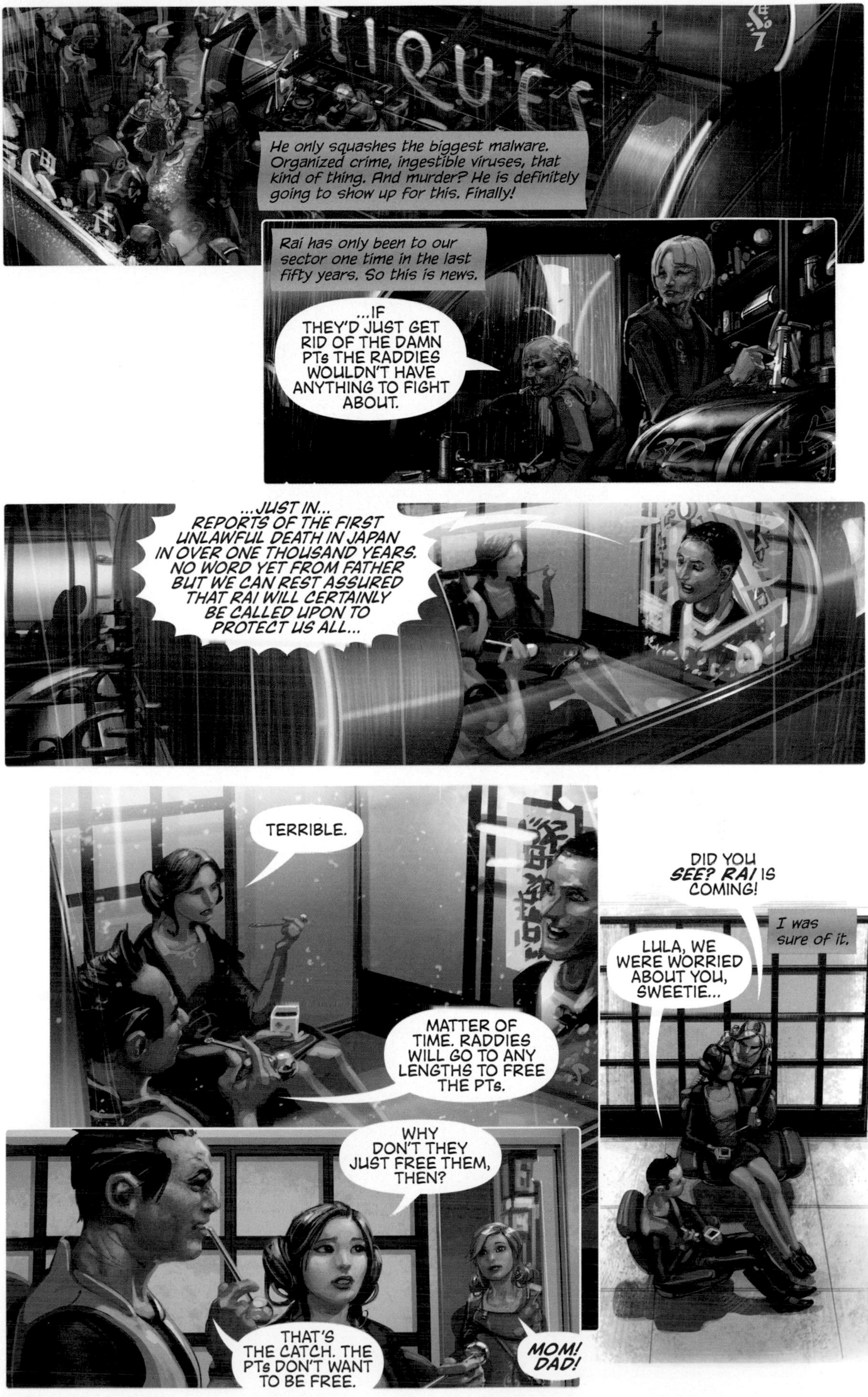
He only squashes the biggest malware. Organized crime, ingestible viruses, that kind of thing. And murder? He is definitely going to show up for this. Finally!
Rai has only been to our sector one time in the last fifty years. So this is news.
...IF THEY'D JUST GET RID OF THE DAMN PTs THE RADDIES WOULDN'T HAVE ANYTHING TO FIGHT ABOUT.
...JUST IN... REPORTS OF THE FIRST UNLAWFUL DEATH IN JAPAN IN OVER ONE THOUSAND YEARS. NO WORD YET FROM FATHER BUT WE CAN REST ASSURED THAT RAI WILL CERTAINLY BE CALLED UPON TO PROTECT US ALL...
TERRIBLE.
MATTER OF TIME. RADDIES WILL GO TO ANY LENGTHS TO FREE THE PTs.
WHY DON'T THEY JUST FREE THEM, THEN?
THAT'S THE CATCH. THE PTs DON'T WANT TO BE FREE.
MOM! DAD!
LULA, WE WERE WORRIED ABOUT YOU, SWEETIE...
DID YOU SEE? RAI IS COMING!
I was sure of it.

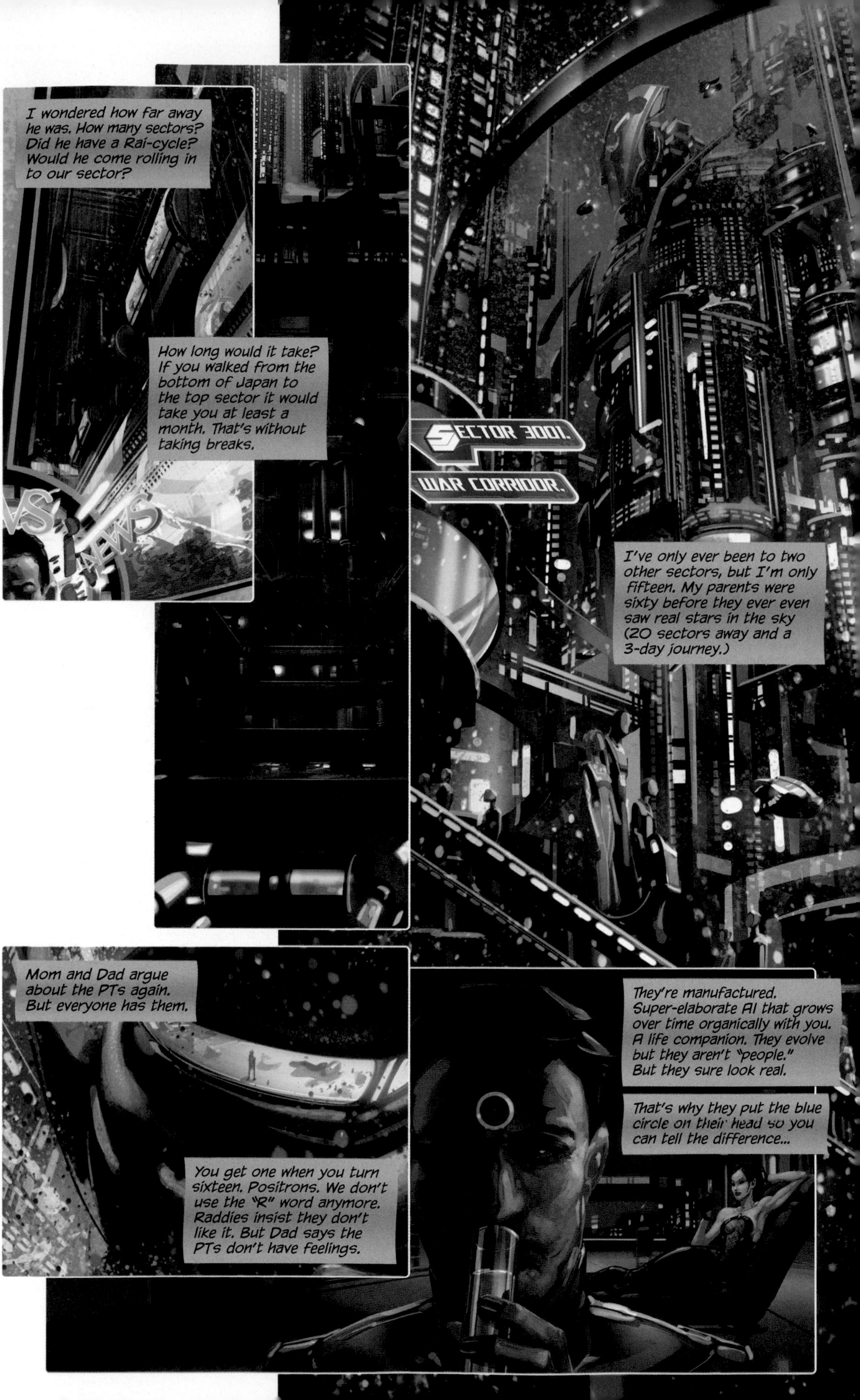

I wondered how far away he was. How many sectors? Did he have a Rai-cycle? Would he come rolling in to our sector?
How long would it take? If you walked from the bottom of Japan to the top sector it would take you at least a month. That's without taking breaks.
SECTOR 3001.
WAR CORRIDOR.
I've only ever been to two other sectors, but I'm only fifteen. My parents were sixty before they ever even saw real stars in the sky (20 sectors away and a 3-day journey.)
Mom and Dad argue about the PTs again. But everyone has them.
You get one when you turn sixteen. Positrons. We don't use the "R" word anymore. Raddies insist they don't like it. But Dad says the PTs don't have feelings.
They're manufactured. Super-elaborate AI that grows over time organically with you. A life companion. They evolve but they aren't "people." But they sure look real.
That's why they put the blue circle on their head so you can tell the difference...

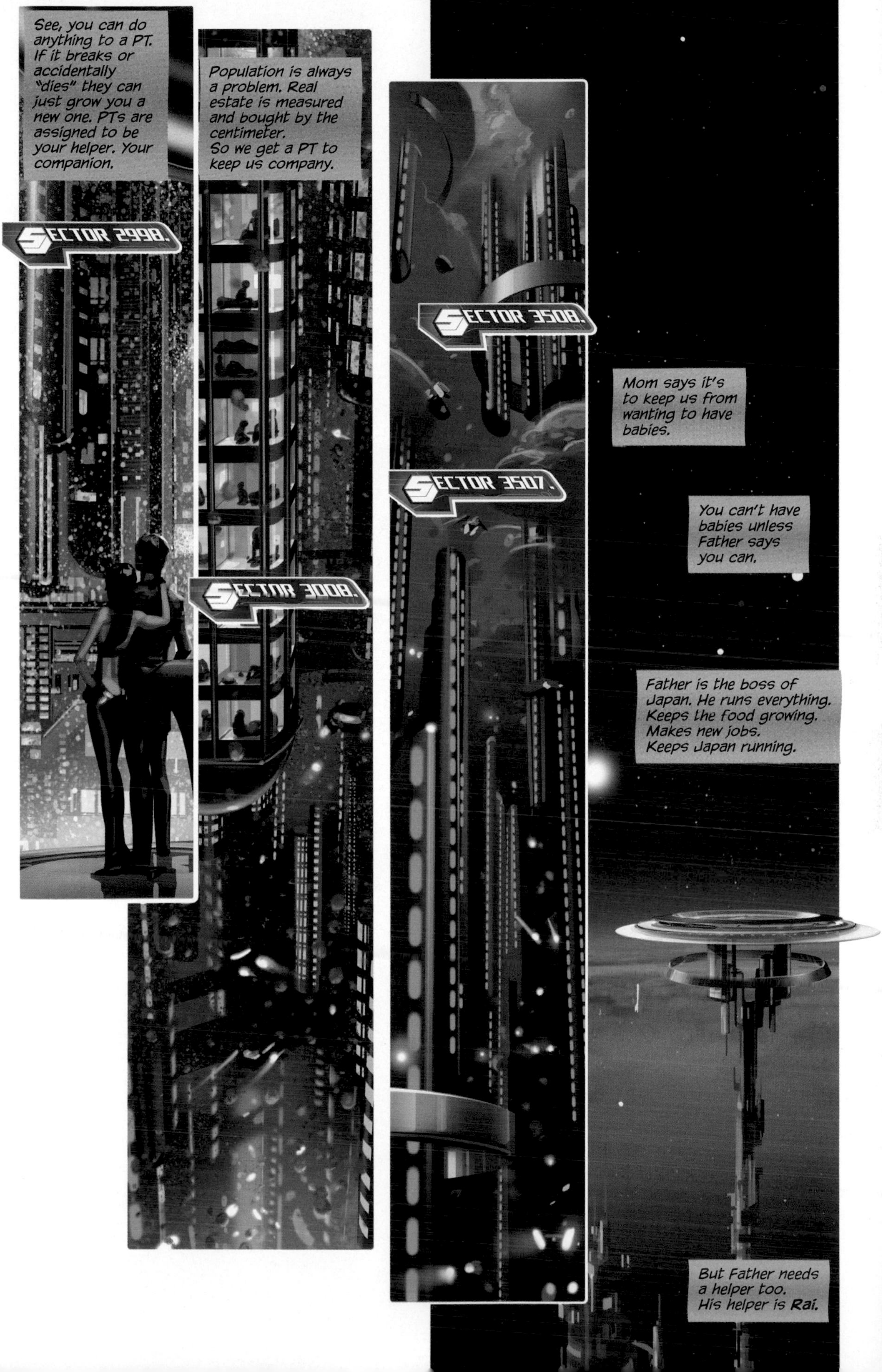
See, you can do anything to a PT. If it breaks or accidentally "dies" they can just grow you a new one. PTs are assigned to be your helper. Your companion.
SECTOR 2998.
Population is always a problem. Real estate is measured and bought by the centimeter.
So we get a PT to keep us company.
SECTOR 3008.
SECTOR 3508.
SECTOR 3507.
Mom says it's to keep us from wanting to have babies.
You can't have babies unless Father says you can.
Father is the boss of Japan. He runs everything. Keeps the food growing. Makes new jobs. Keeps Japan running.
But Father needs a helper too. His helper is Rai.

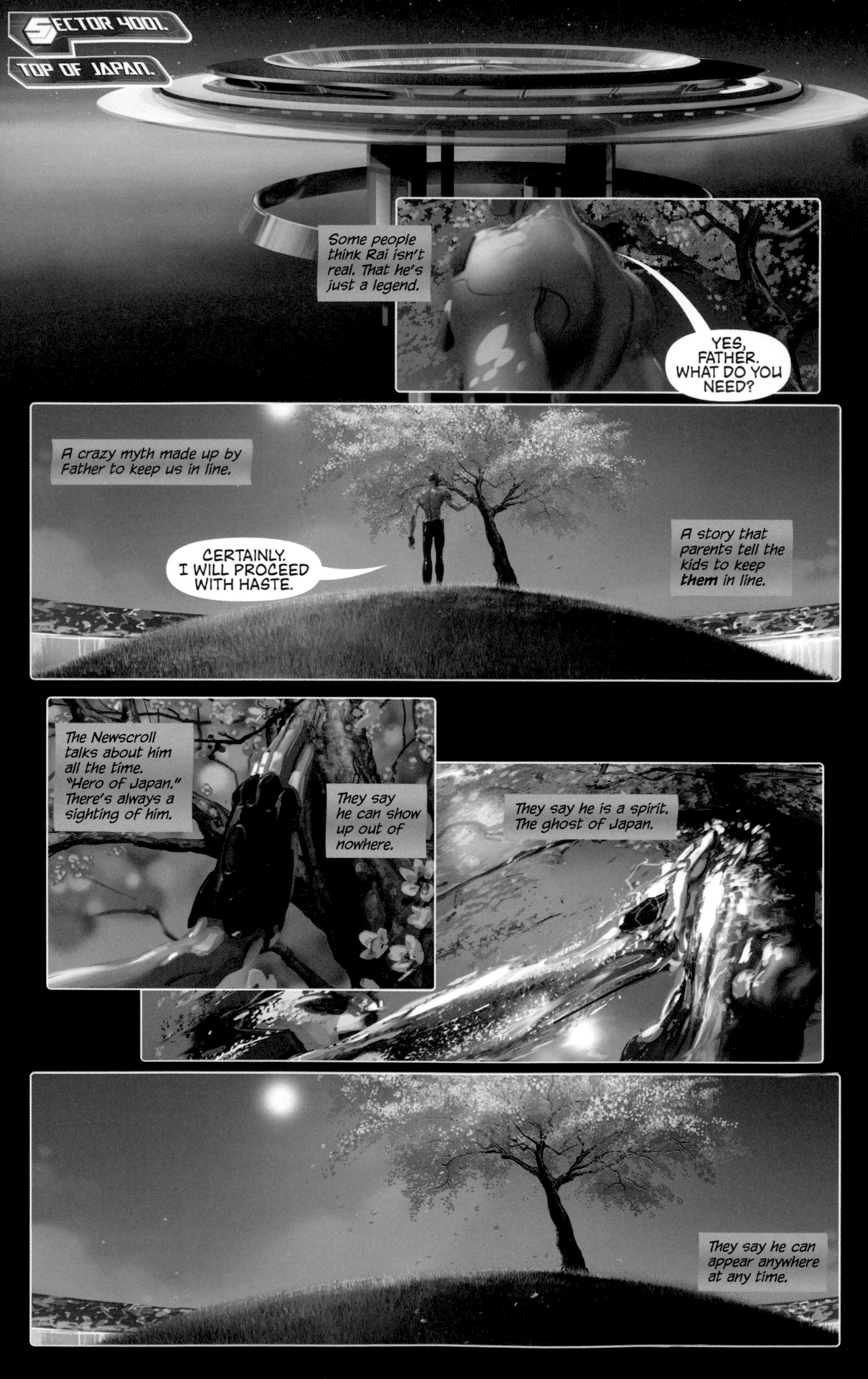
SECTOR 4001.
TOP OF JAPAN.
Some people think Rai isn't real. That he's just a legend.
YES, FATHER. WHAT DO YOU NEED?
A crazy myth made up by Father to keep us in line.
CERTAINLY. I WILL PROCEED WITH HASTE.
A story that parents tell the kids to keep **them** in line.
The Newscroll talks about him all the time. "Hero of Japan." There's always a sighting of him.
They say he can show up out of nowhere.
They say he is a spirit. The ghost of Japan.
They say he can appear anywhere at any time.

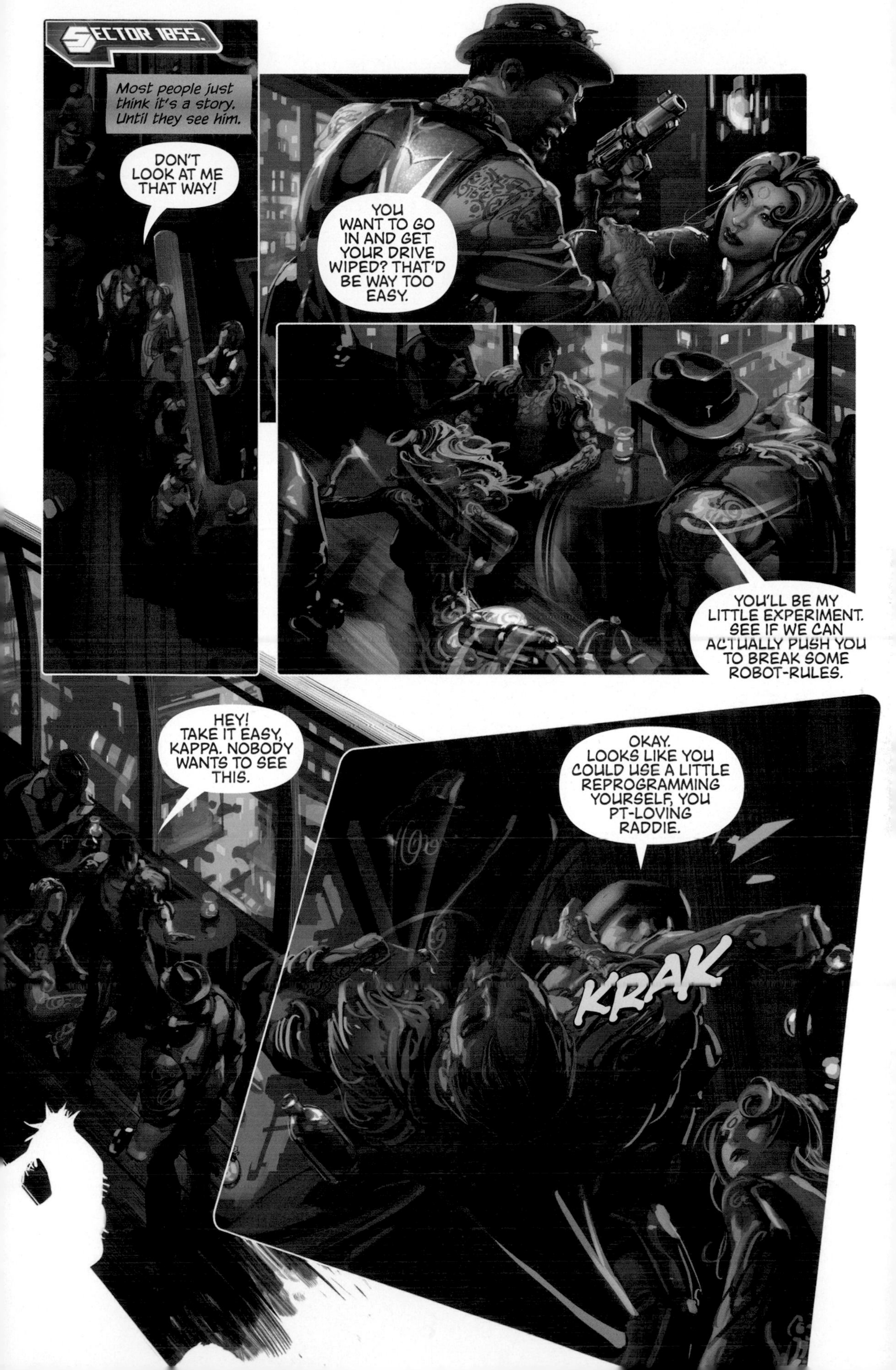
SECTOR 1855.
Most people just think it's a story. Until they see him.
DON'T LOOK AT ME THAT WAY!
YOU WANT TO GO IN AND GET YOUR DRIVE WIPED? THAT'D BE WAY TOO EASY.
YOU'LL BE MY LITTLE EXPERIMENT. SEE IF WE CAN ACTUALLY PUSH YOU TO BREAK SOME ROBOT-RULES.
HEY! TAKE IT EASY, KAPPA. NOBODY WANTS TO SEE THIS.
OKAY. LOOKS LIKE YOU COULD USE A LITTLE REPROGRAMMING YOURSELF, YOU PT-LOVING RADDIE.
KRAK

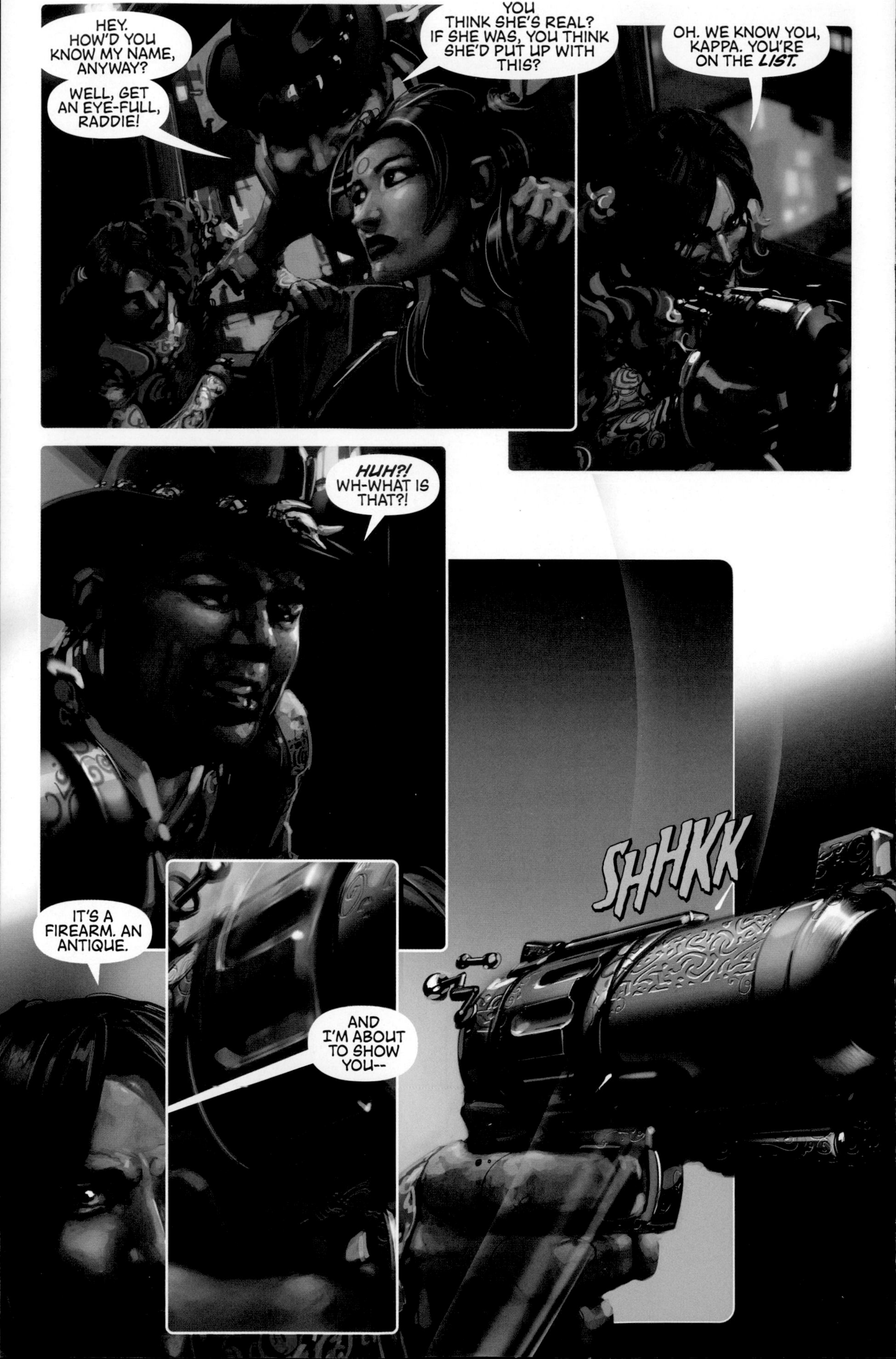
HEY. HOW'D YOU KNOW MY NAME, ANYWAY?
YOU THINK SHE'S REAL? IF SHE WAS, YOU THINK SHE'D PUT UP WITH THIS?
WELL, GET AN EYE-FULL, RADDIE!
OH. WE KNOW YOU, KAPPA. YOU'RE ON THE *LIST.*
HUH?! WH-WHAT IS THAT?!
SHHKK
IT'S A FIREARM. AN ANTIQUE.
AND I'M ABOUT TO SHOW YOU--

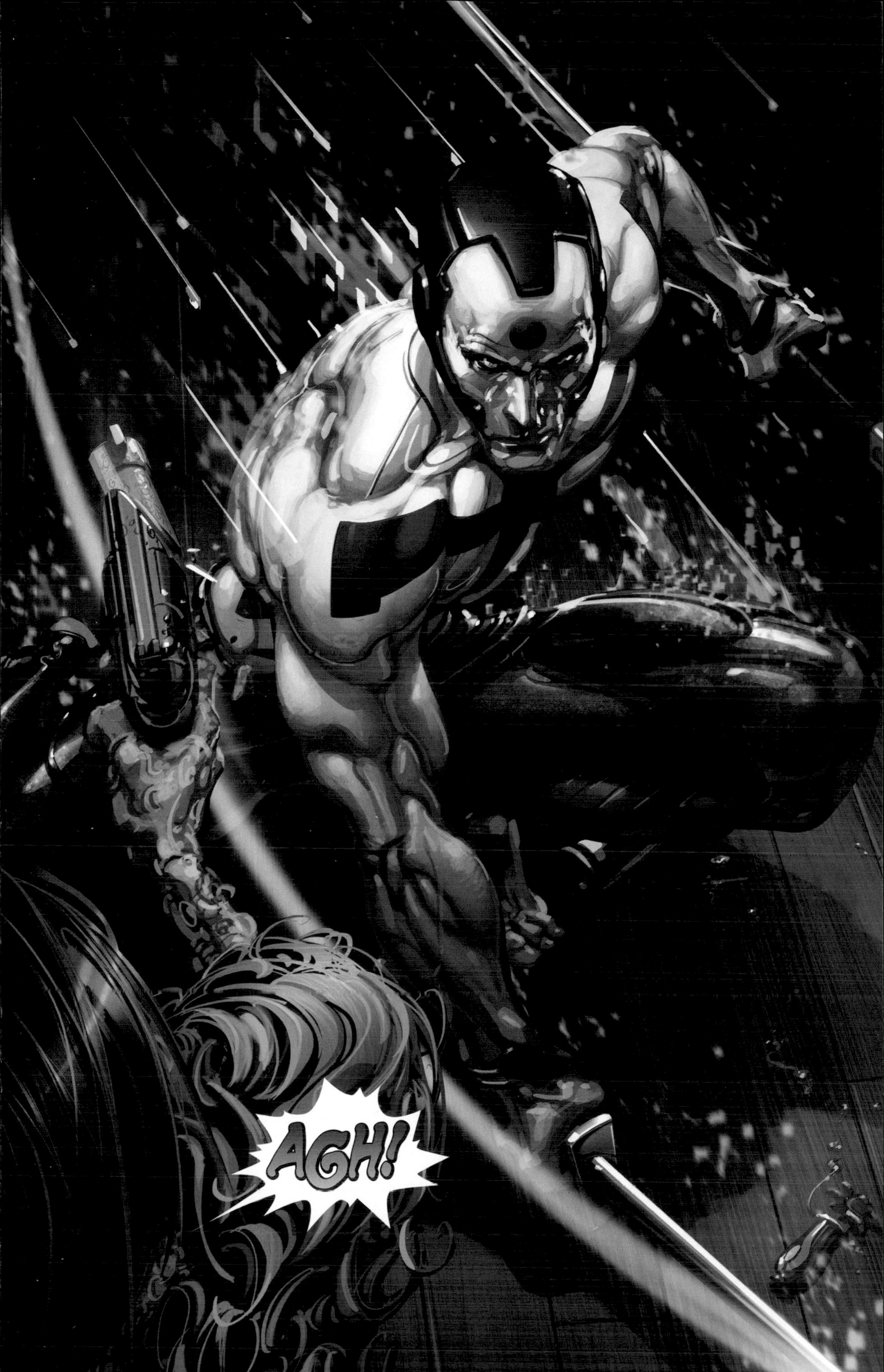
AGH!

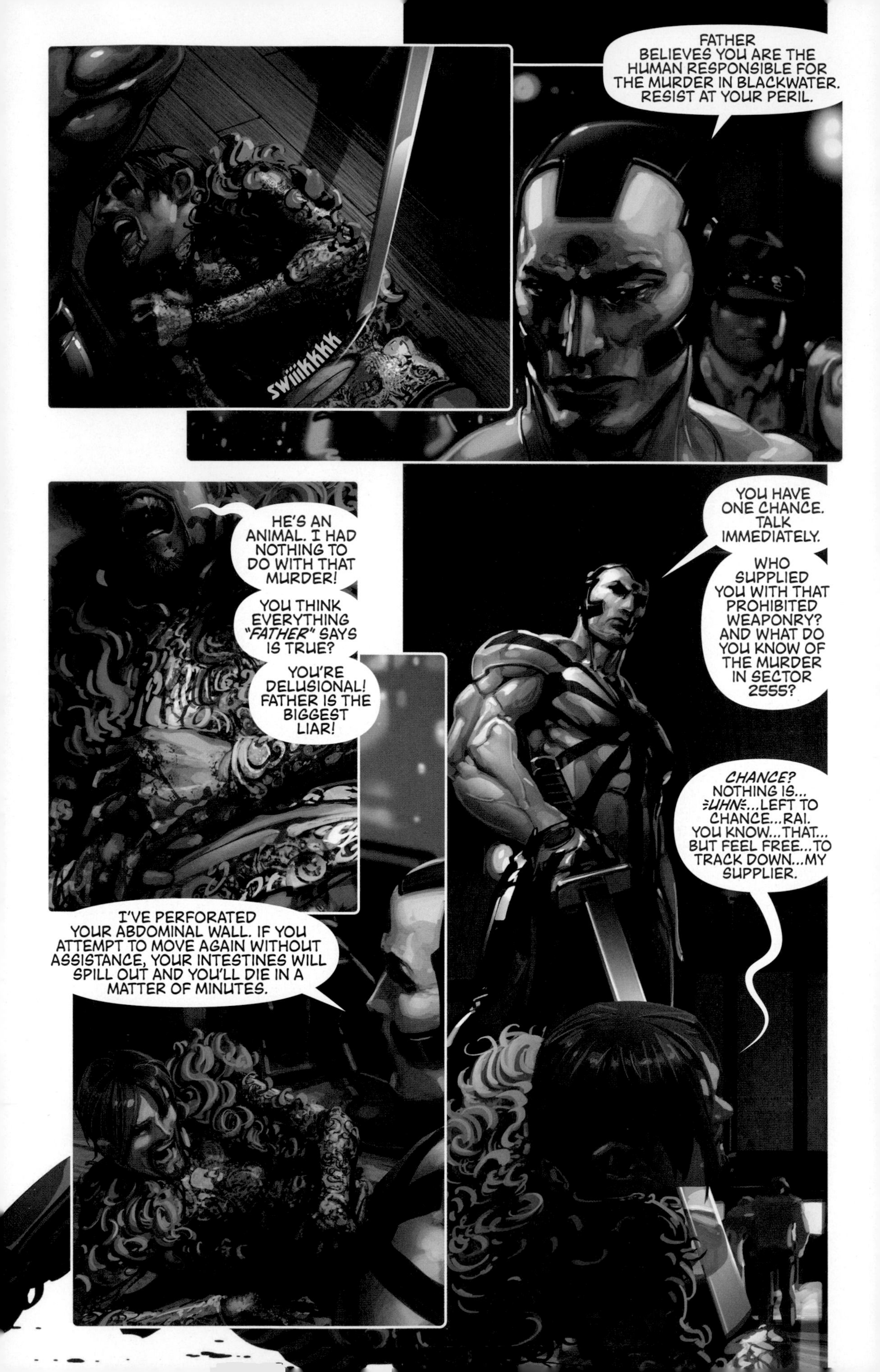
SWIIKKKK
FATHER BELIEVES YOU ARE THE HUMAN RESPONSIBLE FOR THE MURDER IN BLACKWATER. RESIST AT YOUR PERIL.
HE'S AN ANIMAL. I HAD NOTHING TO DO WITH THAT MURDER!
YOU THINK EVERYTHING "FATHER" SAYS IS TRUE?
YOU'RE DELUSIONAL! FATHER IS THE BIGGEST LIAR!
I'VE PERFORATED YOUR ABDOMINAL WALL. IF YOU ATTEMPT TO MOVE AGAIN WITHOUT ASSISTANCE, YOUR INTESTINES WILL SPILL OUT AND YOU'LL DIE IN A MATTER OF MINUTES.
YOU HAVE ONE CHANCE. TALK IMMEDIATELY.
WHO SUPPLIED YOU WITH THAT PROHIBITED WEAPONRY? AND WHAT DO YOU KNOW OF THE MURDER IN SECTOR 2555?
CHANCE? NOTHING IS... =UHN=...LEFT TO CHANCE...RAI. YOU KNOW...THAT... BUT FEEL FREE...TO TRACK DOWN...MY SUPPLIER.

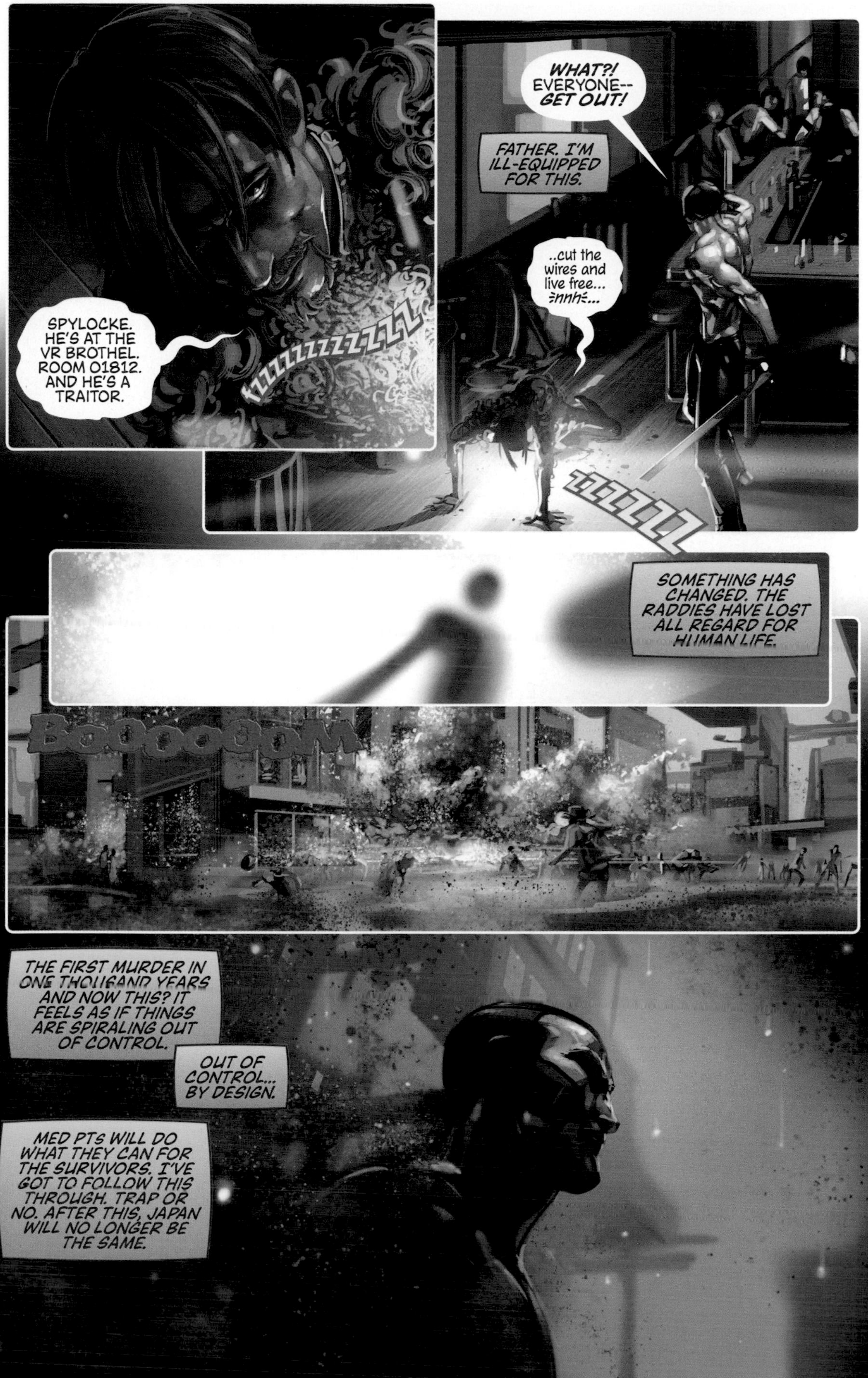
SPYLOCKE. HE'S AT THE VR BROTHEL. ROOM 01812. AND HE'S A TRAITOR.
FZZZZZZZZZZZZZZ
WHAT?! EVERYONE-- GET OUT!
FATHER. I'M ILL-EQUIPPED FOR THIS.
..cut the wires and live free... nnh...
ZZZZZZ
SOMETHING HAS CHANGED. THE RADDIES HAVE LOST ALL REGARD FOR HUMAN LIFE.
BOOOOOOM
THE FIRST MURDER IN ONE THOUSAND YEARS AND NOW THIS? IT FEELS AS IF THINGS ARE SPIRALING OUT OF CONTROL.
OUT OF CONTROL... BY DESIGN.
MED PTS WILL DO WHAT THEY CAN FOR THE SURVIVORS. I'VE GOT TO FOLLOW THIS THROUGH. TRAP OR NO. AFTER THIS, JAPAN WILL NO LONGER BE THE SAME.

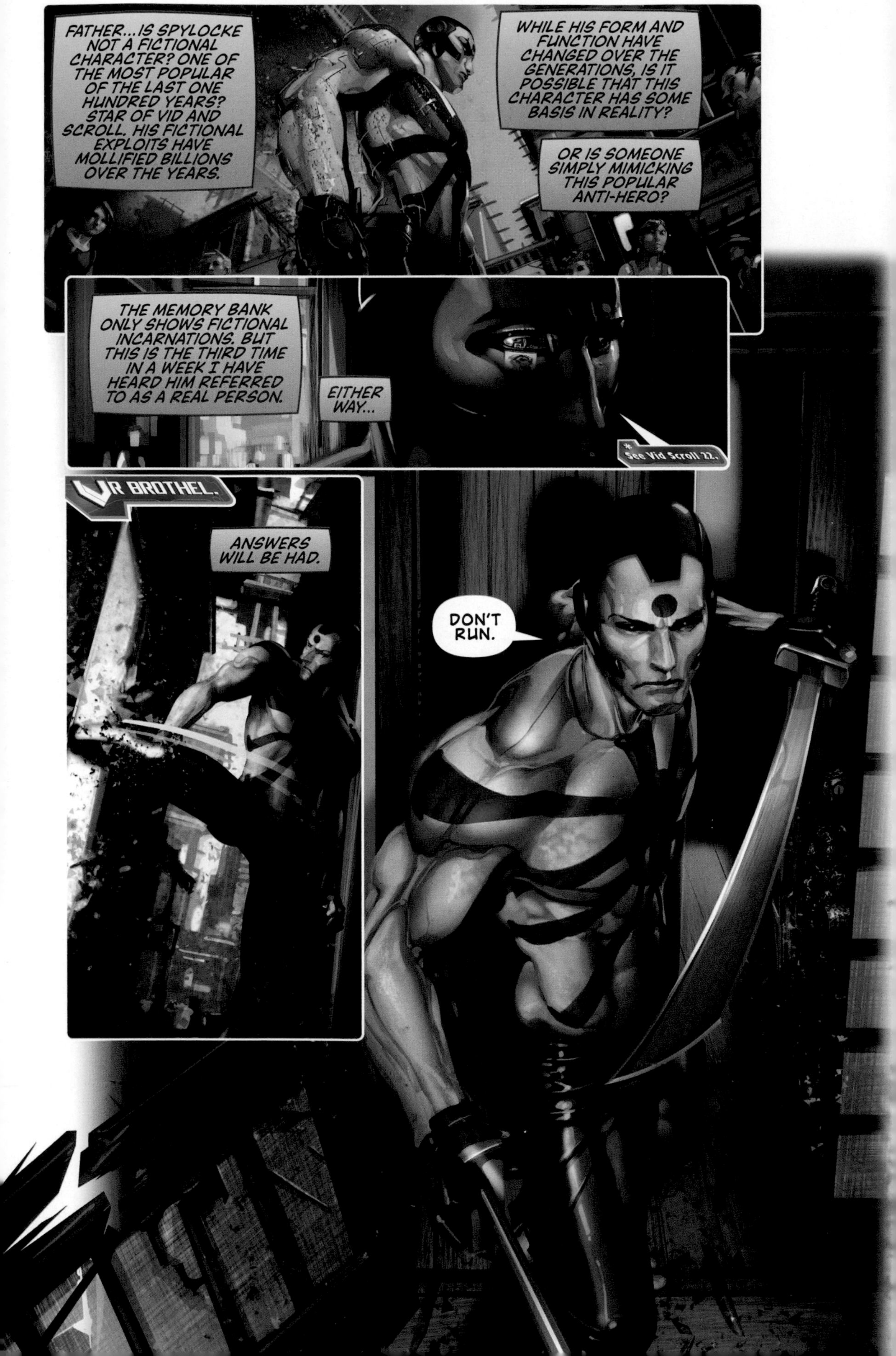
FATHER...IS SPYLOCKE NOT A FICTIONAL CHARACTER? ONE OF THE MOST POPULAR OF THE LAST ONE HUNDRED YEARS? STAR OF VID AND SCROLL. HIS FICTIONAL EXPLOITS HAVE MOLLIFIED BILLIONS OVER THE YEARS.
WHILE HIS FORM AND FUNCTION HAVE CHANGED OVER THE GENERATIONS, IS IT POSSIBLE THAT THIS CHARACTER HAS SOME BASIS IN REALITY?
OR IS SOMEONE SIMPLY MIMICKING THIS POPULAR ANTI-HERO?
THE MEMORY BANK ONLY SHOWS FICTIONAL INCARNATIONS. BUT THIS IS THE THIRD TIME IN A WEEK I HAVE HEARD HIM REFERRED TO AS A REAL PERSON.
EITHER WAY...
* See Vid Scroll 22.
VR BROTHEL.
ANSWERS WILL BE HAD.
DON'T RUN.

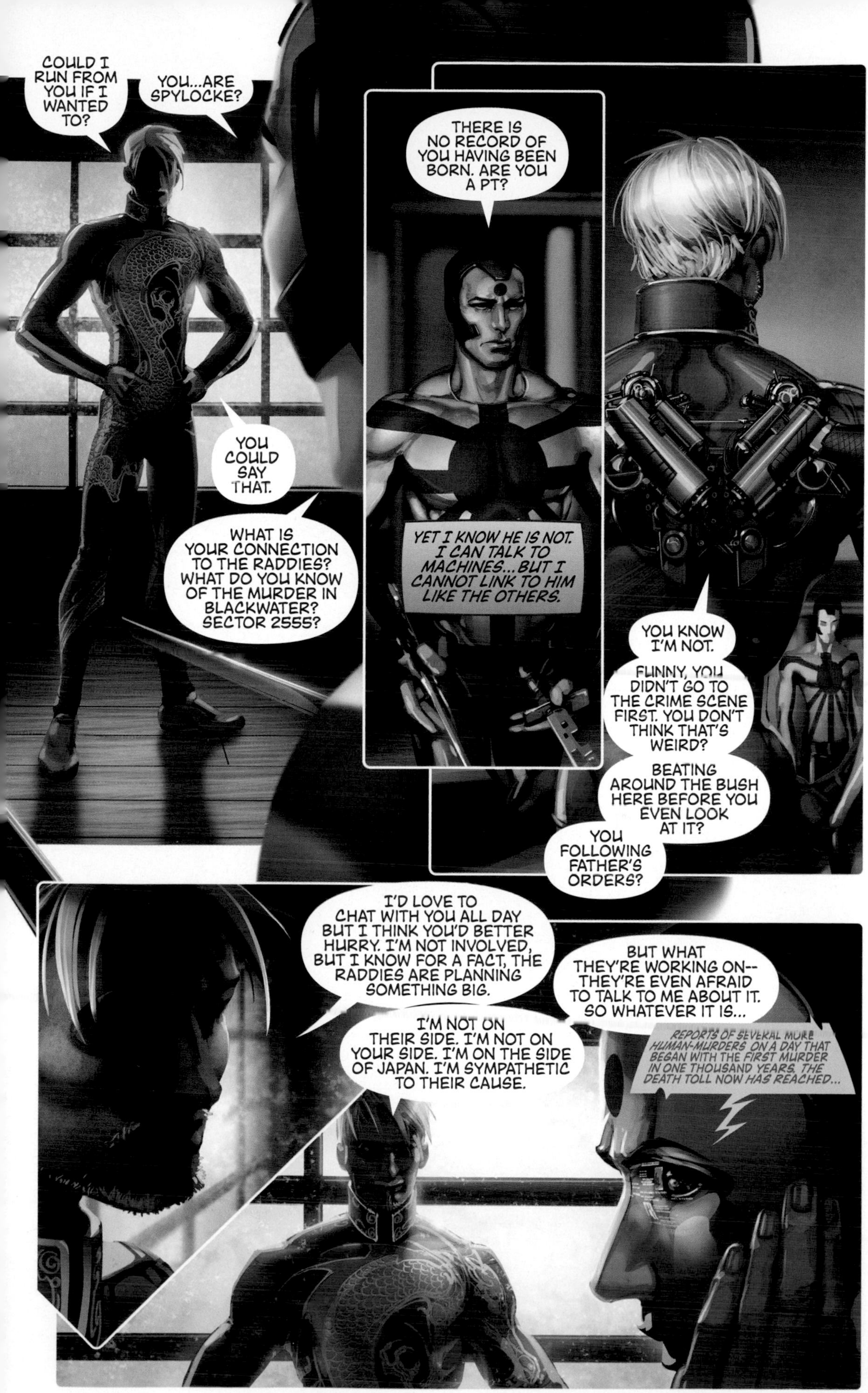
COULD I RUN FROM YOU IF I WANTED TO?
YOU...ARE SPYLOCKE?
YOU COULD SAY THAT.
WHAT IS YOUR CONNECTION TO THE RADDIES? WHAT DO YOU KNOW OF THE MURDER IN BLACKWATER? SECTOR 2555?
THERE IS NO RECORD OF YOU HAVING BEEN BORN. ARE YOU A PT?
YET I KNOW HE IS NOT. I CAN TALK TO MACHINES...BUT I CANNOT LINK TO HIM LIKE THE OTHERS.
YOU KNOW I'M NOT.
FUNNY, YOU DIDN'T GO TO THE CRIME SCENE FIRST. YOU DON'T THINK THAT'S WEIRD?
BEATING AROUND THE BUSH HERE BEFORE YOU EVEN LOOK AT IT?
YOU FOLLOWING FATHER'S ORDERS?
I'D LOVE TO CHAT WITH YOU ALL DAY BUT I THINK YOU'D BETTER HURRY. I'M NOT INVOLVED, BUT I KNOW FOR A FACT, THE RADDIES ARE PLANNING SOMETHING BIG.
I'M NOT ON THEIR SIDE. I'M NOT ON YOUR SIDE. I'M ON THE SIDE OF JAPAN. I'M SYMPATHETIC TO THEIR CAUSE.
BUT WHAT THEY'RE WORKING ON-- THEY'RE EVEN AFRAID TO TALK TO ME ABOUT IT. SO WHATEVER IT IS...
REPORTS OF SEVERAL MORE HUMAN-MURDERS ON A DAY THAT BEGAN WITH THE FIRST MURDER IN ONE THOUSAND YEARS. THE DEATH TOLL NOW HAS REACHED...

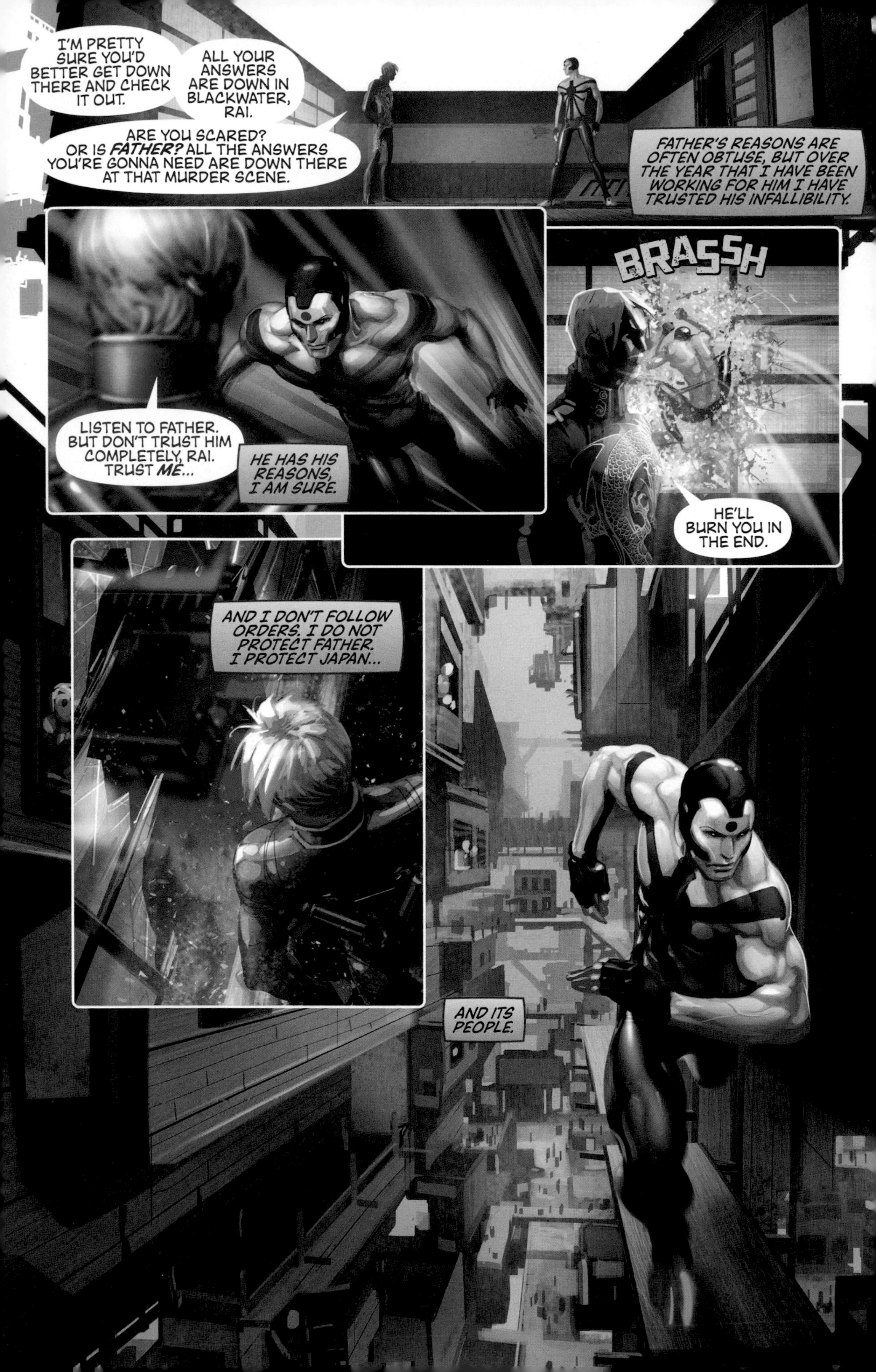
I'M PRETTY SURE YOU'D BETTER GET DOWN THERE AND CHECK IT OUT.
ALL YOUR ANSWERS ARE DOWN IN BLACKWATER, RAI.
ARE YOU SCARED? OR IS FATHER? ALL THE ANSWERS YOU'RE GONNA NEED ARE DOWN THERE AT THAT MURDER SCENE.
FATHER'S REASONS ARE OFTEN OBTUSE, BUT OVER THE YEAR THAT I HAVE BEEN WORKING FOR HIM I HAVE TRUSTED HIS INFALLIBILITY.
LISTEN TO FATHER. BUT DON'T TRUST HIM COMPLETELY, RAI. TRUST ME...
HE HAS HIS REASONS, I AM SURE.
BRASSH
HE'LL BURN YOU IN THE END.
AND I DON'T FOLLOW ORDERS. I DO NOT PROTECT FATHER. I PROTECT JAPAN...
AND ITS PEOPLE.

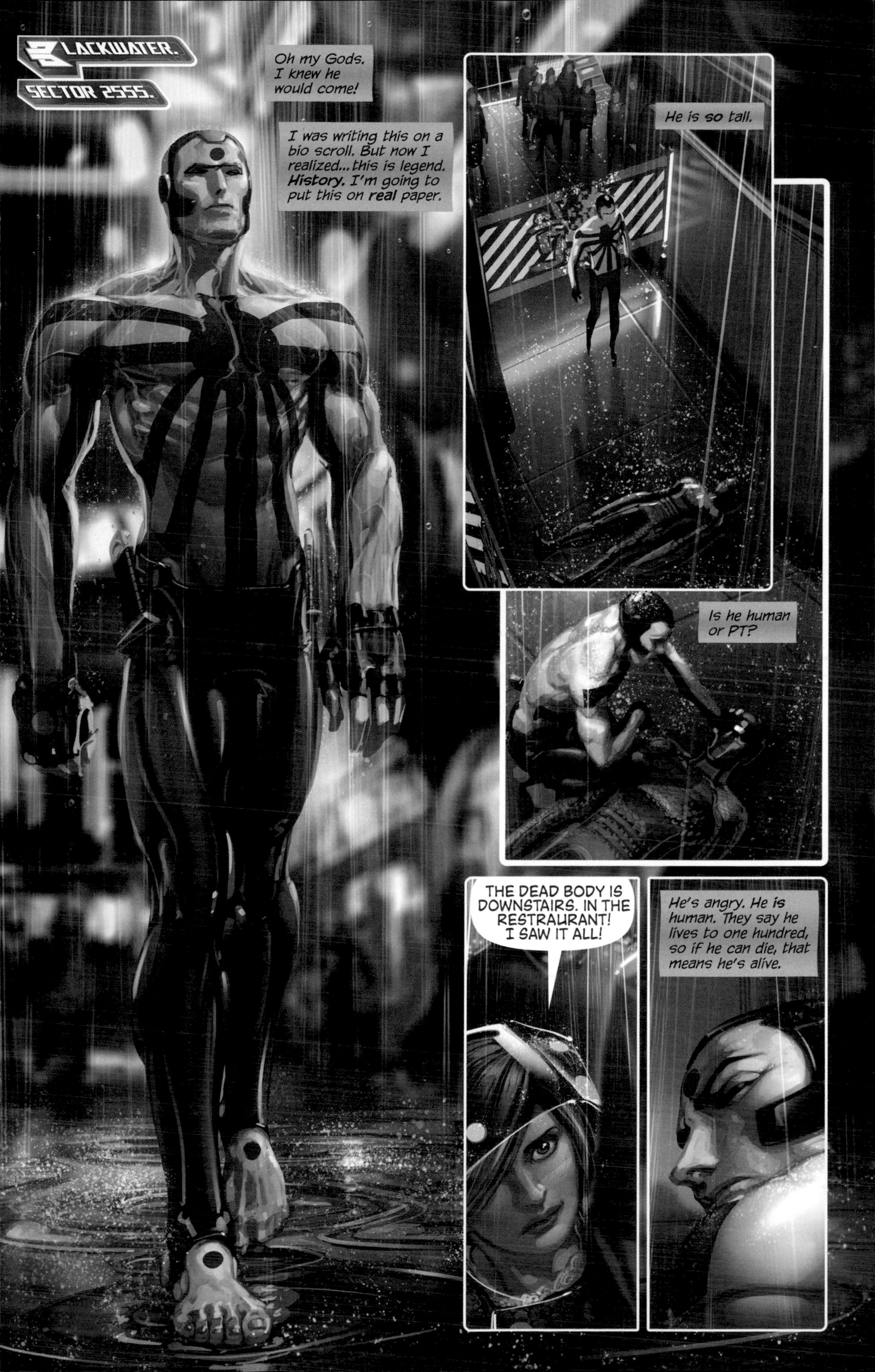
BLACKWATER.
SECTOR 2555.
Oh my Gods. I knew he would come!
I was writing this on a bio scroll. But now I realized...this is legend. History. I'm going to put this on real paper.
He is so tall.
Is he human or PT?
THE DEAD BODY IS DOWNSTAIRS. IN THE RESTRAURANT! I SAW IT ALL!
He's angry. He is human. They say he lives to one hundred, so if he can die, that means he's alive.

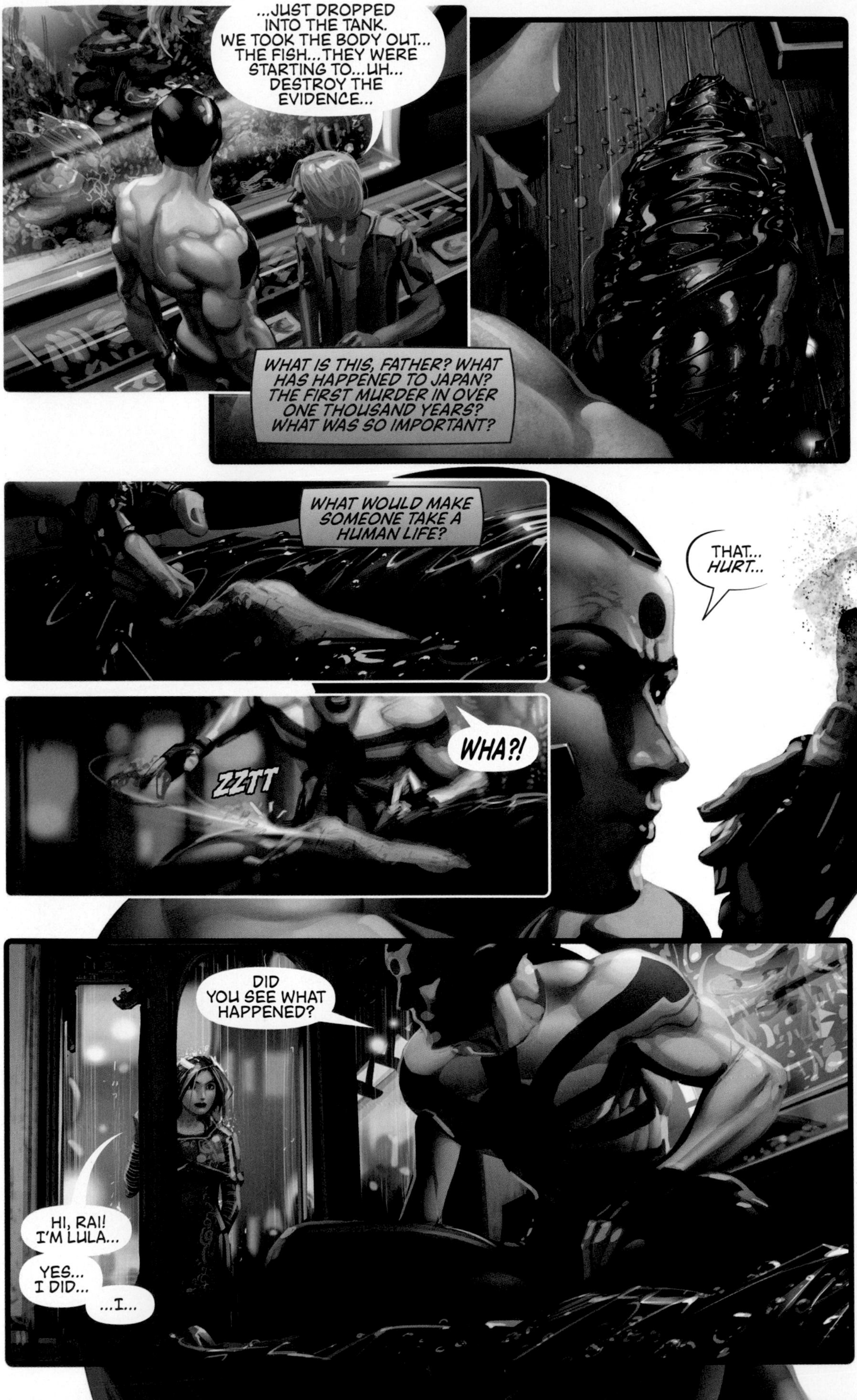
...JUST DROPPED INTO THE TANK. WE TOOK THE BODY OUT... THE FISH...THEY WERE STARTING TO...UH... DESTROY THE EVIDENCE...
WHAT IS THIS, FATHER? WHAT HAS HAPPENED TO JAPAN? THE FIRST MURDER IN OVER ONE THOUSAND YEARS? WHAT WAS SO IMPORTANT?
WHAT WOULD MAKE SOMEONE TAKE A HUMAN LIFE?
ZZTT
WHA?!
THAT... HURT...
DID YOU SEE WHAT HAPPENED?
HI, RAI! I'M LULA...
YES... I DID...
...I...

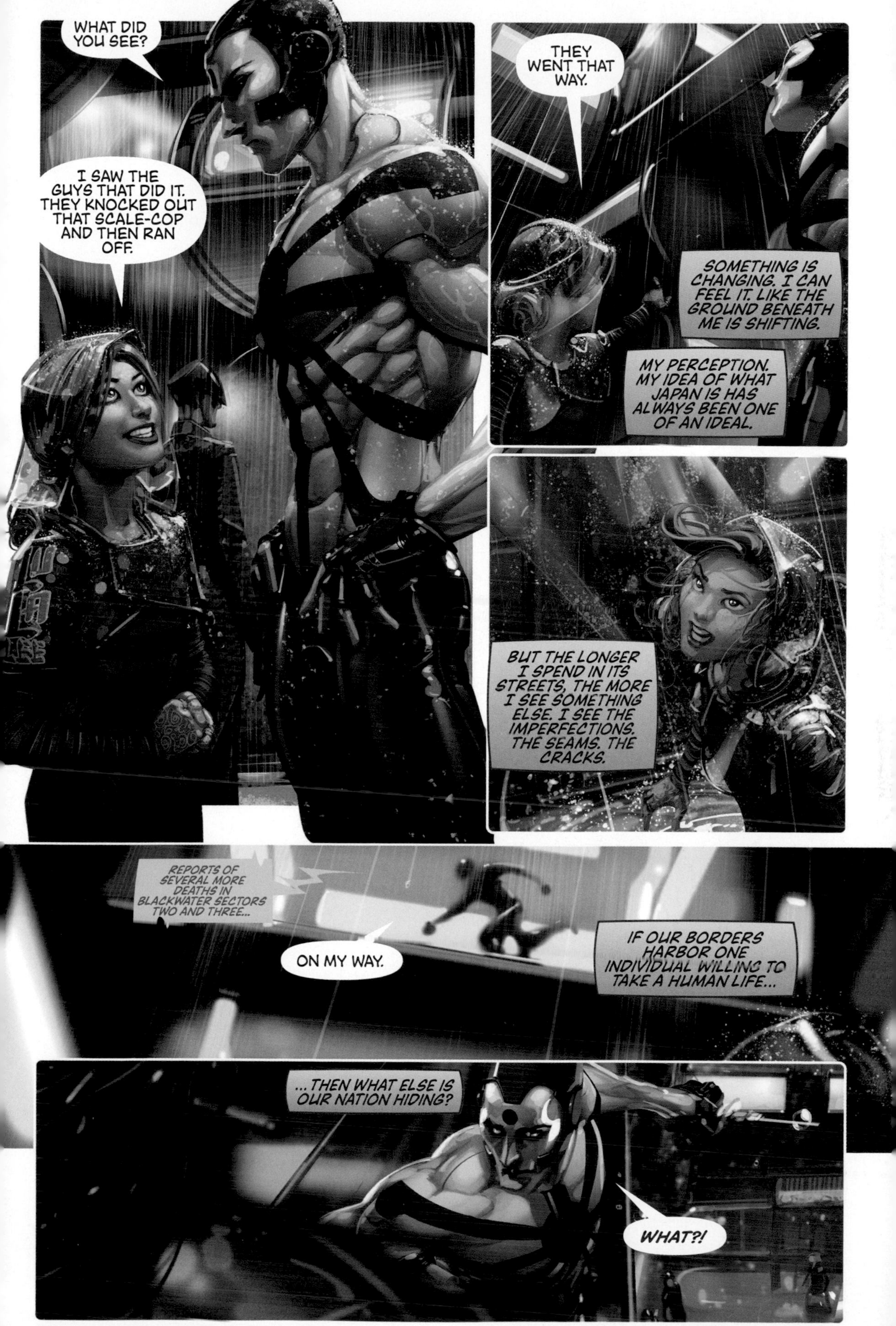
WHAT DID YOU SEE?
I SAW THE GUYS THAT DID IT. THEY KNOCKED OUT THAT SCALE-COP AND THEN RAN OFF.
THEY WENT THAT WAY.
SOMETHING IS CHANGING. I CAN FEEL IT. LIKE THE GROUND BENEATH ME IS SHIFTING.
MY PERCEPTION. MY IDEA OF WHAT JAPAN IS HAS ALWAYS BEEN ONE OF AN IDEAL.
BUT THE LONGER I SPEND IN ITS STREETS, THE MORE I SEE SOMETHING ELSE. I SEE THE IMPERFECTIONS. THE SEAMS. THE CRACKS.
REPORTS OF SEVERAL MORE DEATHS IN BLACKWATER SECTORS TWO AND THREE...
ON MY WAY.
IF OUR BORDERS HARBOR ONE INDIVIDUAL WILLING TO TAKE A HUMAN LIFE...
...THEN WHAT ELSE IS OUR NATION HIDING?
WHAT?!

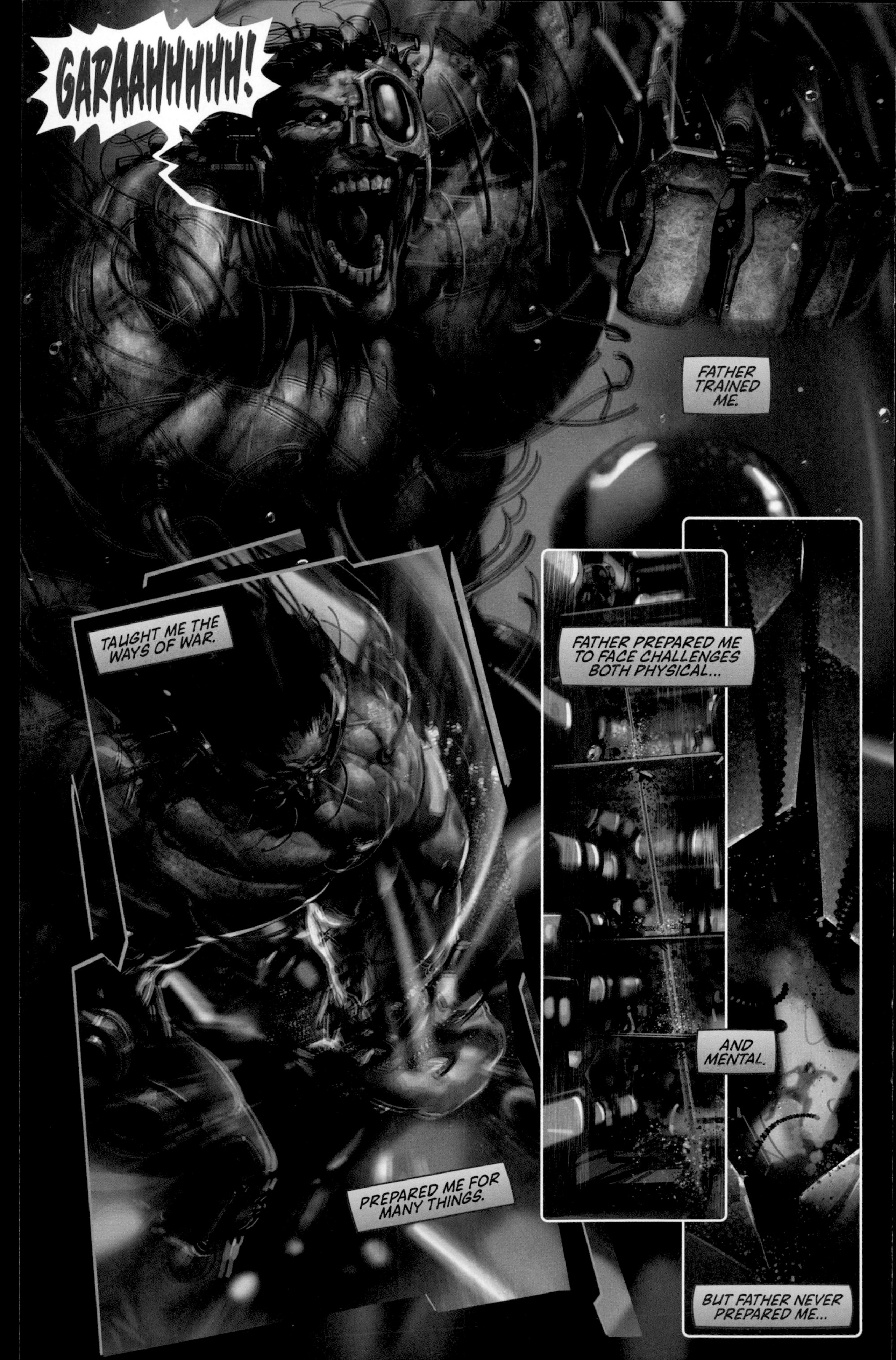
GARAAHHHHH!
FATHER TRAINED ME.
TAUGHT ME THE WAYS OF WAR.
PREPARED ME FOR MANY THINGS.
FATHER PREPARED ME TO FACE CHALLENGES BOTH PHYSICAL...
AND MENTAL.
BUT FATHER NEVER PREPARED ME...

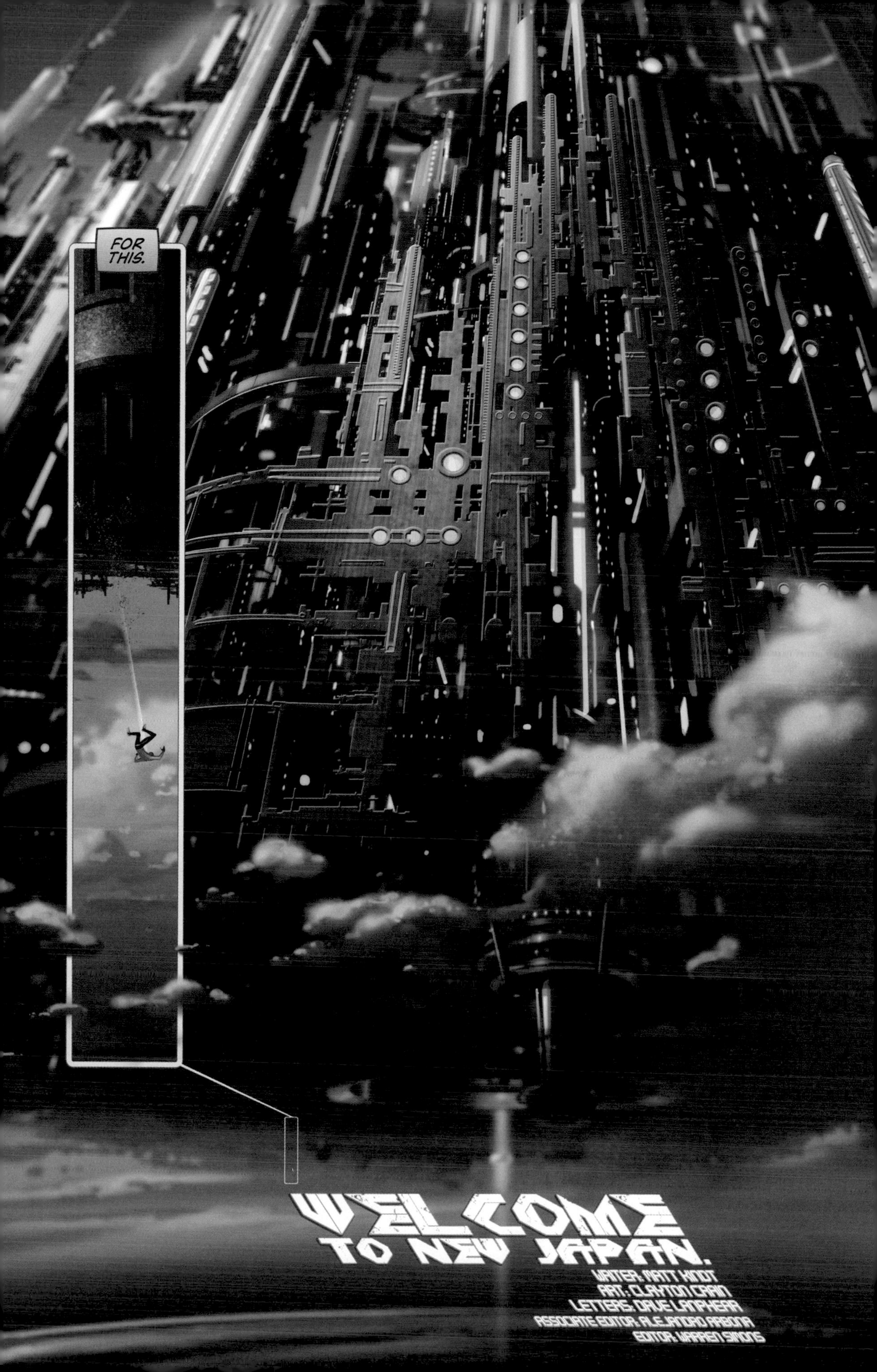
FOR THIS.
WELCOME TO NEW JAPAN.
WRITER: MATT KINDT
ART: CLAYTON CRAIN
LETTERS: DAVE LANPHEAR
ASSOCIATE EDITOR: ALEJANDRO ARBONA
EDITOR: WARREN SIMONS

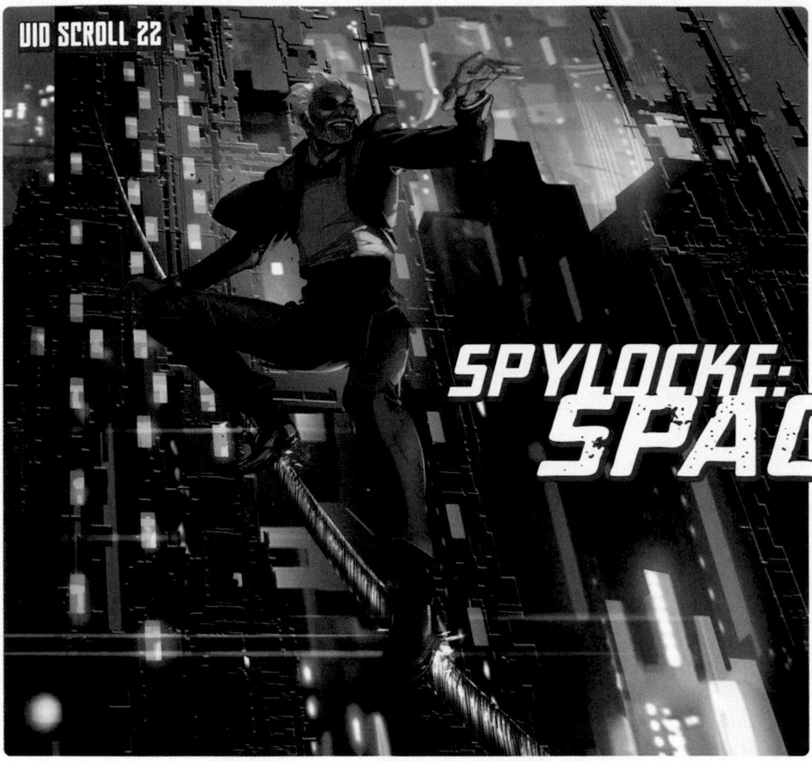
VID SCROLL 22

Spylocke is a fictional hero who may or may not be based on a generation of subversive super-spies. There has been conjecture that Spylocke has real-life historical basis.
True origin, unknown.
In recent years a series of popular vids have been distributed, updating the character for a new generation of viewers.

SPYLOCKE: SPACEFALL

Released 3899. The fate of Japan hangs in the balance as Spylocke must once again sacrifice himself for the safety of the nation. If Japan doesn't unwittingly take him out, the Free Radicals will surely kill him.

SPYLOCKE: DEADEYES

Released 3901. The nation has turned its back on Spylocke while he continues to fight the good fight. The Radicals are at it again, intent on tearing down Japan from the inside...but the only enemy larger than the Radicals is Japan itself. Spylocke must unwillingly use the very training that Japan gave him to fight against it. And at last, the heart-breaking story of Spylocke's lost eye is revealed.

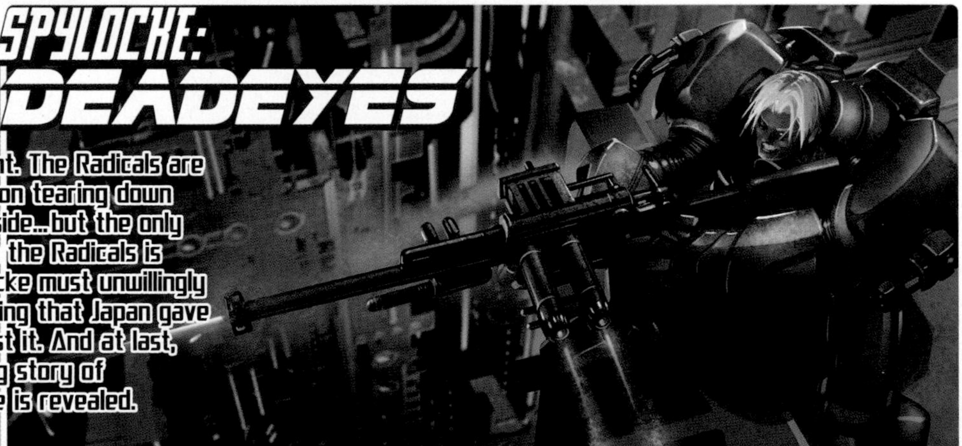

SPYLOCKE: WAR ON TERRA

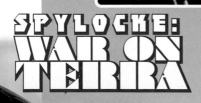

Released 3902. Spylocke is taken off-planet by a Free Radical Terra-beam and finds himself in a world unlike anything he's ever seen.
Spylocke is forced to collaborate with the Positron Metra and their unlikely pairing may be the only thing that can save Japan from invasion.

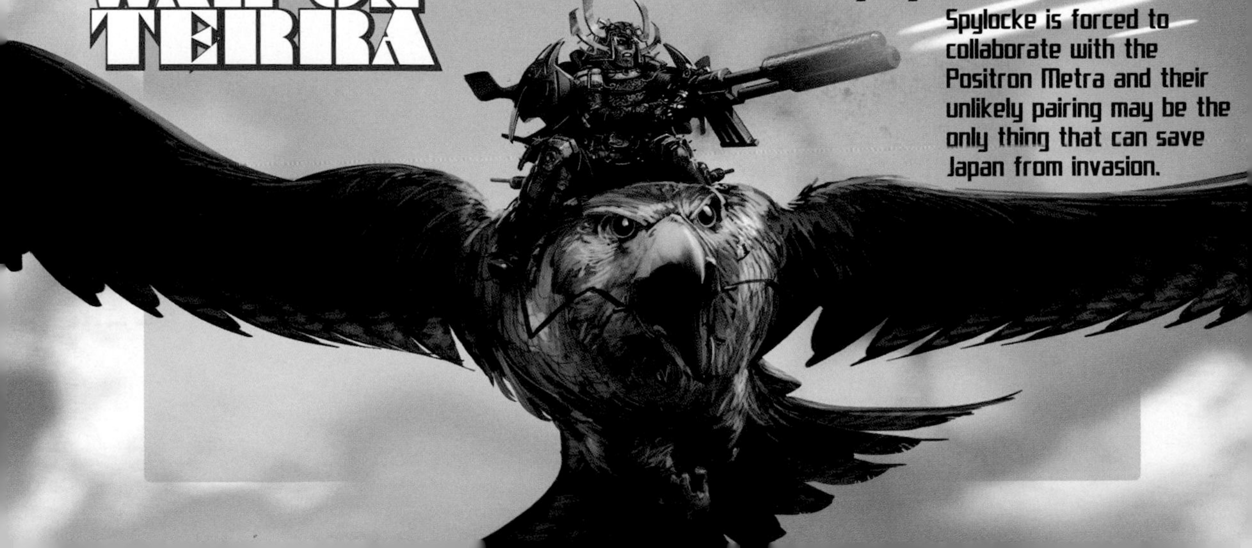

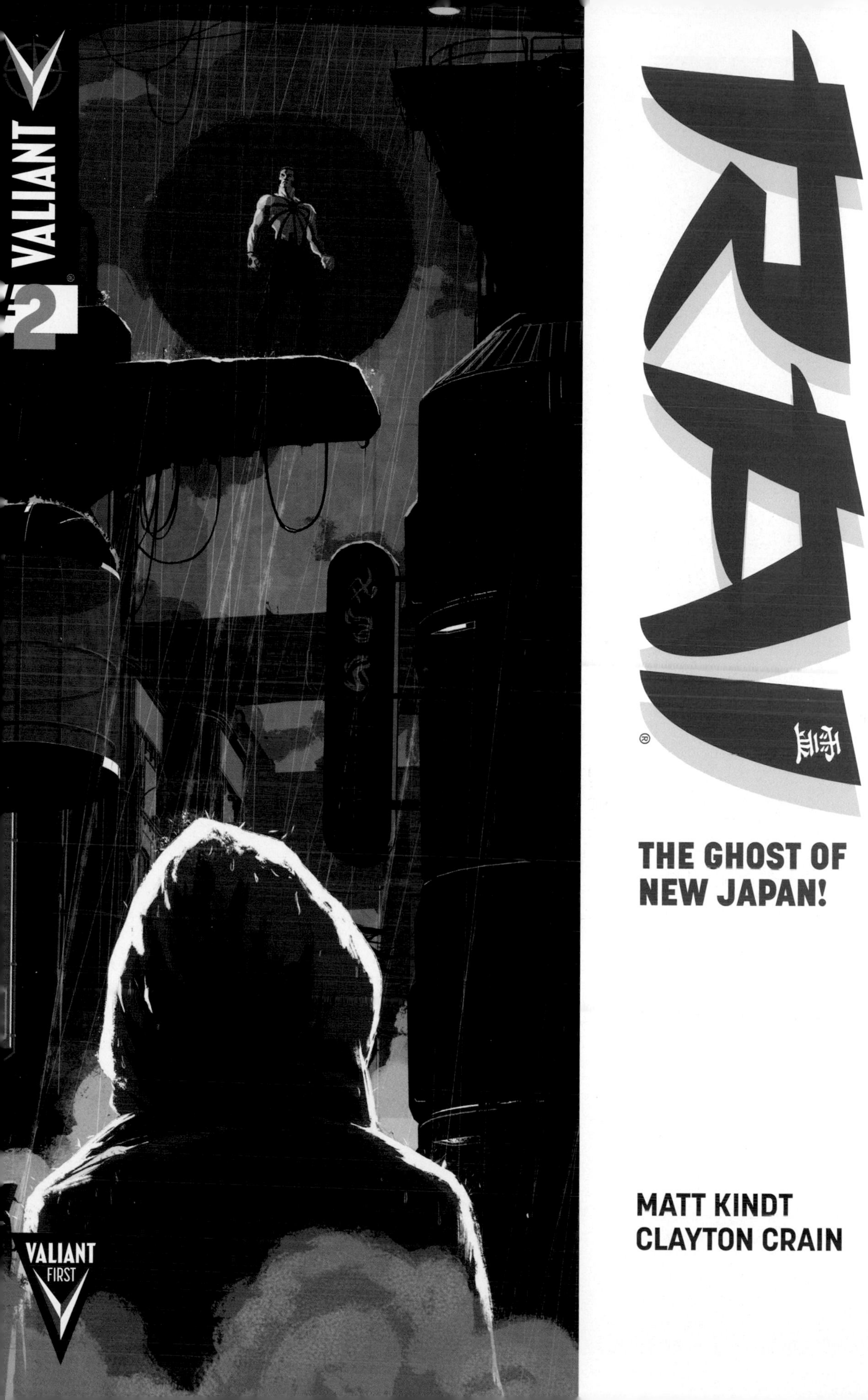
VALIANT
2
VALIANT
FIRST

RAI

THE GHOST OF NEW JAPAN!

MATT KINDT
CLAYTON CRAIN

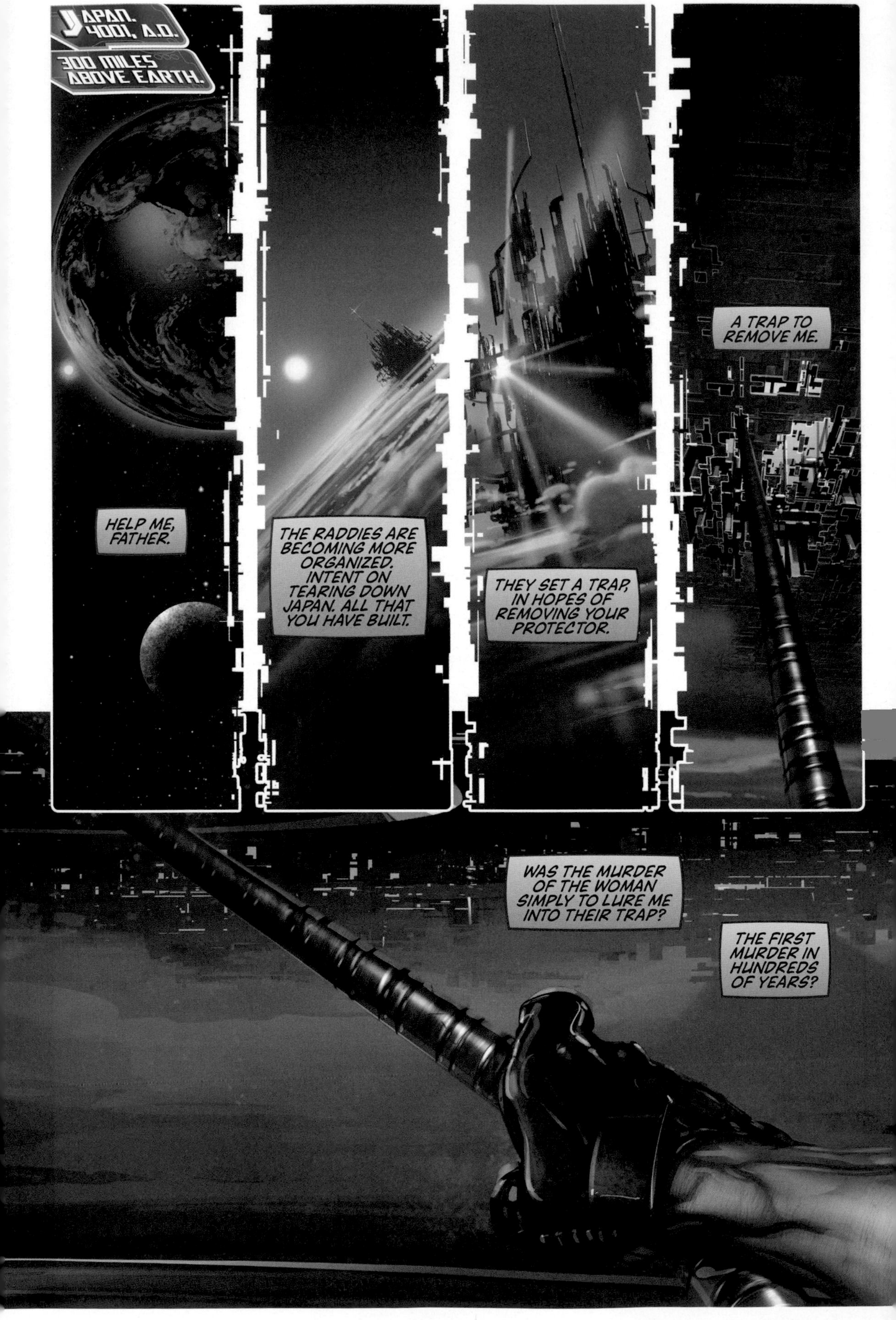
JAPAN. 4001, A.D.
300 MILES ABOVE EARTH.
HELP ME, FATHER.
THE RADDIES ARE BECOMING MORE ORGANIZED. INTENT ON TEARING DOWN JAPAN. ALL THAT YOU HAVE BUILT.
THEY SET A TRAP, IN HOPES OF REMOVING YOUR PROTECTOR.
A TRAP TO REMOVE ME.
WAS THE MURDER OF THE WOMAN SIMPLY TO LURE ME INTO THEIR TRAP?
THE FIRST MURDER IN HUNDREDS OF YEARS?

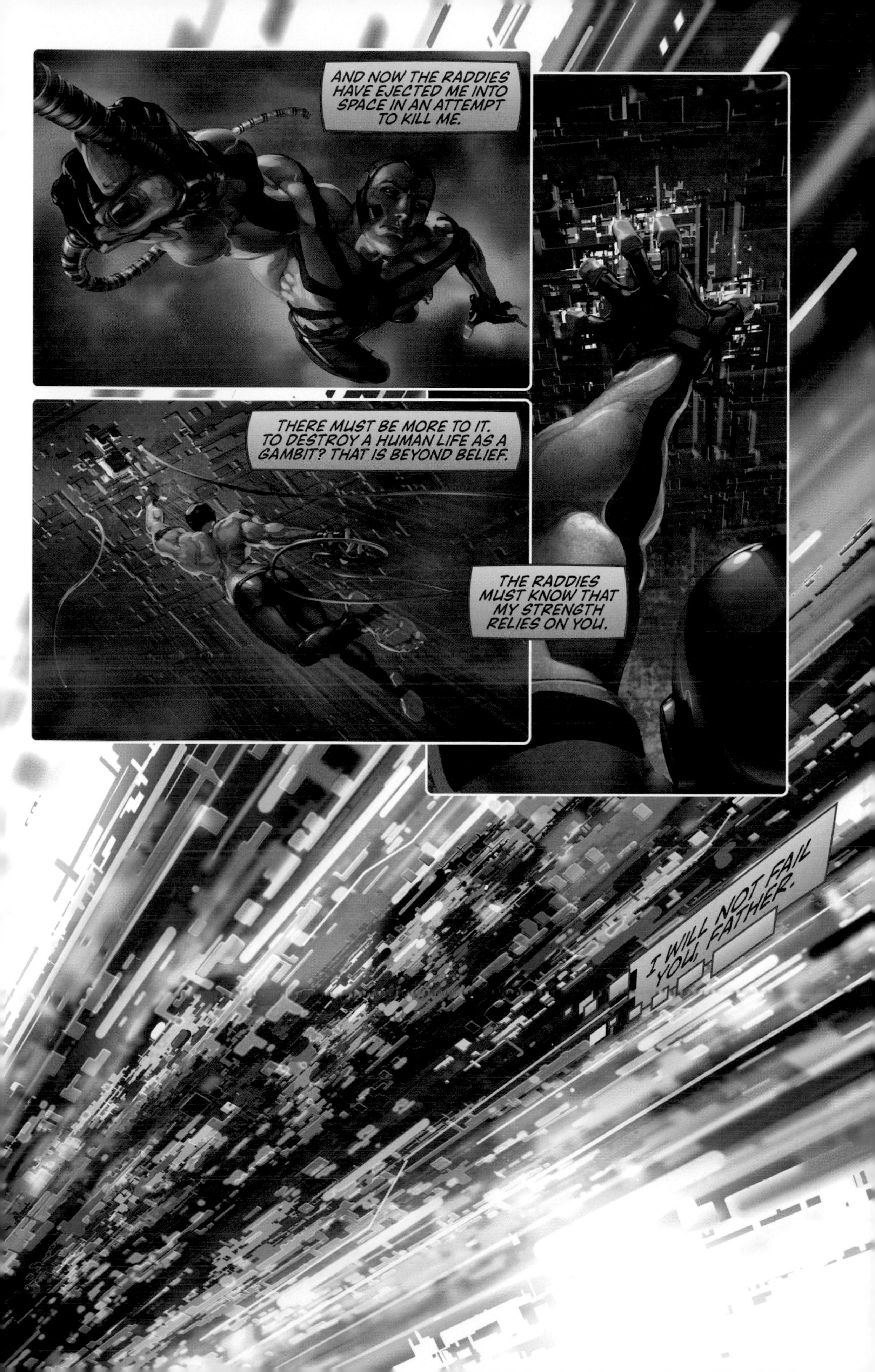
AND NOW THE RADDIES HAVE EJECTED ME INTO SPACE IN AN ATTEMPT TO KILL ME.
THERE MUST BE MORE TO IT. TO DESTROY A HUMAN LIFE AS A GAMBIT? THAT IS BEYOND BELIEF.
THE RADDIES MUST KNOW THAT MY STRENGTH RELIES ON YOU.
I WILL NOT FAIL YOU, FATHER.

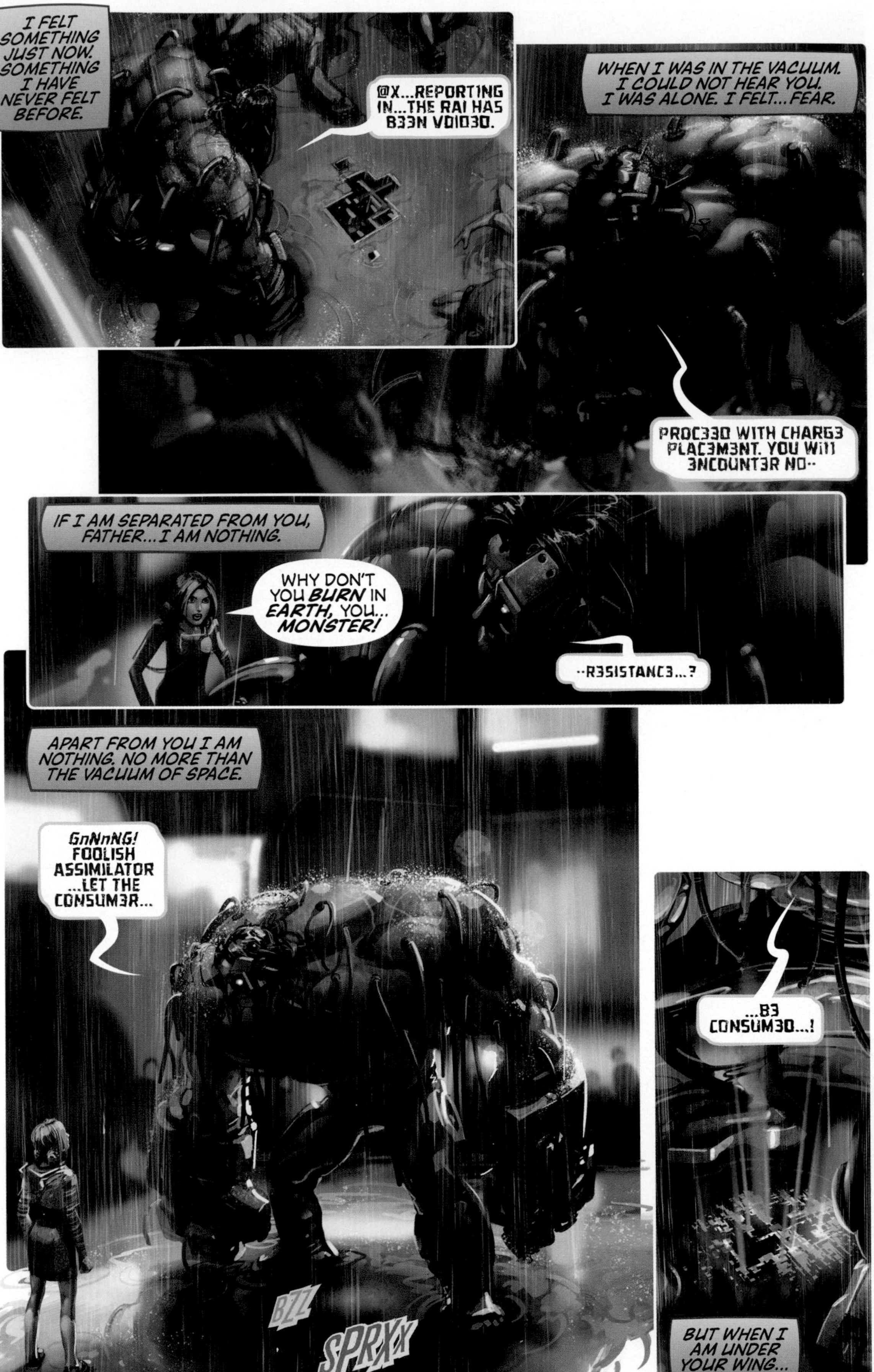
I FELT SOMETHING JUST NOW. SOMETHING I HAVE NEVER FELT BEFORE.
@X...REPORTING IN...THE RAI HAS B33N VOID3D.
WHEN I WAS IN THE VACUUM. I COULD NOT HEAR YOU. I WAS ALONE. I FELT...FEAR.
PROC33D WITH CHARG3 PLAC3M3NT. YOU WI11 3NCOUNT3R NO--
IF I AM SEPARATED FROM YOU, FATHER...I AM NOTHING.
WHY DON'T YOU BURN IN EARTH, YOU... MONSTER!
--R3SISTANC3...?
APART FROM YOU I AM NOTHING. NO MORE THAN THE VACUUM OF SPACE.
GnNnNG! FOOLISH ASSIMILATOR ...LET THE CONSUM3R...
BZZ
SPRXX
...B3 CONSUM3D...!
BUT WHEN I AM UNDER YOUR WING...

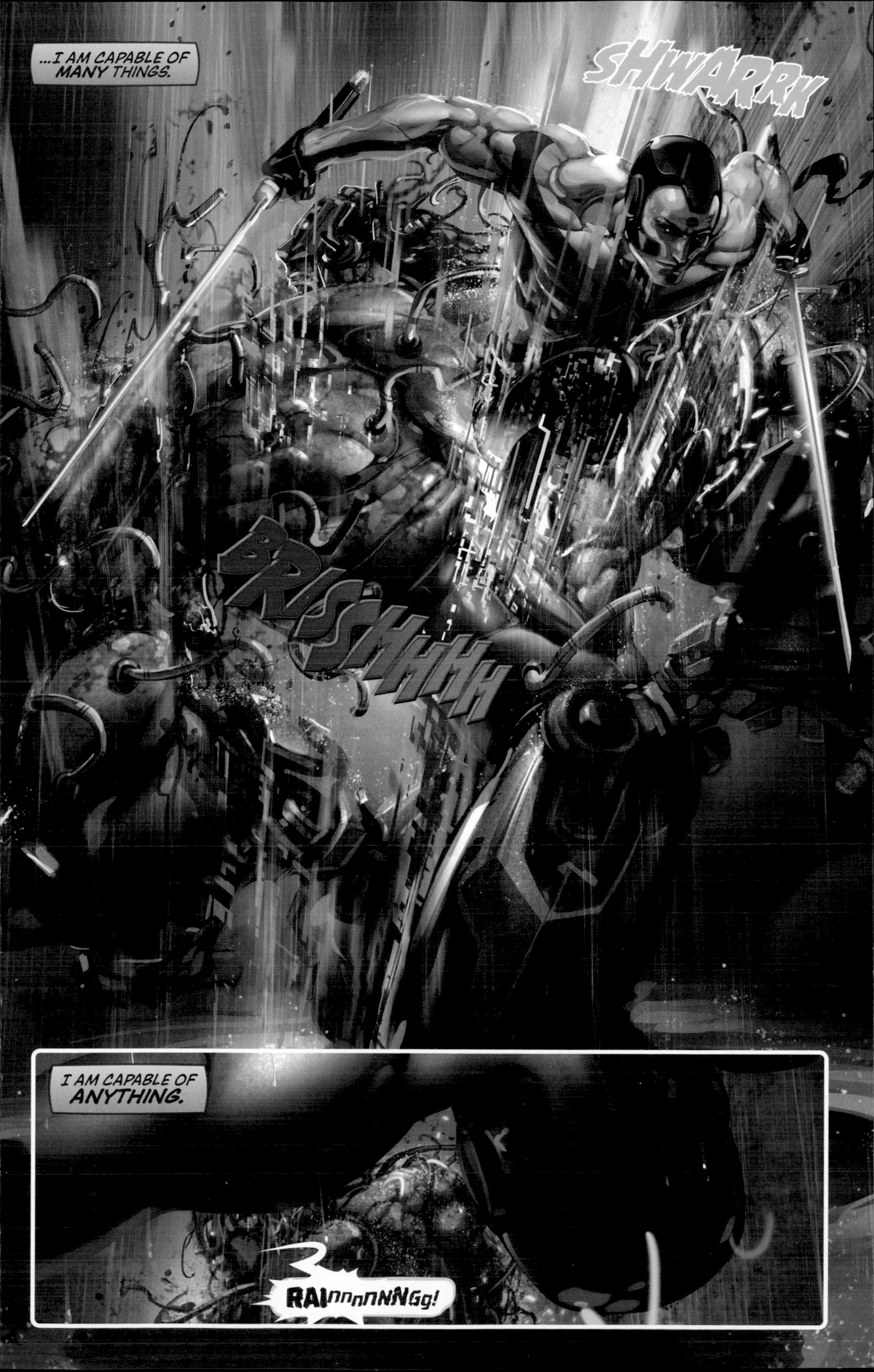
...I AM CAPABLE OF MANY THINGS.
SHWARRRK
BRISHHHH
I AM CAPABLE OF ANYTHING.
RAInnnnNNGg!

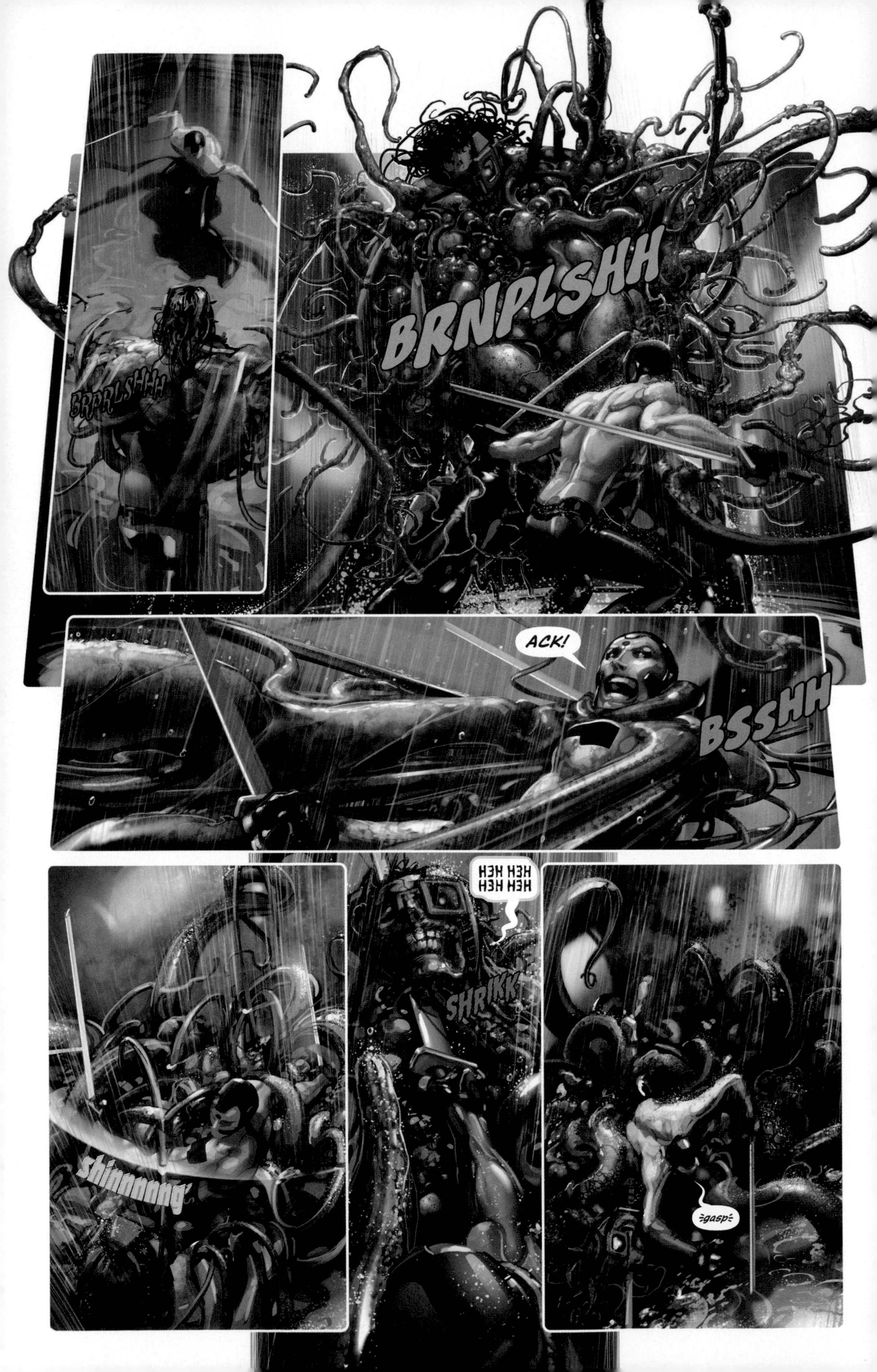

BRPRLSHHH
BRNPLSHH
ACK!
BSSHH
shinnnnng
HEH HEH
HEH HEH
SHRIKK
gasp

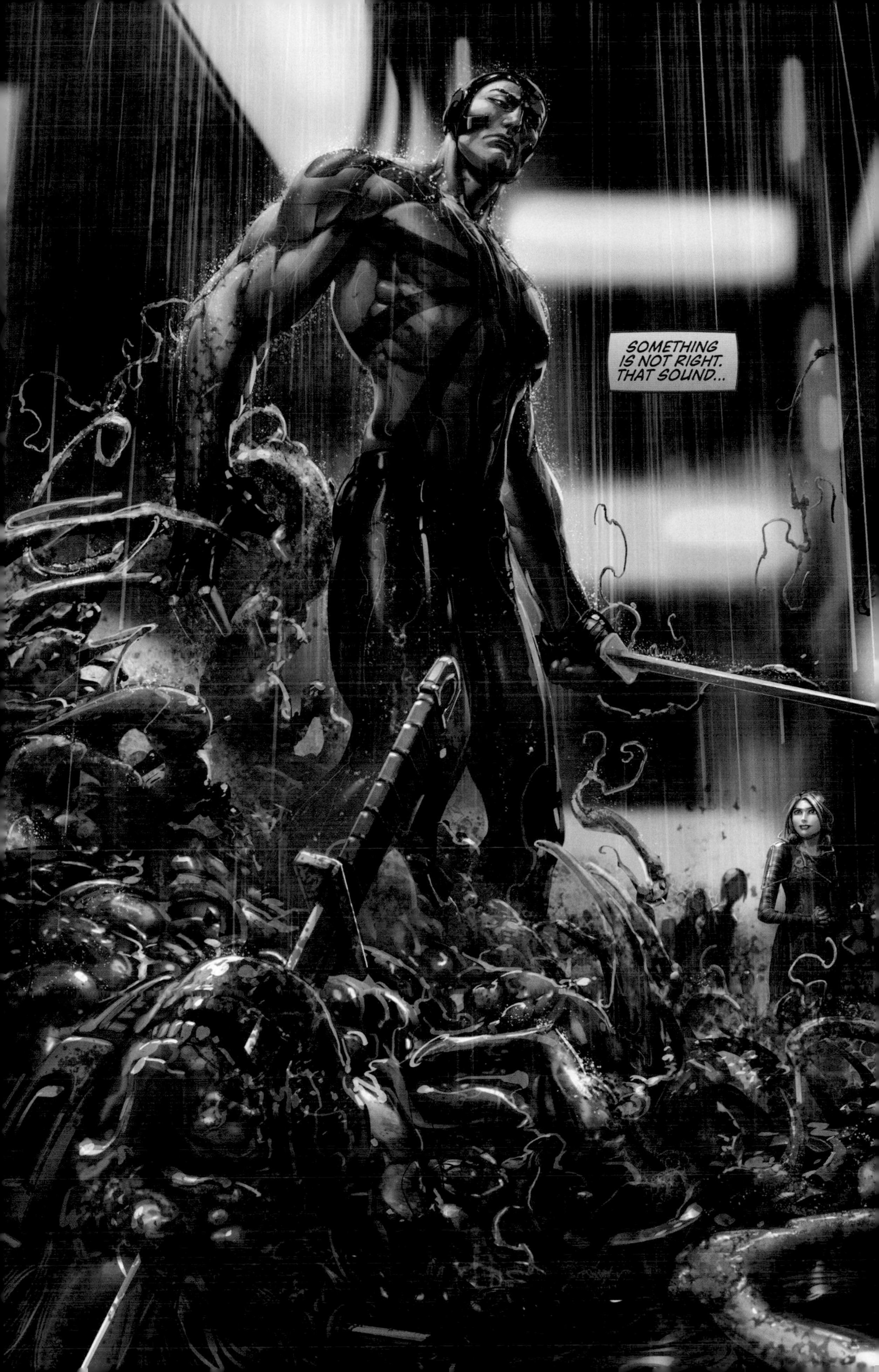
SOMETHING
IS NOT RIGHT.
THAT SOUND...

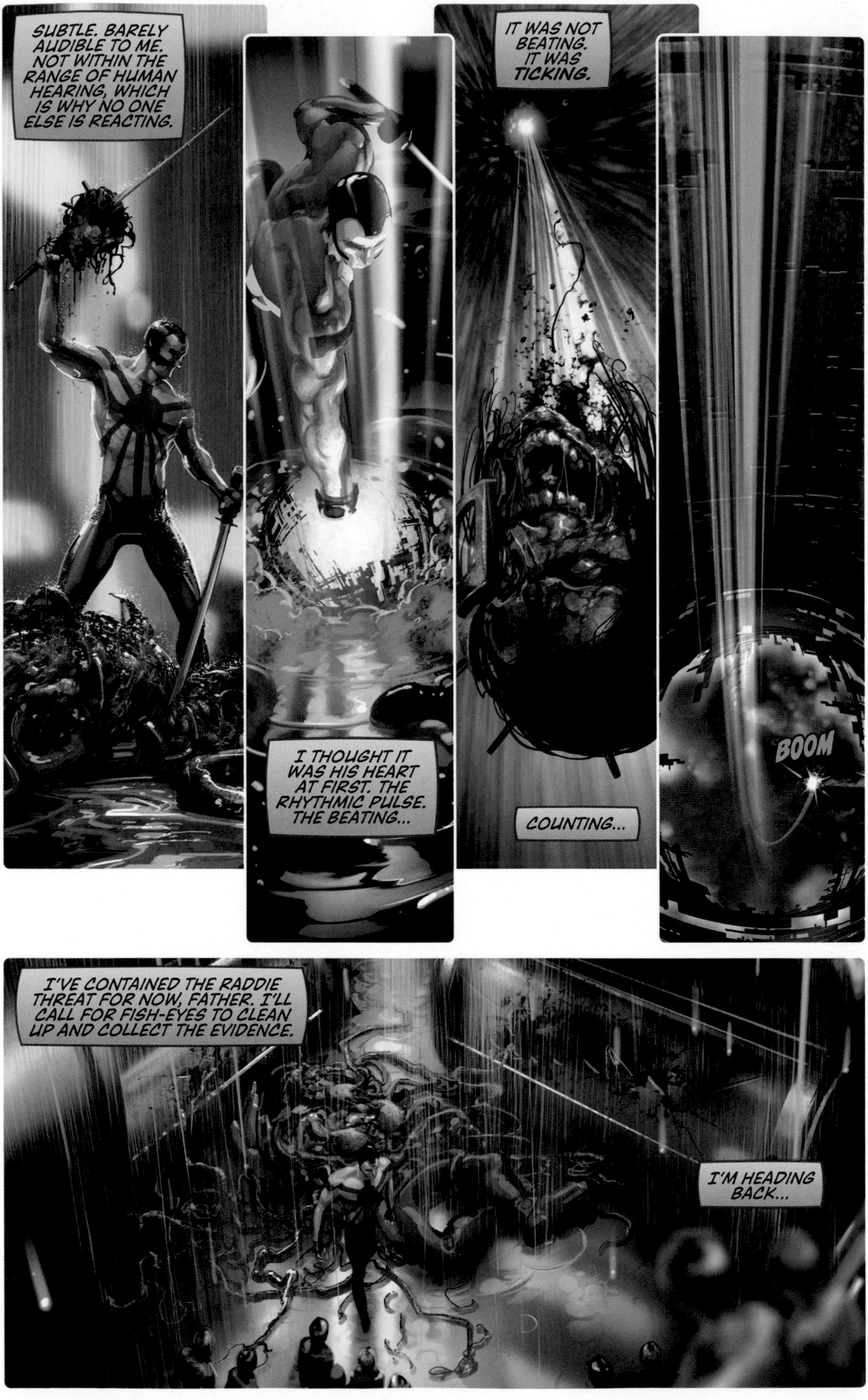
SUBTLE. BARELY AUDIBLE TO ME. NOT WITHIN THE RANGE OF HUMAN HEARING, WHICH IS WHY NO ONE ELSE IS REACTING.
I THOUGHT IT WAS HIS HEART AT FIRST. THE RHYTHMIC PULSE. THE BEATING...
IT WAS NOT BEATING. IT WAS TICKING.
COUNTING...
BOOM
I'VE CONTAINED THE RADDIE THREAT FOR NOW, FATHER. I'LL CALL FOR FISH-EYES TO CLEAN UP AND COLLECT THE EVIDENCE.
I'M HEADING BACK...

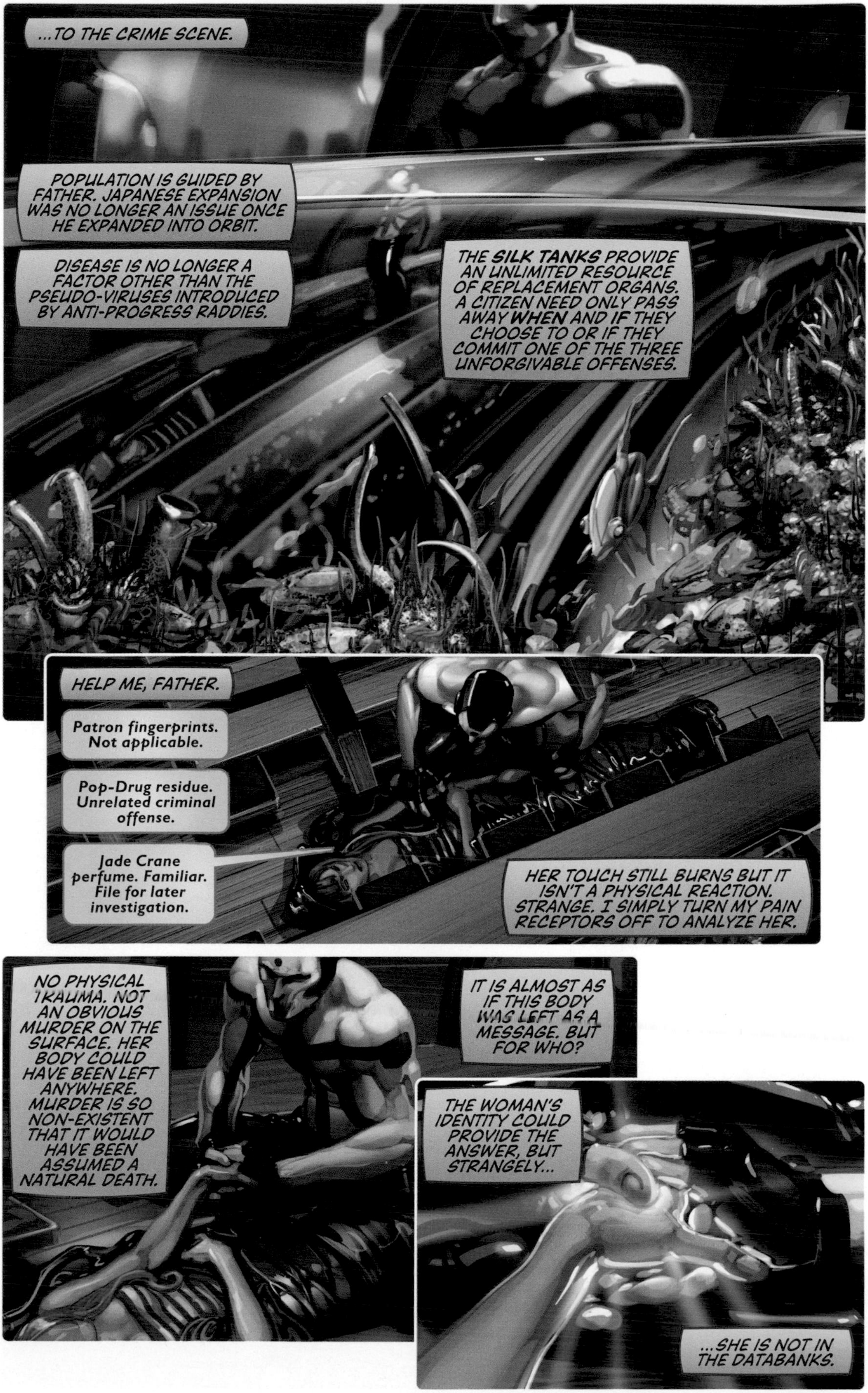
...TO THE CRIME SCENE.
POPULATION IS GUIDED BY FATHER. JAPANESE EXPANSION WAS NO LONGER AN ISSUE ONCE HE EXPANDED INTO ORBIT.
DISEASE IS NO LONGER A FACTOR OTHER THAN THE PSEUDO-VIRUSES INTRODUCED BY ANTI-PROGRESS RADDIES.
THE SILK TANKS PROVIDE AN UNLIMITED RESOURCE OF REPLACEMENT ORGANS. A CITIZEN NEED ONLY PASS AWAY WHEN AND IF THEY CHOOSE TO OR IF THEY COMMIT ONE OF THE THREE UNFORGIVABLE OFFENSES.
HELP ME, FATHER.
Patron fingerprints. Not applicable.
Pop-Drug residue. Unrelated criminal offense.
Jade Crane perfume. Familiar. File for later investigation.
HER TOUCH STILL BURNS BUT IT ISN'T A PHYSICAL REACTION. STRANGE. I SIMPLY TURN MY PAIN RECEPTORS OFF TO ANALYZE HER.
NO PHYSICAL TRAUMA. NOT AN OBVIOUS MURDER ON THE SURFACE. HER BODY COULD HAVE BEEN LEFT ANYWHERE. MURDER IS SO NON-EXISTENT THAT IT WOULD HAVE BEEN ASSUMED A NATURAL DEATH.
IT IS ALMOST AS IF THIS BODY WAS LEFT AS A MESSAGE. BUT FOR WHO?
THE WOMAN'S IDENTITY COULD PROVIDE THE ANSWER, BUT STRANGELY...
...SHE IS NOT IN THE DATABANKS.

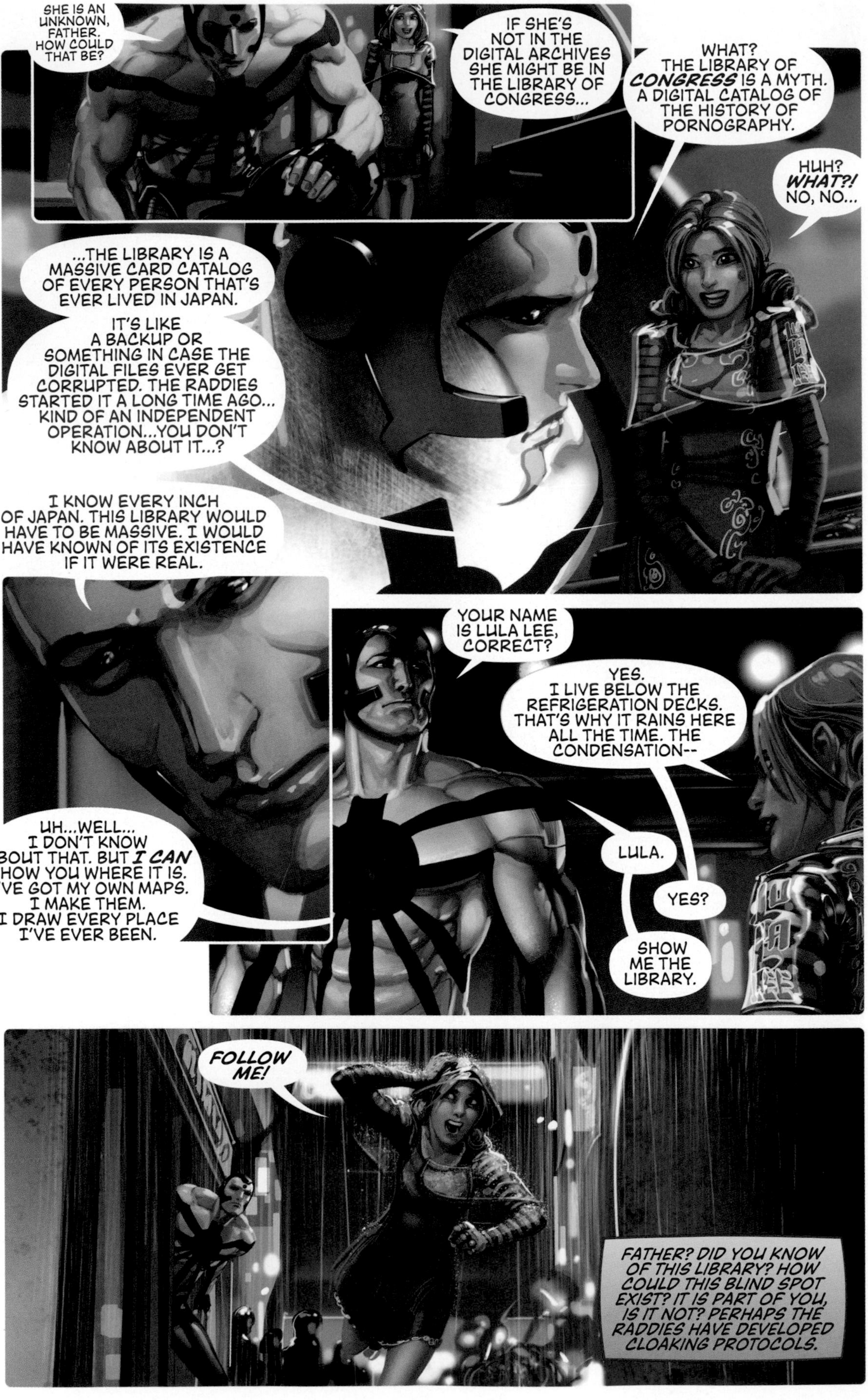
SHE IS AN UNKNOWN, FATHER. HOW COULD THAT BE?
IF SHE'S NOT IN THE DIGITAL ARCHIVES SHE MIGHT BE IN THE LIBRARY OF CONGRESS...
WHAT? THE LIBRARY OF CONGRESS IS A MYTH. A DIGITAL CATALOG OF THE HISTORY OF PORNOGRAPHY.
HUH? WHAT?! NO, NO...
...THE LIBRARY IS A MASSIVE CARD CATALOG OF EVERY PERSON THAT'S EVER LIVED IN JAPAN.
IT'S LIKE A BACKUP OR SOMETHING IN CASE THE DIGITAL FILES EVER GET CORRUPTED. THE RADDIES STARTED IT A LONG TIME AGO... KIND OF AN INDEPENDENT OPERATION...YOU DON'T KNOW ABOUT IT...?
I KNOW EVERY INCH OF JAPAN. THIS LIBRARY WOULD HAVE TO BE MASSIVE. I WOULD HAVE KNOWN OF ITS EXISTENCE IF IT WERE REAL.
UH...WELL... I DON'T KNOW ABOUT THAT. BUT I CAN SHOW YOU WHERE IT IS. I'VE GOT MY OWN MAPS. I MAKE THEM. I DRAW EVERY PLACE I'VE EVER BEEN.
YOUR NAME IS LULA LEE, CORRECT?
YES. I LIVE BELOW THE REFRIGERATION DECKS. THAT'S WHY IT RAINS HERE ALL THE TIME. THE CONDENSATION--
LULA.
YES?
SHOW ME THE LIBRARY.
FOLLOW ME!
FATHER? DID YOU KNOW OF THIS LIBRARY? HOW COULD THIS BLIND SPOT EXIST? IT IS PART OF YOU, IS IT NOT? PERHAPS THE RADDIES HAVE DEVELOPED CLOAKING PROTOCOLS.

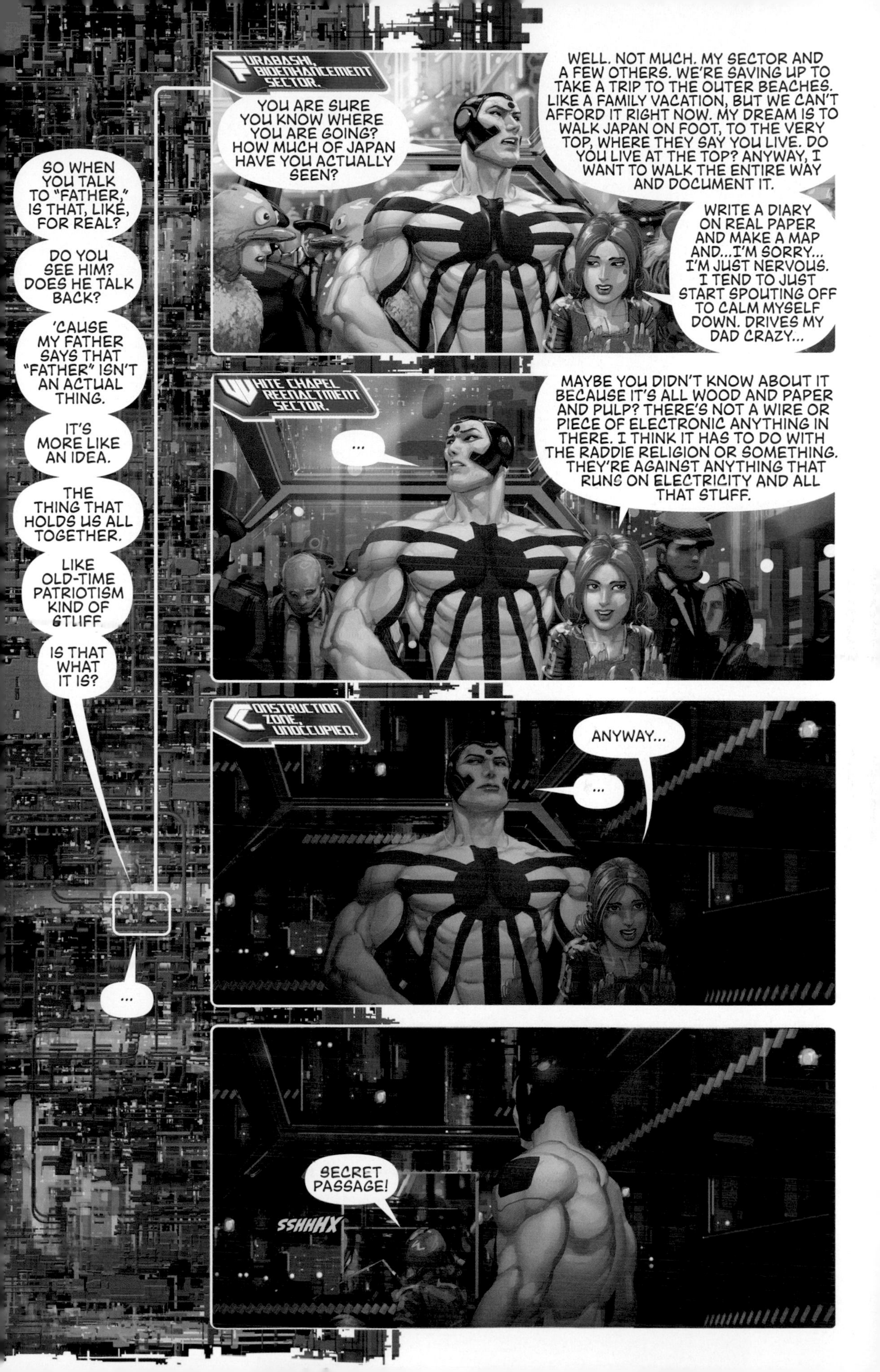
FURABASHI, BIOENHANCEMENT SECTOR.
YOU ARE SURE YOU KNOW WHERE YOU ARE GOING? HOW MUCH OF JAPAN HAVE YOU ACTUALLY SEEN?
WELL. NOT MUCH. MY SECTOR AND A FEW OTHERS. WE'RE SAVING UP TO TAKE A TRIP TO THE OUTER BEACHES. LIKE A FAMILY VACATION, BUT WE CAN'T AFFORD IT RIGHT NOW. MY DREAM IS TO WALK JAPAN ON FOOT, TO THE VERY TOP, WHERE THEY SAY YOU LIVE. DO YOU LIVE AT THE TOP? ANYWAY, I WANT TO WALK THE ENTIRE WAY AND DOCUMENT IT.
WRITE A DIARY ON REAL PAPER AND MAKE A MAP AND...I'M SORRY... I'M JUST NERVOUS. I TEND TO JUST START SPOUTING OFF TO CALM MYSELF DOWN. DRIVES MY DAD CRAZY...
WHITE CHAPEL REENACTMENT SECTOR.
...
MAYBE YOU DIDN'T KNOW ABOUT IT BECAUSE IT'S ALL WOOD AND PAPER AND PULP? THERE'S NOT A WIRE OR PIECE OF ELECTRONIC ANYTHING IN THERE. I THINK IT HAS TO DO WITH THE RADDIE RELIGION OR SOMETHING. THEY'RE AGAINST ANYTHING THAT RUNS ON ELECTRICITY AND ALL THAT STUFF.
CONSTRUCTION ZONE, UNOCCUPIED.
ANYWAY...
...
SO WHEN YOU TALK TO "FATHER," IS THAT, LIKE, FOR REAL?
DO YOU SEE HIM? DOES HE TALK BACK?
'CAUSE MY FATHER SAYS THAT "FATHER" ISN'T AN ACTUAL THING.
IT'S MORE LIKE AN IDEA.
THE THING THAT HOLDS US ALL TOGETHER.
LIKE OLD-TIME PATRIOTISM KIND OF STUFF.
IS THAT WHAT IT IS?
...
SECRET PASSAGE!
SSHHHX

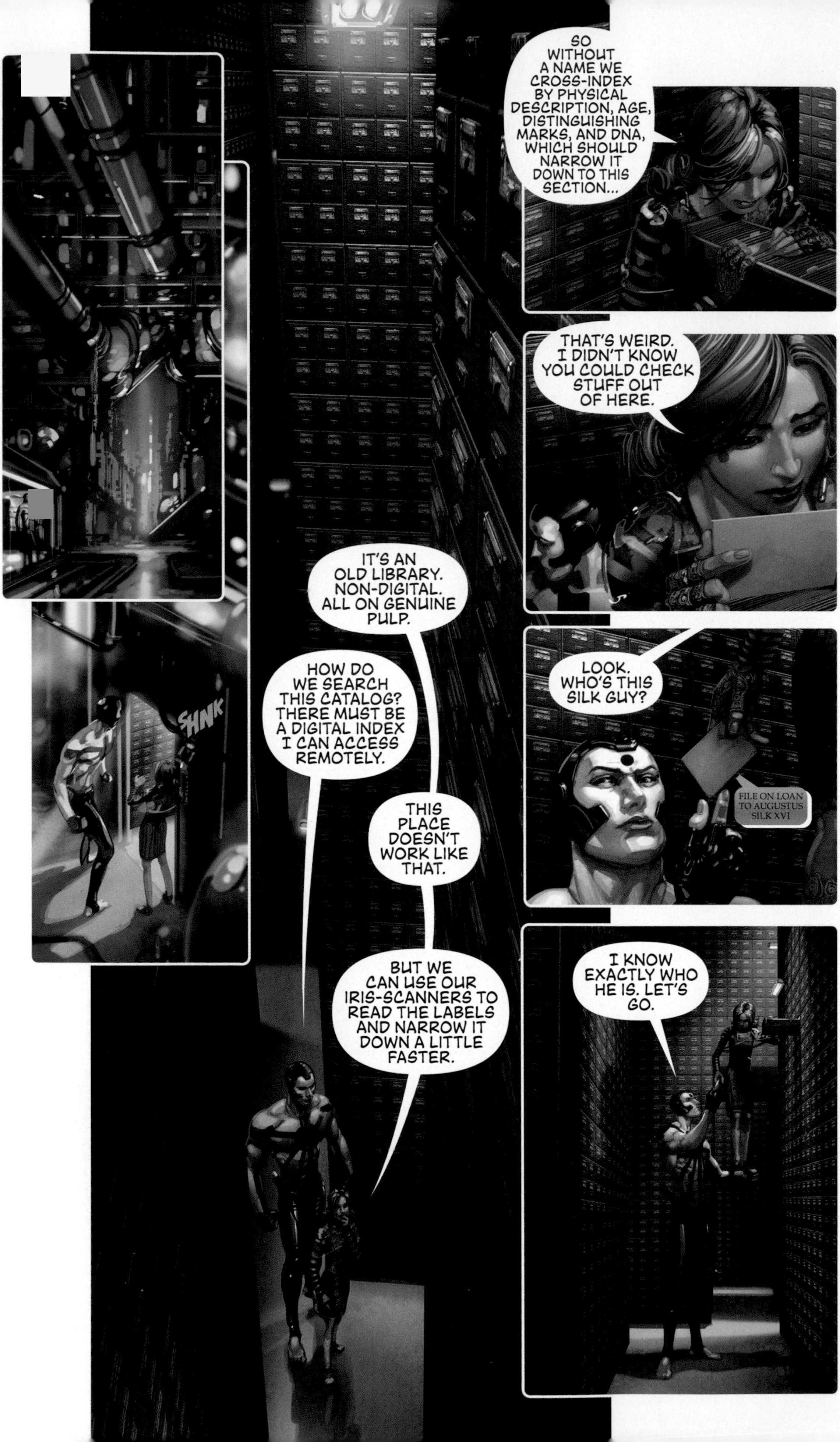

SHNK
SO WITHOUT A NAME WE CROSS-INDEX BY PHYSICAL DESCRIPTION, AGE, DISTINGUISHING MARKS, AND DNA, WHICH SHOULD NARROW IT DOWN TO THIS SECTION...
THAT'S WEIRD. I DIDN'T KNOW YOU COULD CHECK STUFF OUT OF HERE.
LOOK. WHO'S THIS SILK GUY?
FILE ON LOAN TO AUGUSTUS SILK XVI
I KNOW EXACTLY WHO HE IS. LET'S GO.
IT'S AN OLD LIBRARY. NON-DIGITAL. ALL ON GENUINE PULP.
HOW DO WE SEARCH THIS CATALOG? THERE MUST BE A DIGITAL INDEX I CAN ACCESS REMOTELY.
THIS PLACE DOESN'T WORK LIKE THAT.
BUT WE CAN USE OUR IRIS-SCANNERS TO READ THE LABELS AND NARROW IT DOWN A LITTLE FASTER.

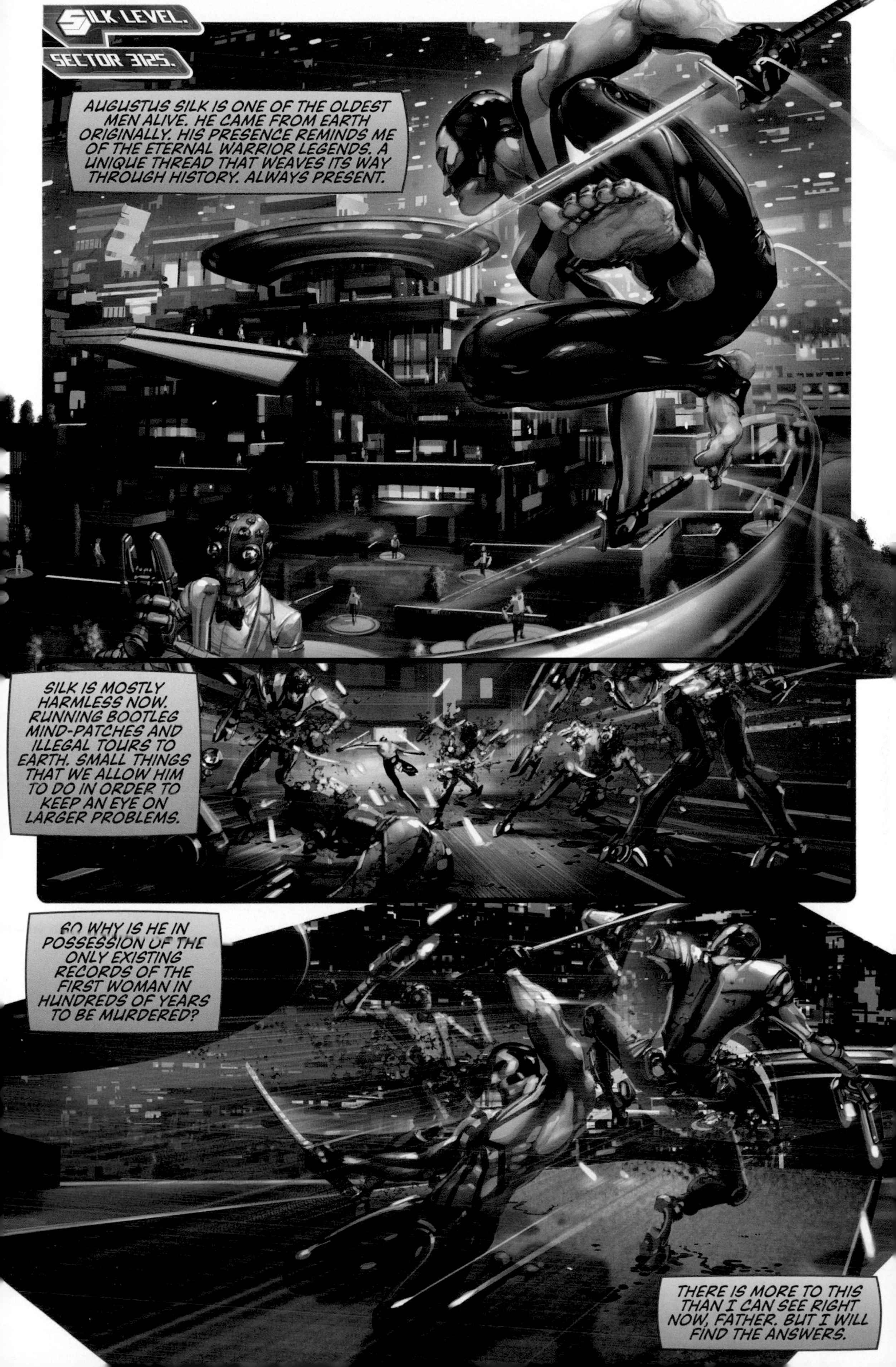
SILK LEVEL.
SECTOR 3125.
AUGUSTUS SILK IS ONE OF THE OLDEST MEN ALIVE. HE CAME FROM EARTH ORIGINALLY. HIS PRESENCE REMINDS ME OF THE ETERNAL WARRIOR LEGENDS. A UNIQUE THREAD THAT WEAVES ITS WAY THROUGH HISTORY. ALWAYS PRESENT.
SILK IS MOSTLY HARMLESS NOW. RUNNING BOOTLEG MIND-PATCHES AND ILLEGAL TOURS TO EARTH. SMALL THINGS THAT WE ALLOW HIM TO DO IN ORDER TO KEEP AN EYE ON LARGER PROBLEMS.
SO WHY IS HE IN POSSESSION OF THE ONLY EXISTING RECORDS OF THE FIRST WOMAN IN HUNDREDS OF YEARS TO BE MURDERED?
THERE IS MORE TO THIS THAN I CAN SEE RIGHT NOW, FATHER. BUT I WILL FIND THE ANSWERS.

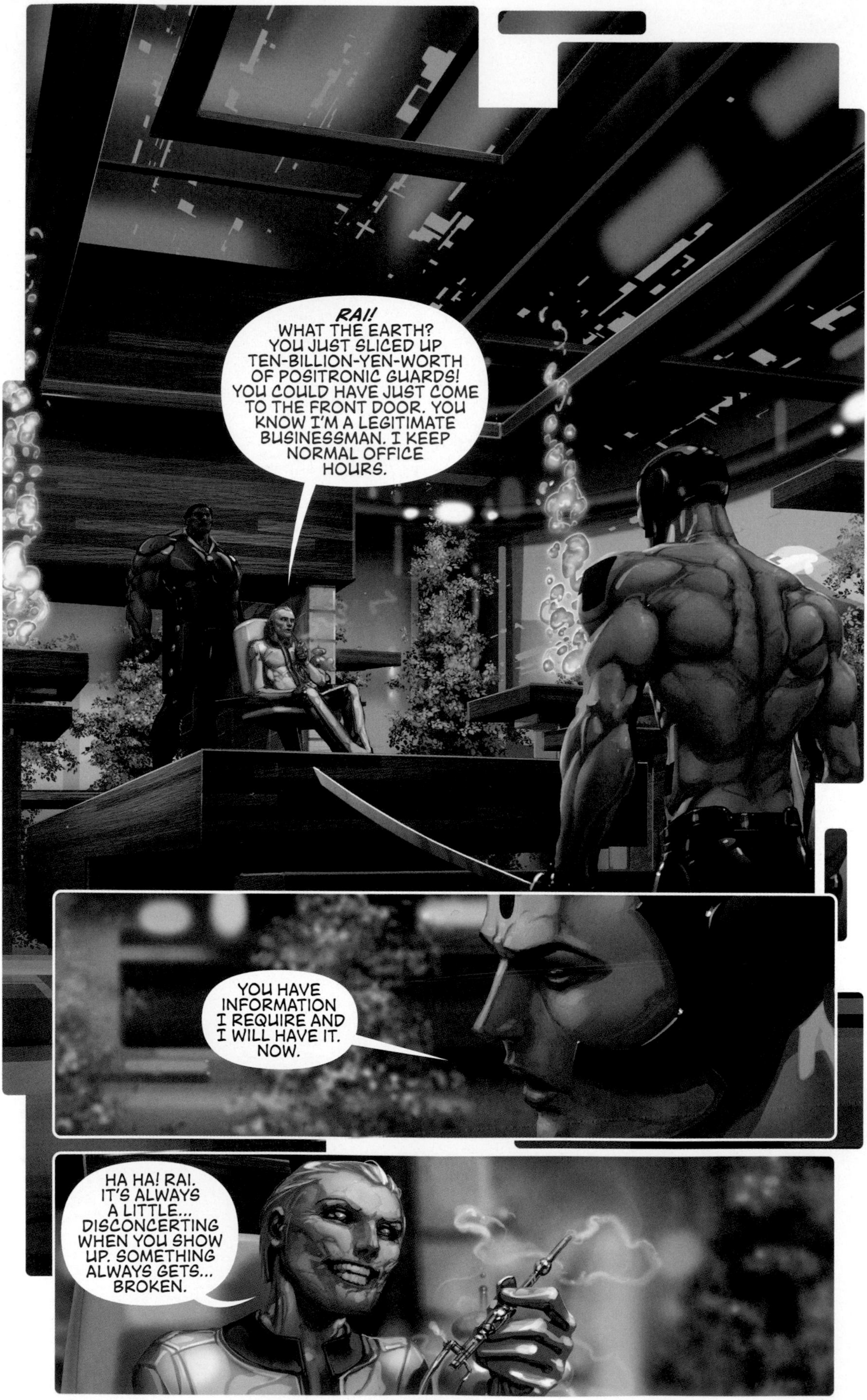
RAI! WHAT THE EARTH? YOU JUST SLICED UP TEN-BILLION-YEN-WORTH OF POSITRONIC GUARDS! YOU COULD HAVE JUST COME TO THE FRONT DOOR. YOU KNOW I'M A LEGITIMATE BUSINESSMAN. I KEEP NORMAL OFFICE HOURS.
YOU HAVE INFORMATION I REQUIRE AND I WILL HAVE IT. NOW.
HA HA! RAI. IT'S ALWAYS A LITTLE... DISCONCERTING WHEN YOU SHOW UP. SOMETHING ALWAYS GETS... BROKEN.

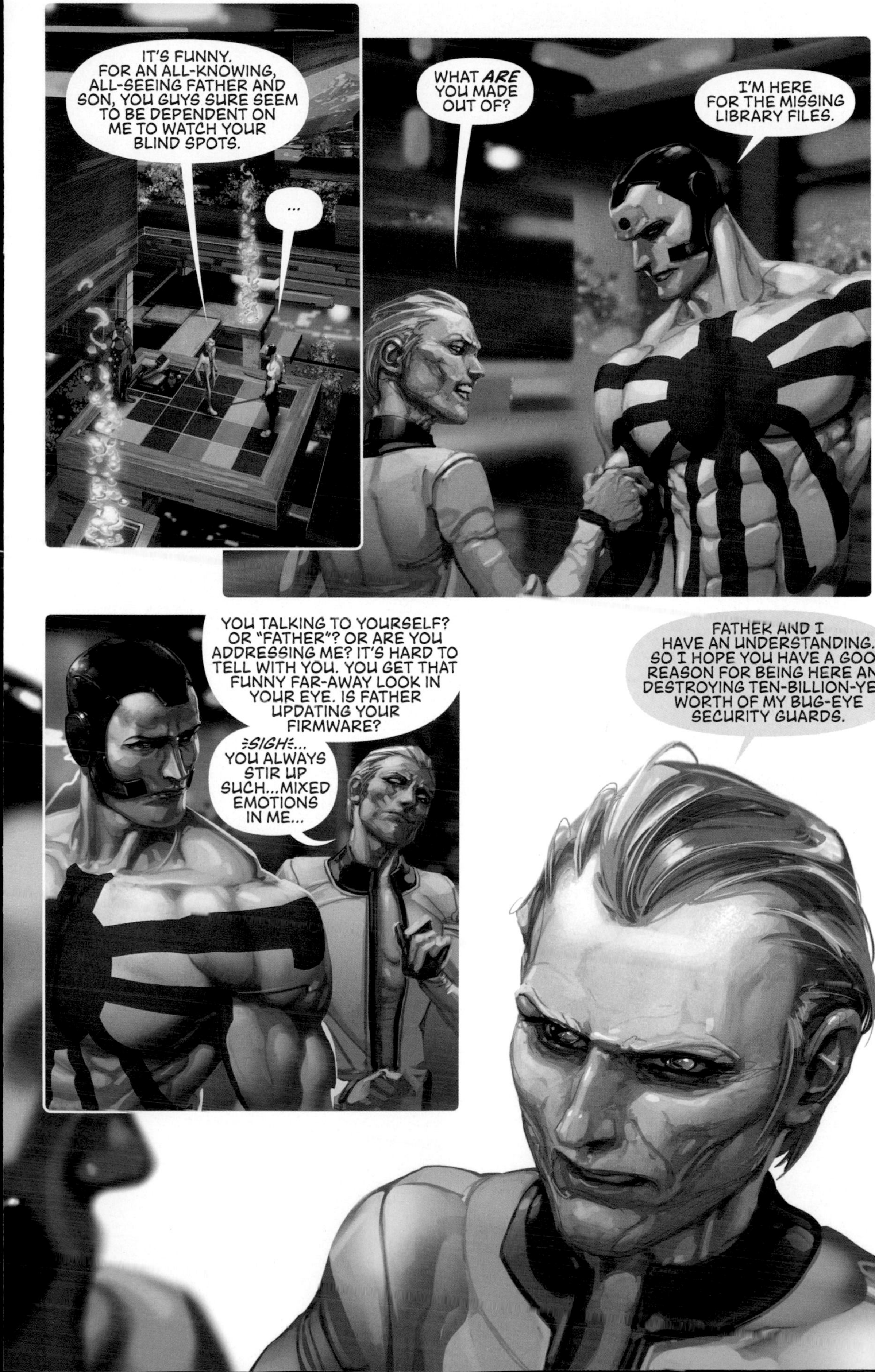
IT'S FUNNY. FOR AN ALL-KNOWING, ALL-SEEING FATHER AND SON, YOU GUYS SURE SEEM TO BE DEPENDENT ON ME TO WATCH YOUR BLIND SPOTS.
...
WHAT ARE YOU MADE OUT OF?
I'M HERE FOR THE MISSING LIBRARY FILES.
YOU TALKING TO YOURSELF? OR "FATHER"? OR ARE YOU ADDRESSING ME? IT'S HARD TO TELL WITH YOU. YOU GET THAT FUNNY FAR-AWAY LOOK IN YOUR EYE. IS FATHER UPDATING YOUR FIRMWARE?
=SIGH=... YOU ALWAYS STIR UP SUCH...MIXED EMOTIONS IN ME...
FATHER AND I HAVE AN UNDERSTANDING. SO I HOPE YOU HAVE A GOOD REASON FOR BEING HERE AND DESTROYING TEN-BILLION-YEN-WORTH OF MY BUG-EYE SECURITY GUARDS.

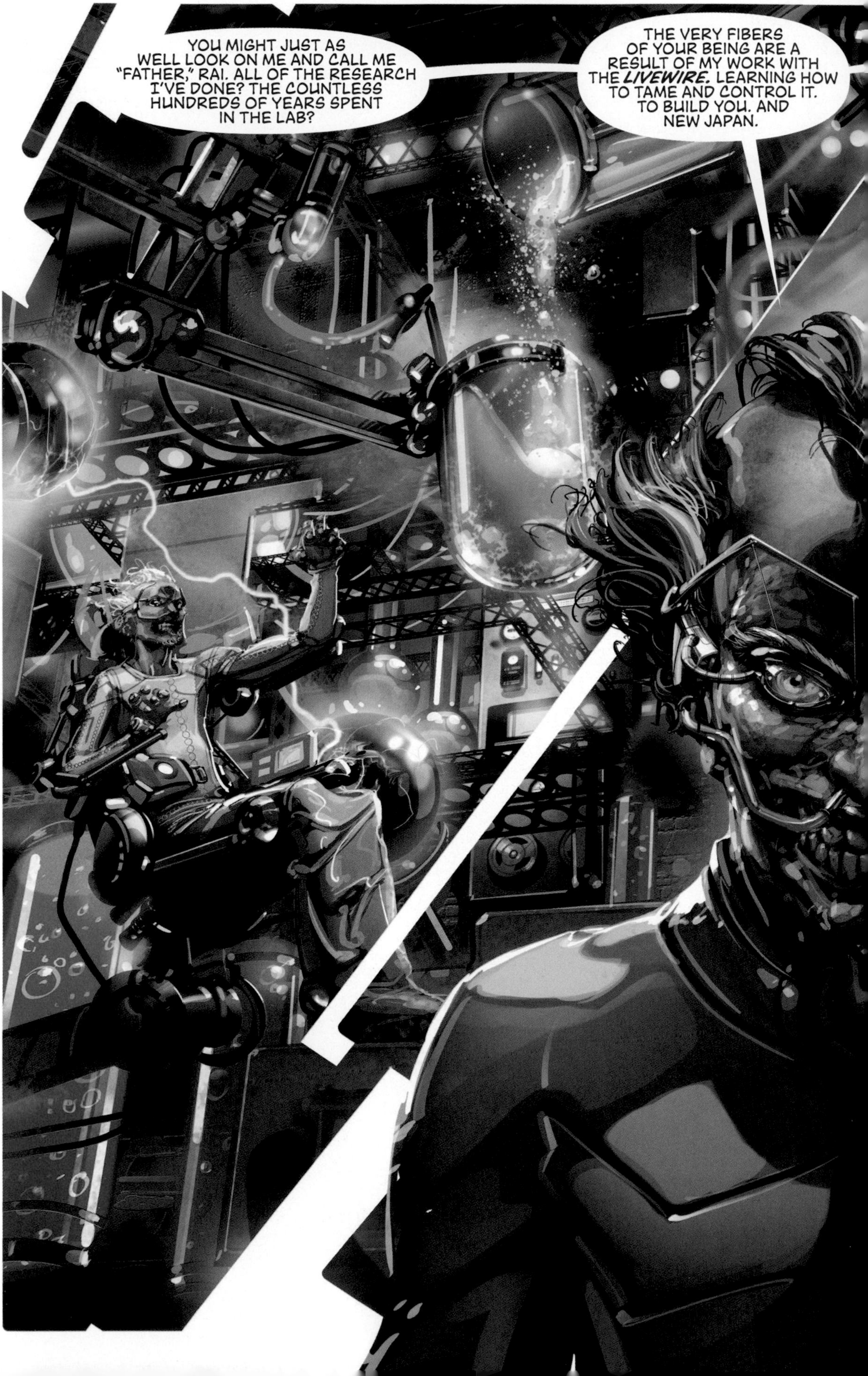
YOU MIGHT JUST AS WELL LOOK ON ME AND CALL ME "FATHER," RAI. ALL OF THE RESEARCH I'VE DONE? THE COUNTLESS HUNDREDS OF YEARS SPENT IN THE LAB?
THE VERY FIBERS OF YOUR BEING ARE A RESULT OF MY WORK WITH THE *LIVEWIRE.* LEARNING HOW TO TAME AND CONTROL IT. TO BUILD YOU. AND NEW JAPAN.

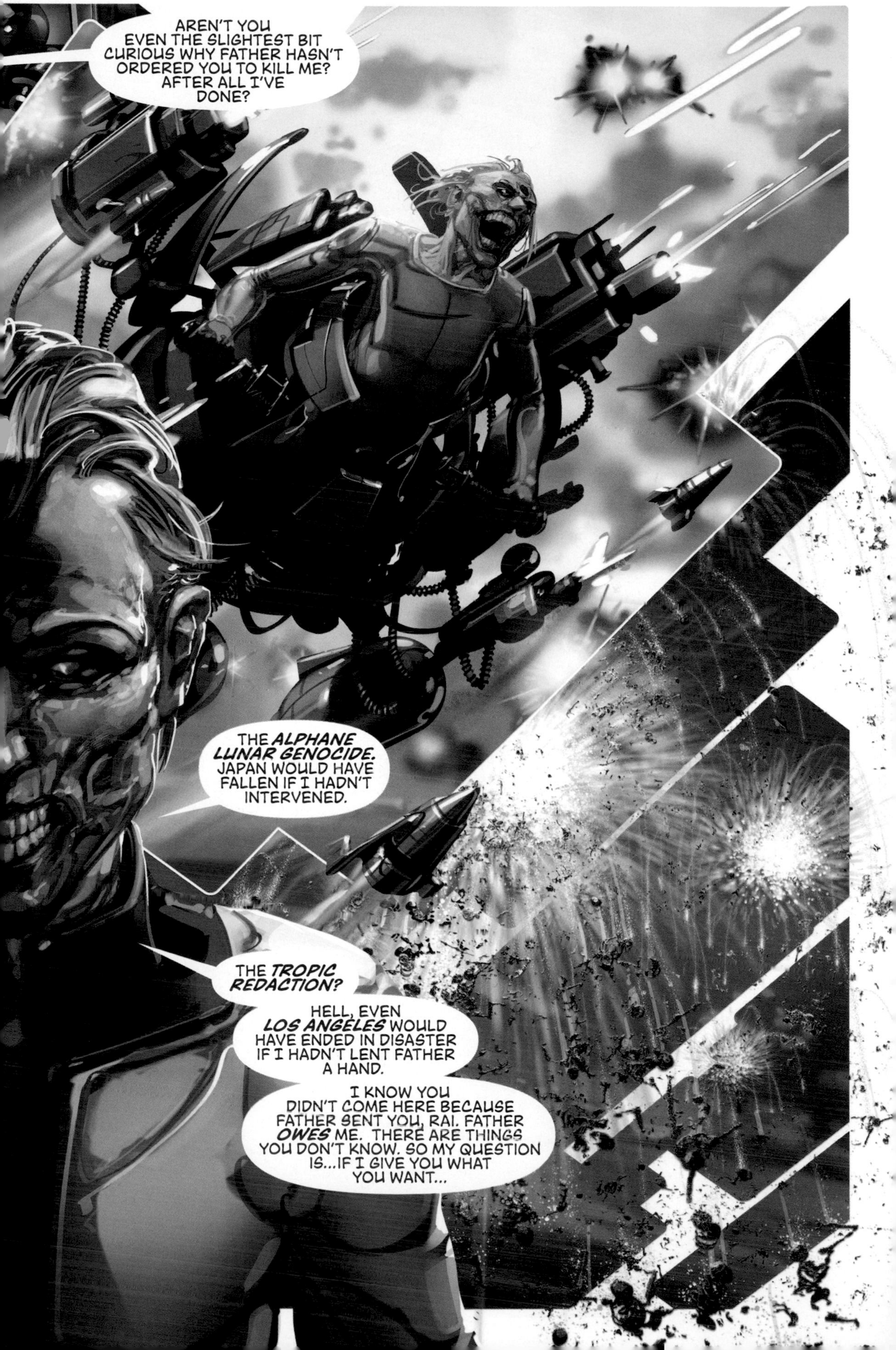
AREN'T YOU EVEN THE SLIGHTEST BIT CURIOUS WHY FATHER HASN'T ORDERED YOU TO KILL ME? AFTER ALL I'VE DONE?
THE ALPHANE LUNAR GENOCIDE. JAPAN WOULD HAVE FALLEN IF I HADN'T INTERVENED.
THE TROPIC REDACTION?
HELL, EVEN LOS ANGELES WOULD HAVE ENDED IN DISASTER IF I HADN'T LENT FATHER A HAND.
I KNOW YOU DIDN'T COME HERE BECAUSE FATHER SENT YOU, RAI. FATHER OWES ME. THERE ARE THINGS YOU DON'T KNOW. SO MY QUESTION IS...IF I GIVE YOU WHAT YOU WANT...

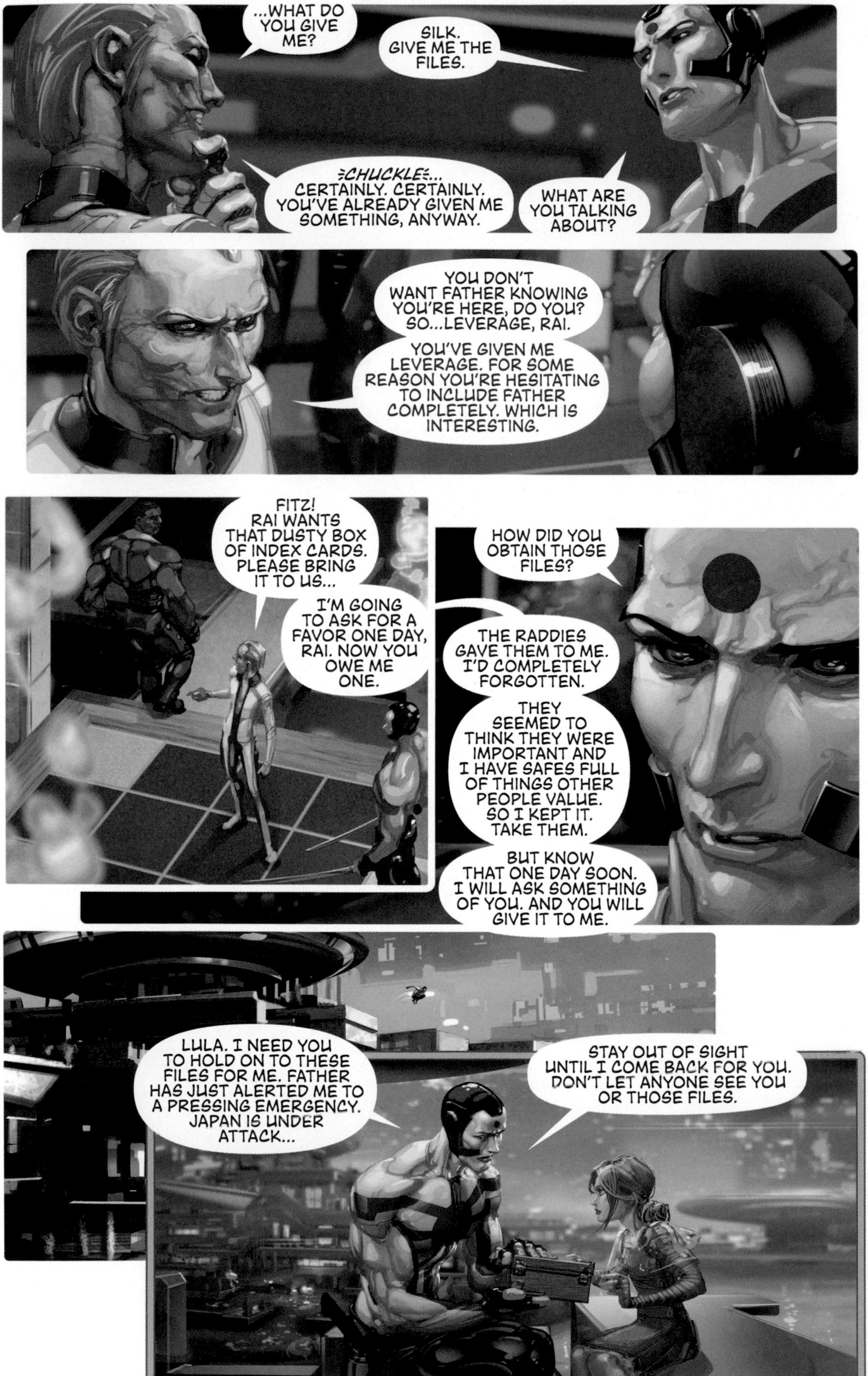
...WHAT DO YOU GIVE ME?
SILK. GIVE ME THE FILES.
CHUCKLE... CERTAINLY. CERTAINLY. YOU'VE ALREADY GIVEN ME SOMETHING, ANYWAY.
WHAT ARE YOU TALKING ABOUT?
YOU DON'T WANT FATHER KNOWING YOU'RE HERE, DO YOU? SO...LEVERAGE, RAI.
YOU'VE GIVEN ME LEVERAGE. FOR SOME REASON YOU'RE HESITATING TO INCLUDE FATHER COMPLETELY. WHICH IS INTERESTING.
FITZ! RAI WANTS THAT DUSTY BOX OF INDEX CARDS. PLEASE BRING IT TO US...
I'M GOING TO ASK FOR A FAVOR ONE DAY, RAI. NOW YOU OWE ME ONE.
HOW DID YOU OBTAIN THOSE FILES?
THE RADDIES GAVE THEM TO ME. I'D COMPLETELY FORGOTTEN.
THEY SEEMED TO THINK THEY WERE IMPORTANT AND I HAVE SAFES FULL OF THINGS OTHER PEOPLE VALUE. SO I KEPT IT. TAKE THEM.
BUT KNOW THAT ONE DAY SOON. I WILL ASK SOMETHING OF YOU. AND YOU WILL GIVE IT TO ME.
LULA. I NEED YOU TO HOLD ON TO THESE FILES FOR ME. FATHER HAS JUST ALERTED ME TO A PRESSING EMERGENCY. JAPAN IS UNDER ATTACK...
STAY OUT OF SIGHT UNTIL I COME BACK FOR YOU. DON'T LET ANYONE SEE YOU OR THOSE FILES.

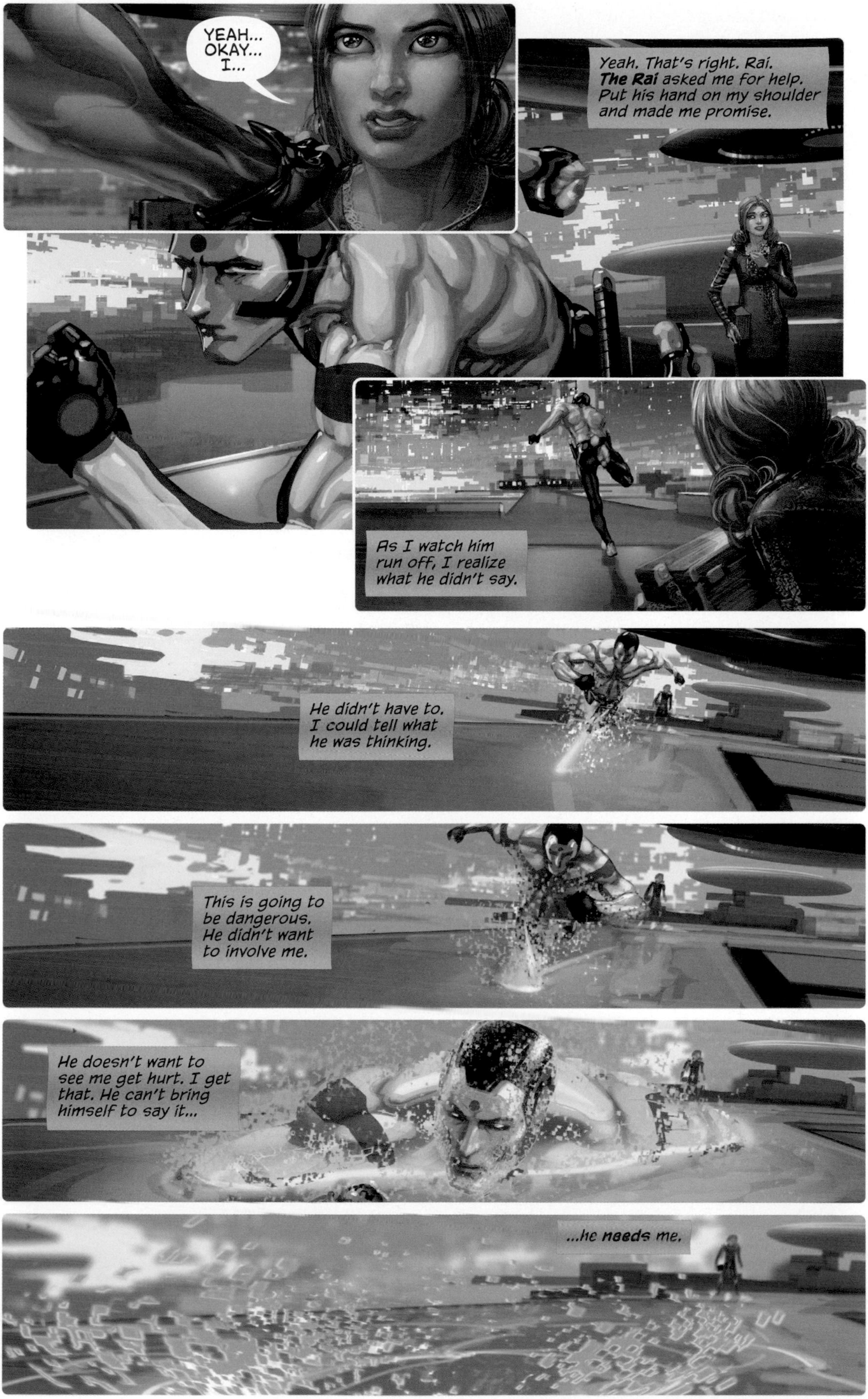
YEAH... OKAY... I...
Yeah. That's right. Rai. **The Rai** asked me for help. Put his hand on my shoulder and made me promise.
As I watch him run off, I realize what he didn't say.
He didn't have to. I could tell what he was thinking.
This is going to be dangerous. He didn't want to involve me.
He doesn't want to see me get hurt. I get that. He can't bring himself to say it...
...he **needs** me.

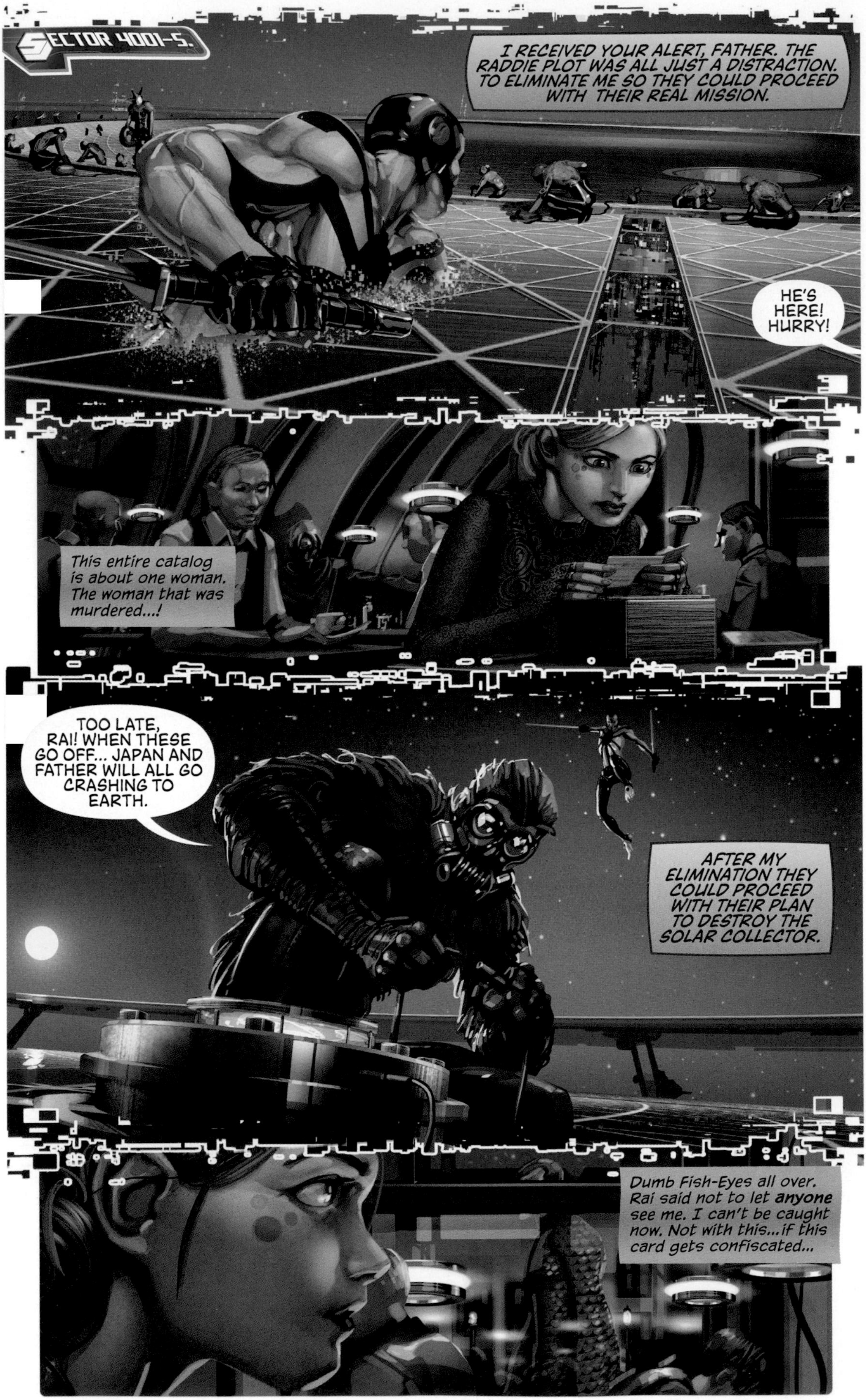
SECTOR 4001-S.
I RECEIVED YOUR ALERT, FATHER. THE RADDIE PLOT WAS ALL JUST A DISTRACTION. TO ELIMINATE ME SO THEY COULD PROCEED WITH THEIR REAL MISSION.
HE'S HERE! HURRY!
This entire catalog is about one woman. The woman that was murdered...!
TOO LATE, RAI! WHEN THESE GO OFF... JAPAN AND FATHER WILL ALL GO CRASHING TO EARTH.
AFTER MY ELIMINATION THEY COULD PROCEED WITH THEIR PLAN TO DESTROY THE SOLAR COLLECTOR.
Dumb Fish-Eyes all over. Rai said not to let anyone see me. I can't be caught now. Not with this...if this card gets confiscated...

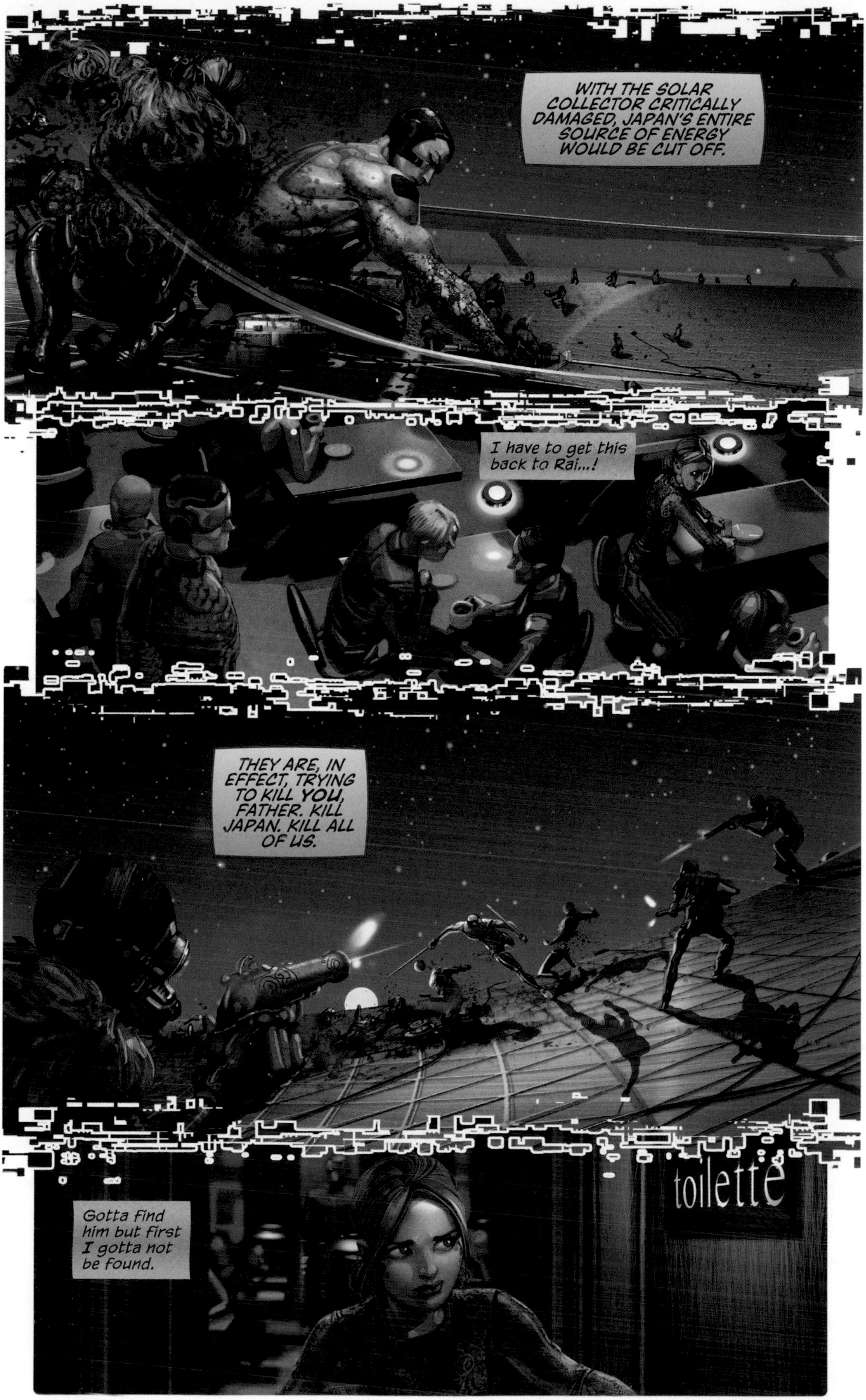
WITH THE SOLAR COLLECTOR CRITICALLY DAMAGED, JAPAN'S ENTIRE SOURCE OF ENERGY WOULD BE CUT OFF.
I have to get this back to Rai...!
THEY ARE, IN EFFECT, TRYING TO KILL YOU, FATHER. KILL JAPAN. KILL ALL OF US.
toilette
Gotta find him but first I gotta not be found.

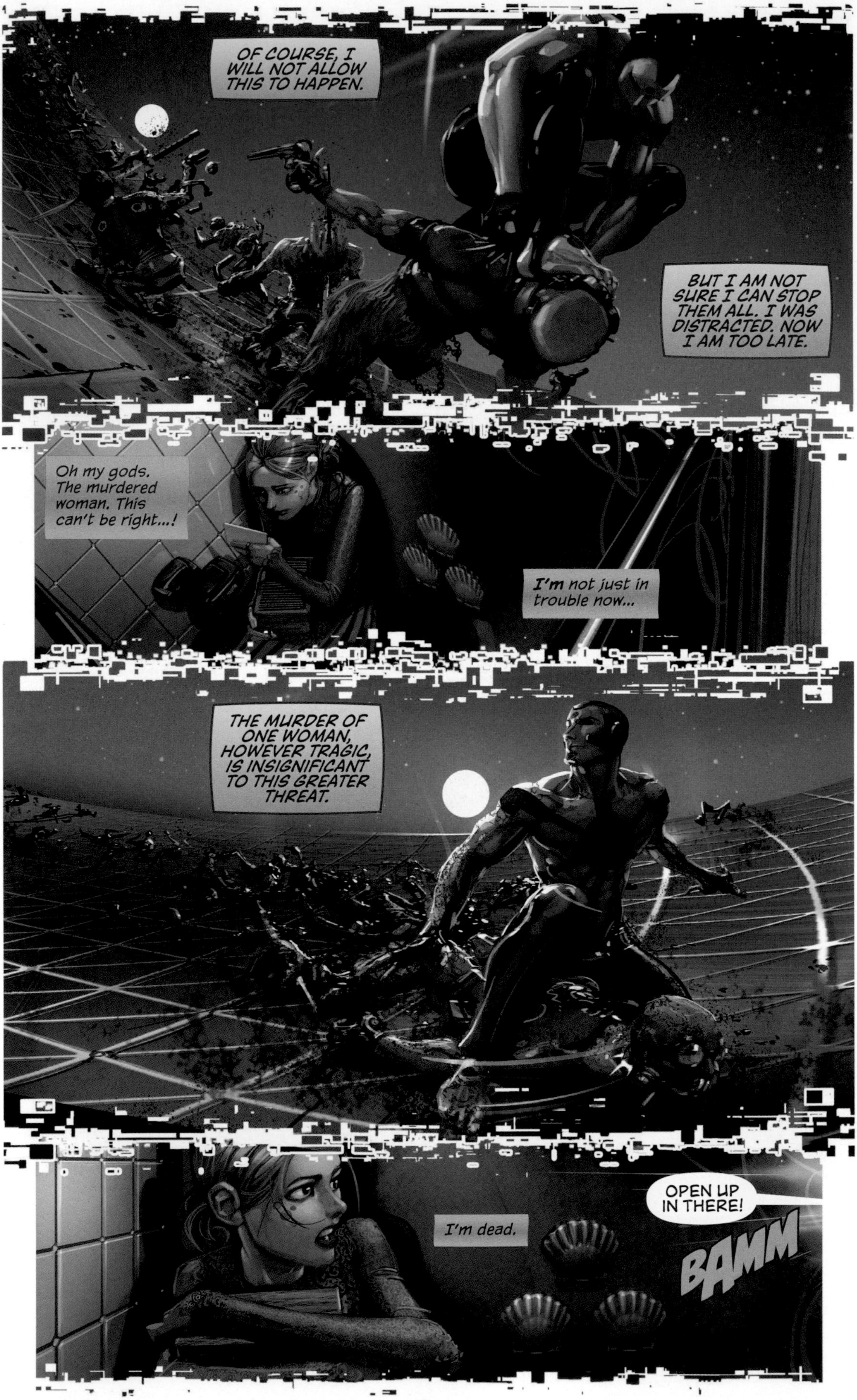
OF COURSE, I WILL NOT ALLOW THIS TO HAPPEN.
BUT I AM NOT SURE I CAN STOP THEM ALL. I WAS DISTRACTED. NOW I AM TOO LATE.
Oh my gods. The murdered woman. This can't be right...!
I'm not just in trouble now...
THE MURDER OF ONE WOMAN, HOWEVER TRAGIC, IS INSIGNIFICANT TO THIS GREATER THREAT.
I'm dead.
OPEN UP IN THERE!
BAMM

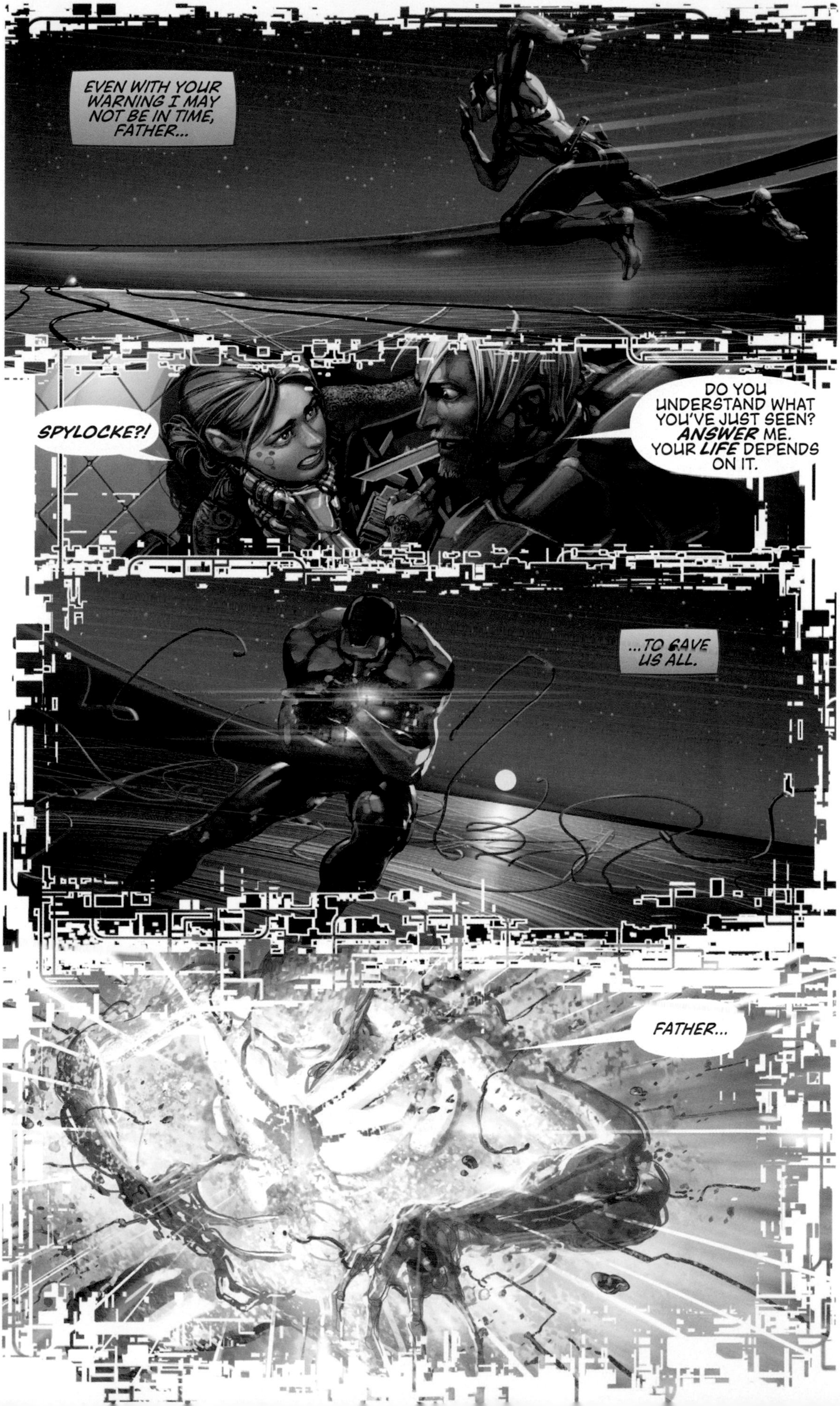
EVEN WITH YOUR WARNING I MAY NOT BE IN TIME, FATHER...
SPYLOCKE?!
DO YOU UNDERSTAND WHAT YOU'VE JUST SEEN? ANSWER ME. YOUR LIFE DEPENDS ON IT.
...TO SAVE US ALL.
FATHER...

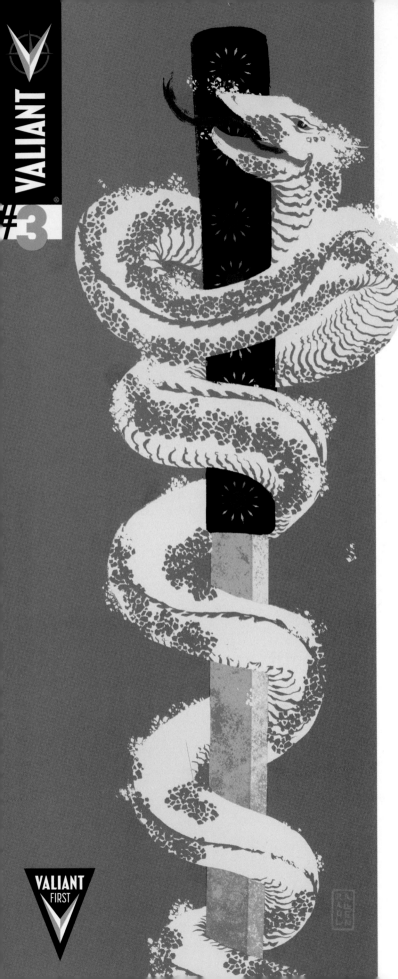

RAI

41st CENTURY REVOLUTION!

MATT KINDT
CLAYTON CRAIN

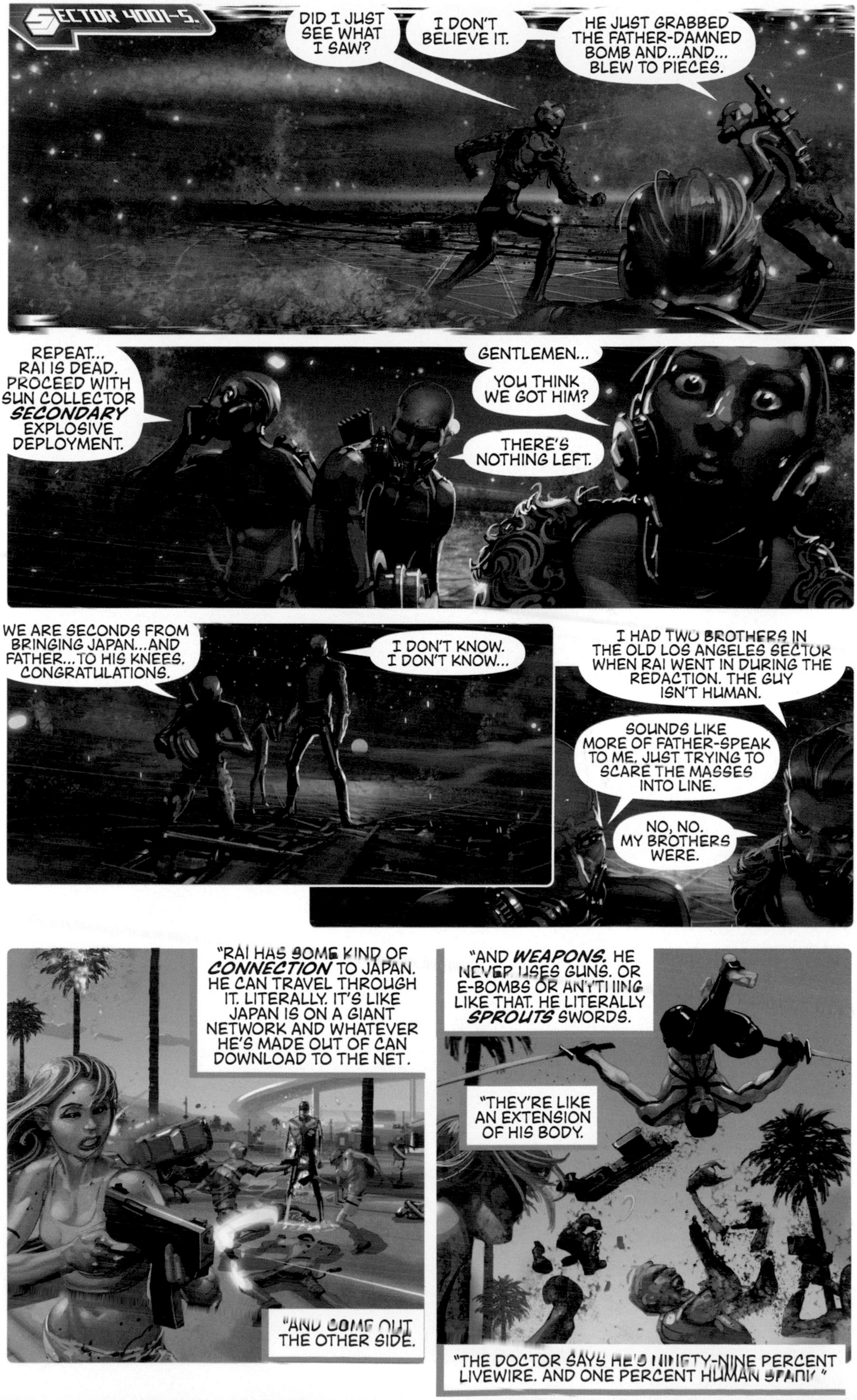
SECTOR 4001-S.
DID I JUST SEE WHAT I SAW?
I DON'T BELIEVE IT.
HE JUST GRABBED THE FATHER-DAMNED BOMB AND...AND... BLEW TO PIECES.
REPEAT... RAI IS DEAD. PROCEED WITH SUN COLLECTOR SECONDARY EXPLOSIVE DEPLOYMENT.
GENTLEMEN...
YOU THINK WE GOT HIM?
THERE'S NOTHING LEFT.
WE ARE SECONDS FROM BRINGING JAPAN...AND FATHER...TO HIS KNEES. CONGRATULATIONS.
I DON'T KNOW. I DON'T KNOW...
I HAD TWO BROTHERS IN THE OLD LOS ANGELES SECTOR WHEN RAI WENT IN DURING THE REDACTION. THE GUY ISN'T HUMAN.
SOUNDS LIKE MORE OF FATHER-SPEAK TO ME. JUST TRYING TO SCARE THE MASSES INTO LINE.
NO, NO. MY BROTHERS WERE.
"RAI HAS SOME KIND OF CONNECTION TO JAPAN. HE CAN TRAVEL THROUGH IT. LITERALLY. IT'S LIKE JAPAN IS ON A GIANT NETWORK AND WHATEVER HE'S MADE OUT OF CAN DOWNLOAD TO THE NET.
"AND COME OUT THE OTHER SIDE.
"AND WEAPONS. HE NEVER USES GUNS. OR E-BOMBS OR ANYTHING LIKE THAT. HE LITERALLY SPROUTS SWORDS.
"THEY'RE LIKE AN EXTENSION OF HIS BODY.
"THE DOCTOR SAYS HE'S NINETY-NINE PERCENT LIVEWIRE. AND ONE PERCENT HUMAN SPARK."

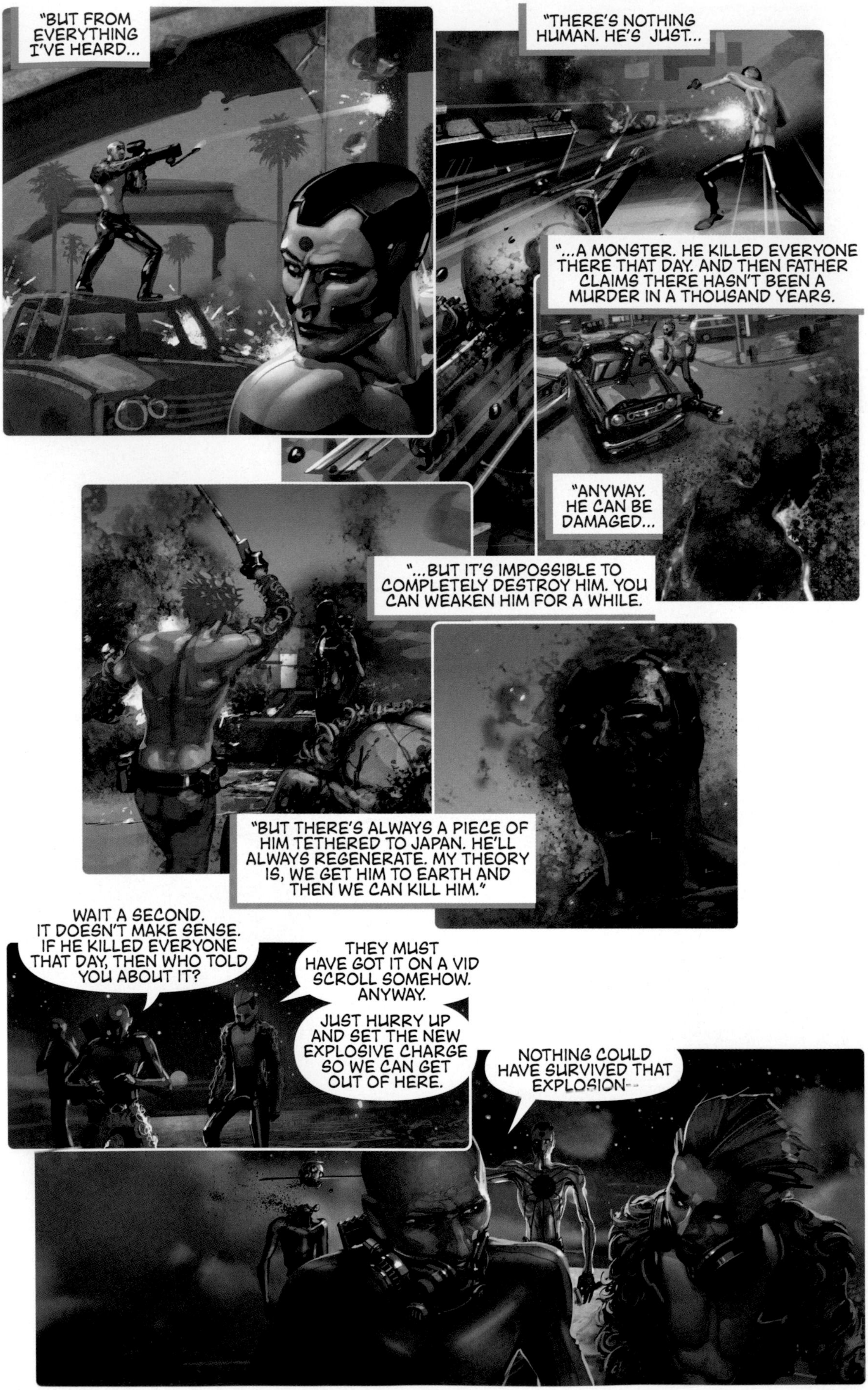
"BUT FROM EVERYTHING I'VE HEARD...
"THERE'S NOTHING HUMAN. HE'S JUST...
"...A MONSTER. HE KILLED EVERYONE THERE THAT DAY. AND THEN FATHER CLAIMS THERE HASN'T BEEN A MURDER IN A THOUSAND YEARS.
"ANYWAY. HE CAN BE DAMAGED...
"...BUT IT'S IMPOSSIBLE TO COMPLETELY DESTROY HIM. YOU CAN WEAKEN HIM FOR A WHILE.
"BUT THERE'S ALWAYS A PIECE OF HIM TETHERED TO JAPAN. HE'LL ALWAYS REGENERATE. MY THEORY IS, WE GET HIM TO EARTH AND THEN WE CAN KILL HIM."
WAIT A SECOND. IT DOESN'T MAKE SENSE. IF HE KILLED EVERYONE THAT DAY, THEN WHO TOLD YOU ABOUT IT?
THEY MUST HAVE GOT IT ON A VID SCROLL SOMEHOW. ANYWAY.
JUST HURRY UP AND SET THE NEW EXPLOSIVE CHARGE SO WE CAN GET OUT OF HERE.
NOTHING COULD HAVE SURVIVED THAT EXPLOSION--

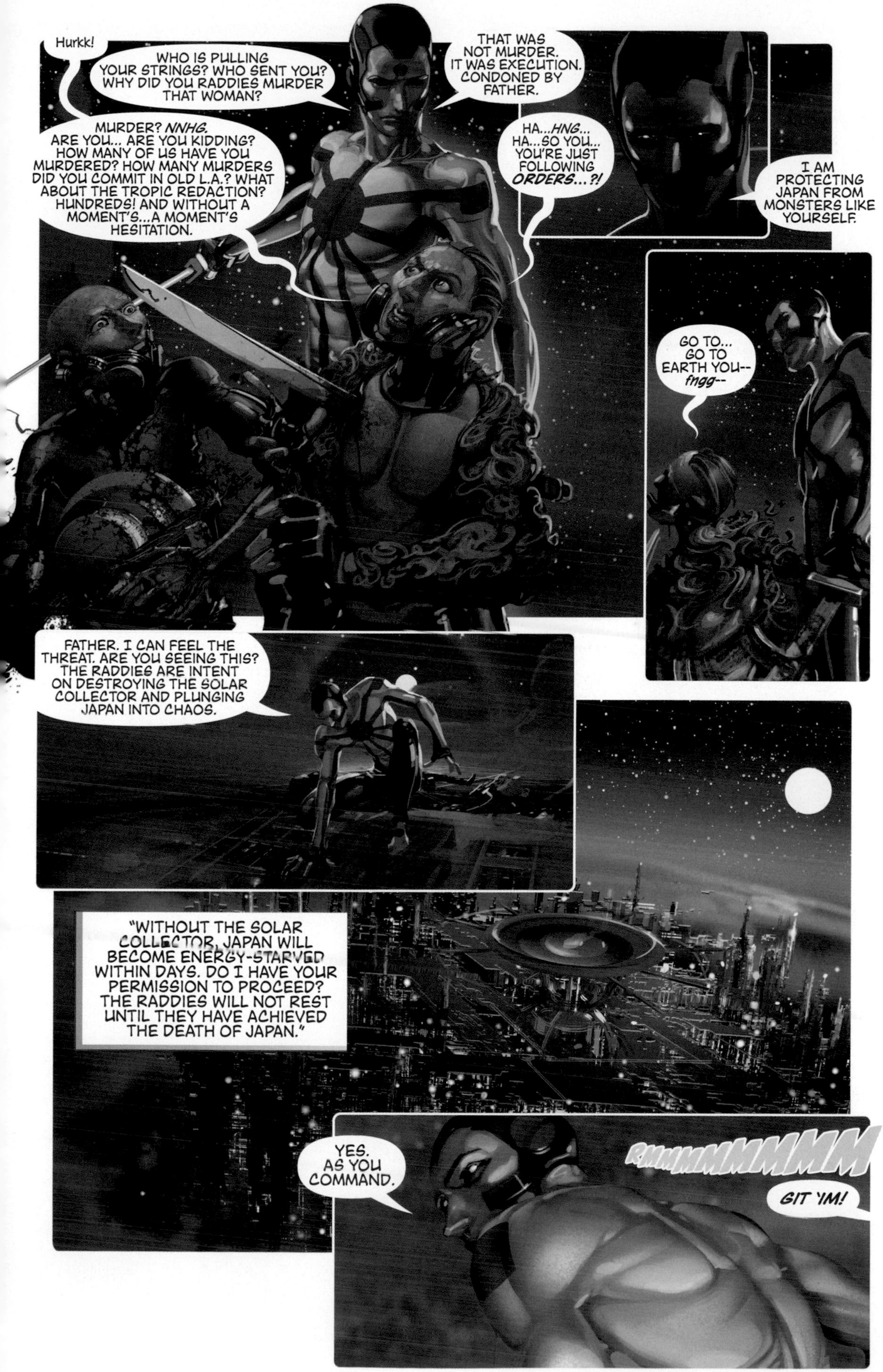
Hurkk!
WHO IS PULLING YOUR STRINGS? WHO SENT YOU? WHY DID YOU RADDIES MURDER THAT WOMAN?
MURDER? NNHG. ARE YOU... ARE YOU KIDDING? HOW MANY OF US HAVE YOU MURDERED? HOW MANY MURDERS DID YOU COMMIT IN OLD L.A.? WHAT ABOUT THE TROPIC REDACTION? HUNDREDS! AND WITHOUT A MOMENT'S...A MOMENT'S HESITATION.
THAT WAS NOT MURDER. IT WAS EXECUTION. CONDONED BY FATHER.
HA...HNG... HA...SO YOU... YOU'RE JUST FOLLOWING ORDERS...?!
I AM PROTECTING JAPAN FROM MONSTERS LIKE YOURSELF.
GO TO... GO TO EARTH YOU-- fngg--
FATHER. I CAN FEEL THE THREAT. ARE YOU SEEING THIS? THE RADDIES ARE INTENT ON DESTROYING THE SOLAR COLLECTOR AND PLUNGING JAPAN INTO CHAOS.
"WITHOUT THE SOLAR COLLECTOR, JAPAN WILL BECOME ENERGY-STARVED WITHIN DAYS. DO I HAVE YOUR PERMISSION TO PROCEED? THE RADDIES WILL NOT REST UNTIL THEY HAVE ACHIEVED THE DEATH OF JAPAN."
YES. AS YOU COMMAND.
RMMMMMMMMMM
GIT 'IM!

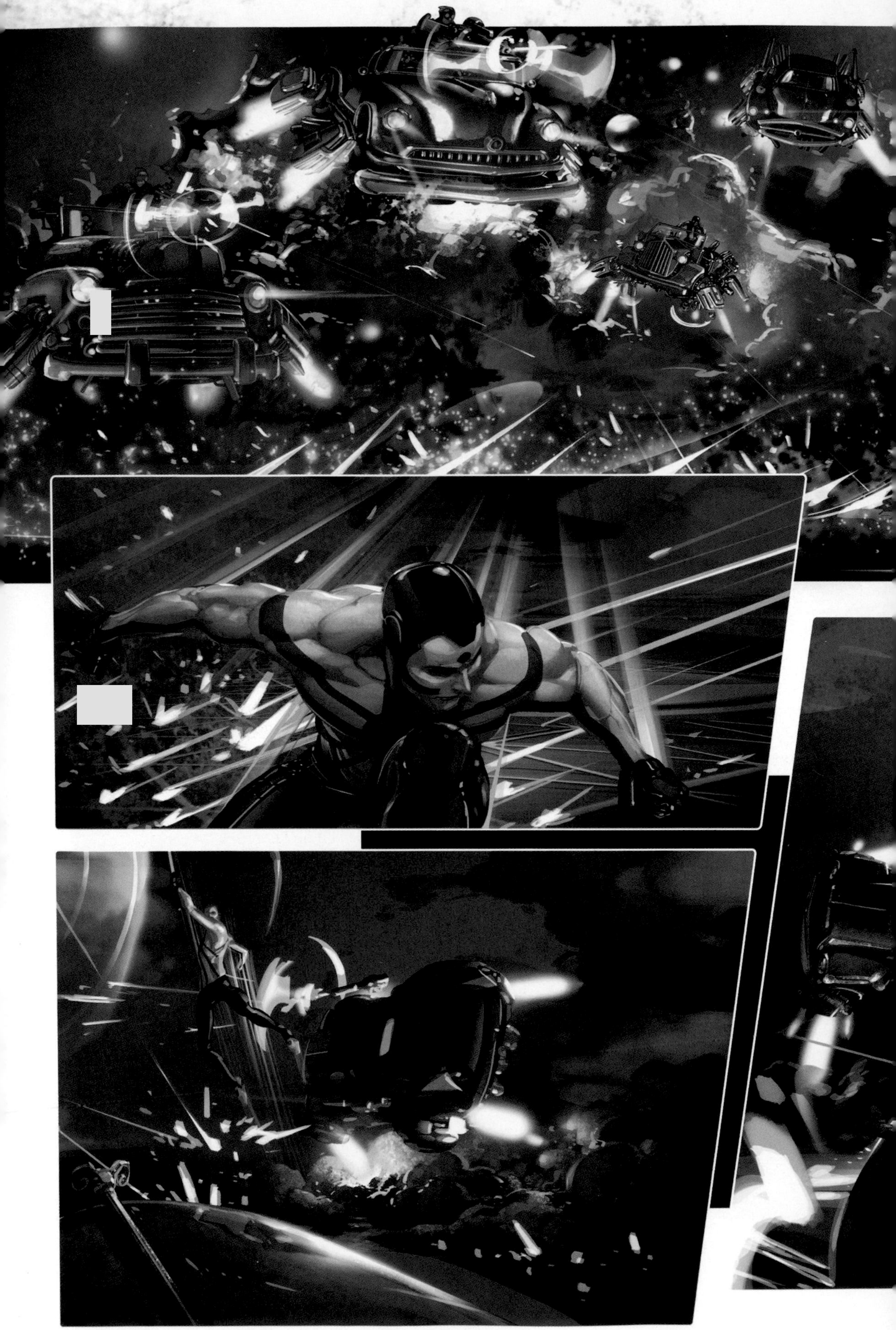

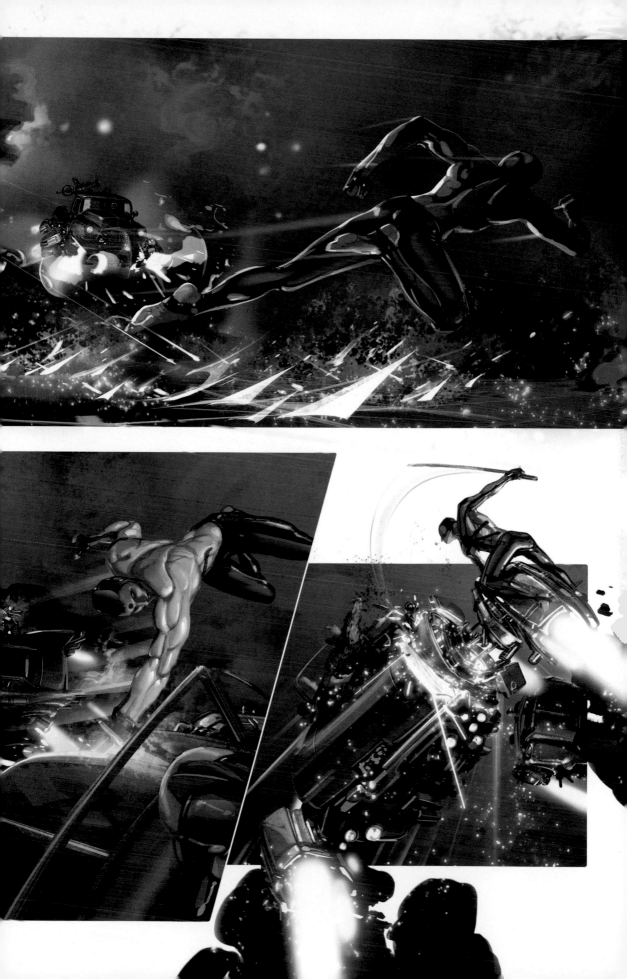

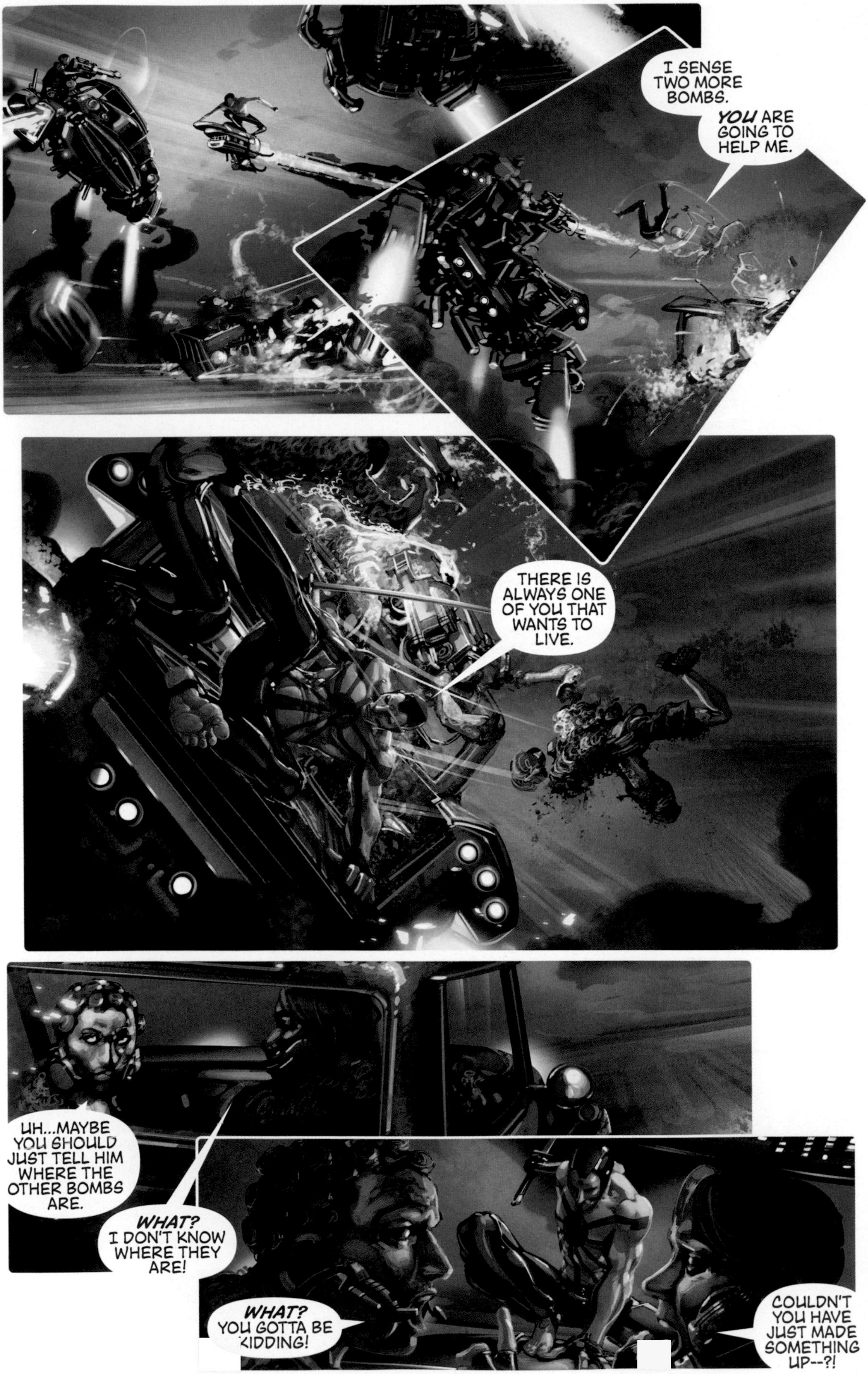
I SENSE TWO MORE BOMBS.
YOU ARE GOING TO HELP ME.
THERE IS ALWAYS ONE OF YOU THAT WANTS TO LIVE.
UH...MAYBE YOU SHOULD JUST TELL HIM WHERE THE OTHER BOMBS ARE.
WHAT? I DON'T KNOW WHERE THEY ARE!
WHAT? YOU GOTTA BE KIDDING!
COULDN'T YOU HAVE JUST MADE SOMETHING UP--?!

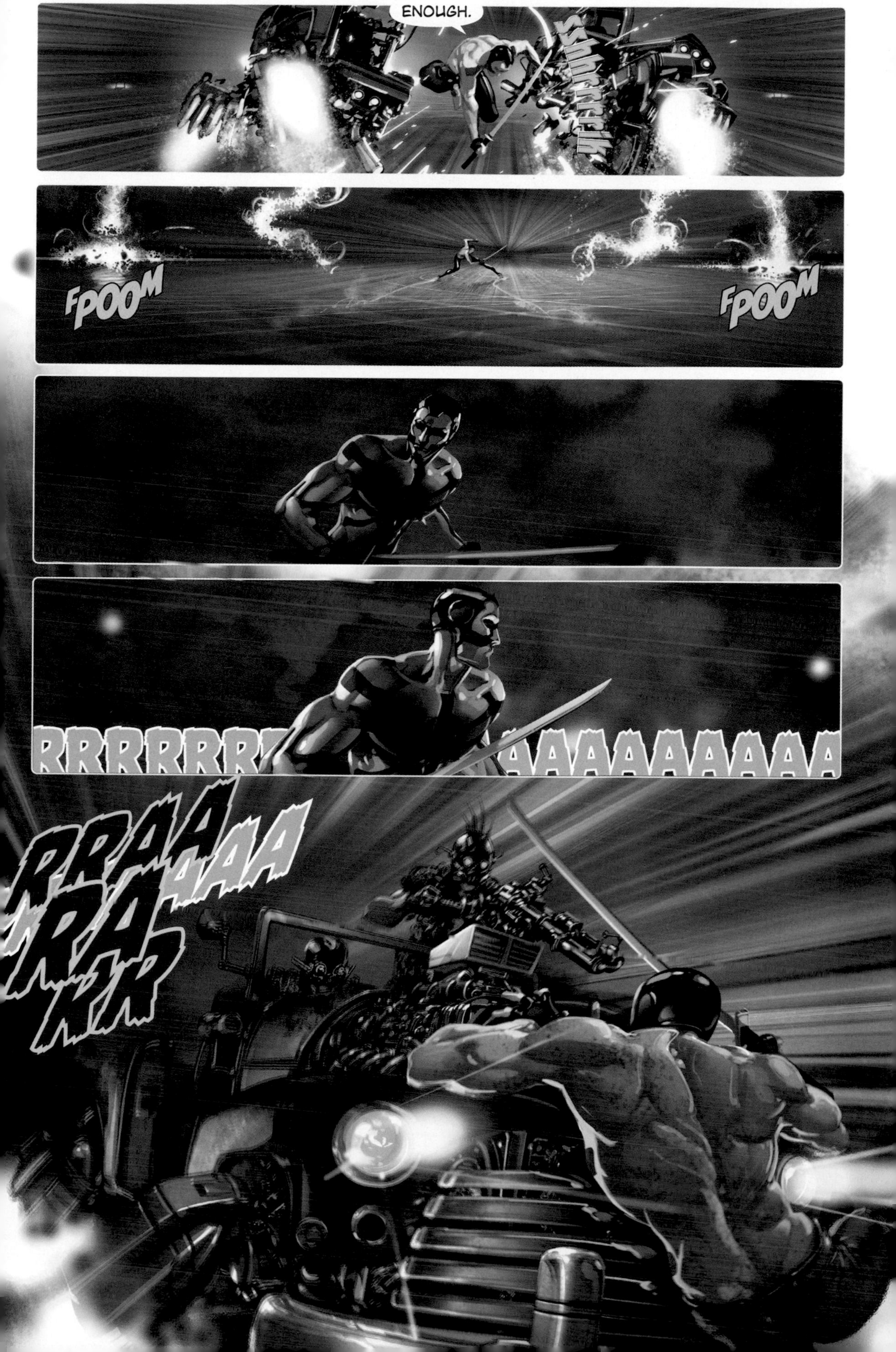
ENOUGH.
SHHRRRK
FPOOM
FPOOM
RRRRRRR
AAAAAAAAAA
RRAAAAAAA
RA
RR

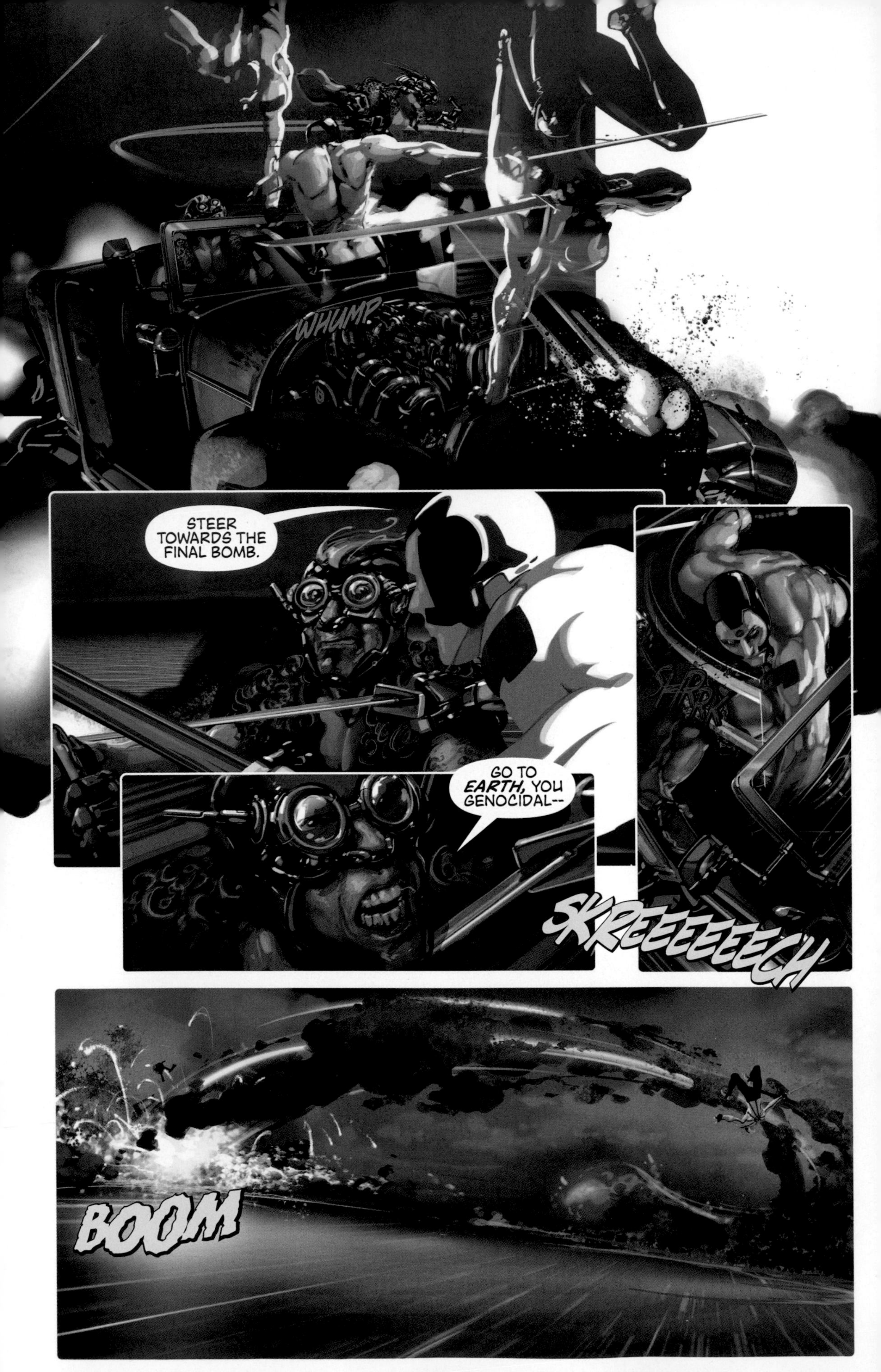
WHUMP
STEER TOWARDS THE FINAL BOMB.
SHRRK
GO TO EARTH, YOU GENOCIDAL--
SKREEEEEEECH
BOOM

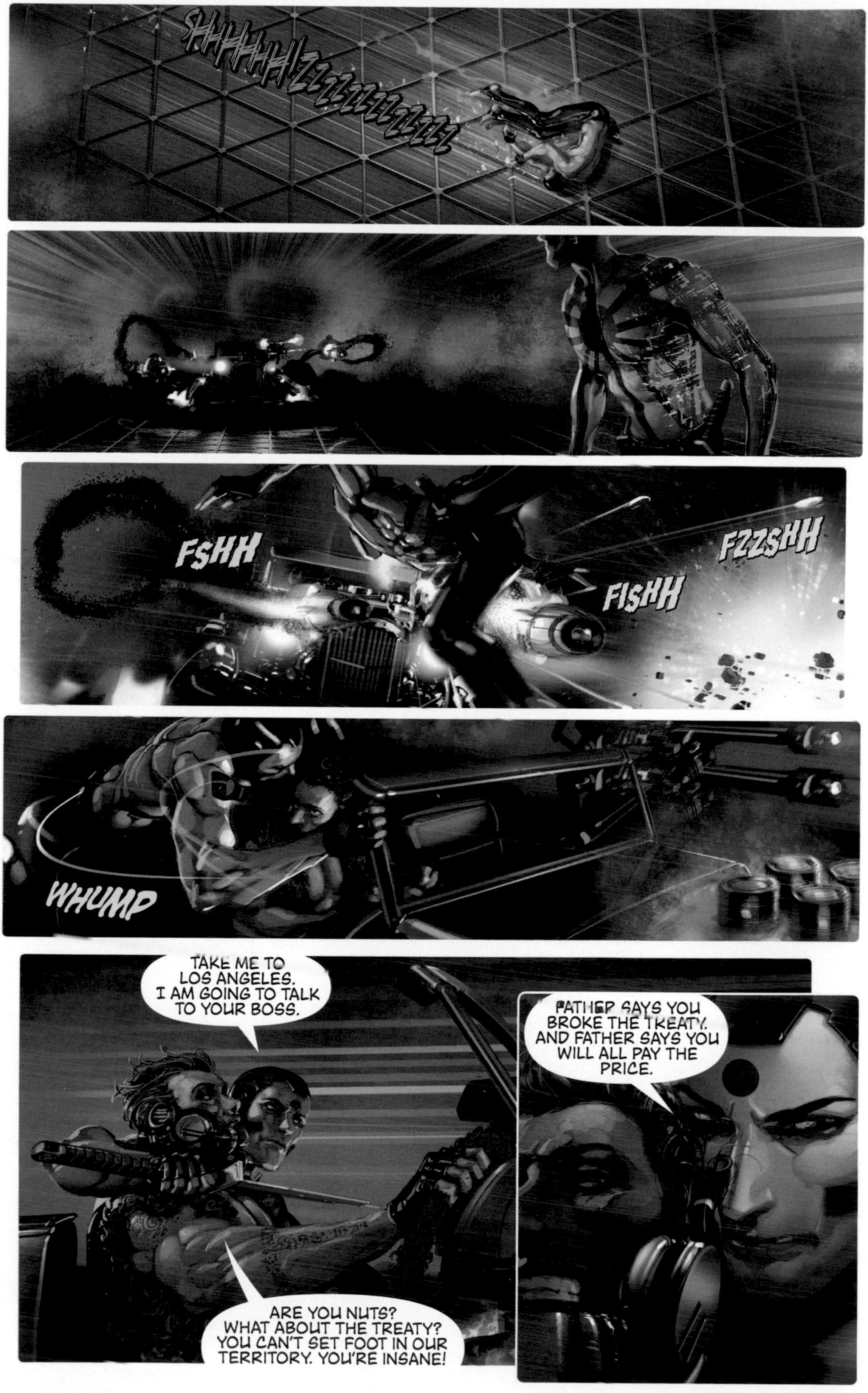
SHHHHHHIZZZZZZZZZZZZ
FSHH
FZZSHH
FISHH
WHUMP
TAKE ME TO LOS ANGELES. I AM GOING TO TALK TO YOUR BOSS.
ARE YOU NUTS? WHAT ABOUT THE TREATY? YOU CAN'T SET FOOT IN OUR TERRITORY. YOU'RE INSANE!
FATHER SAYS YOU BROKE THE TREATY. AND FATHER SAYS YOU WILL ALL PAY THE PRICE.

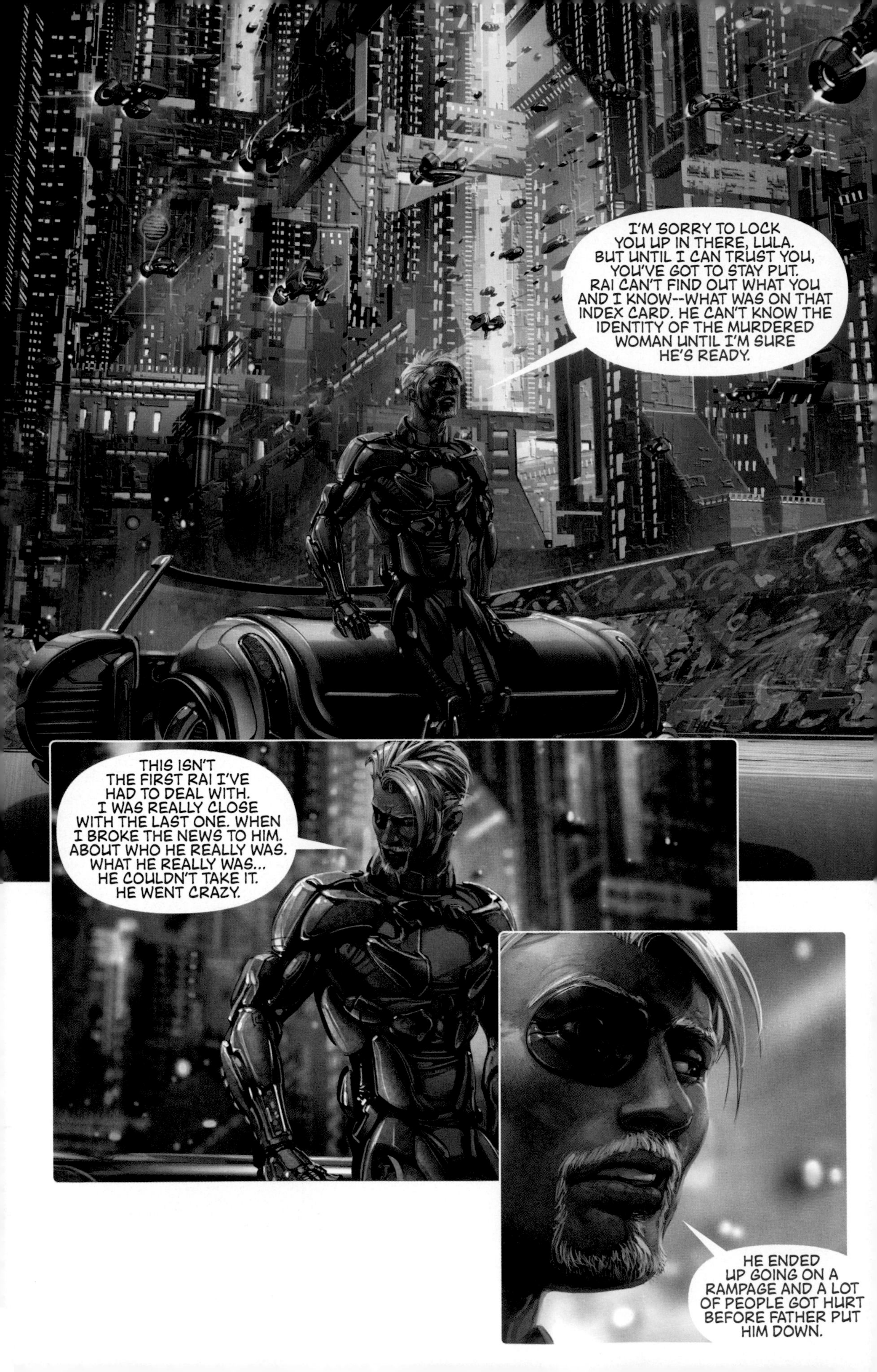
I'M SORRY TO LOCK YOU UP IN THERE, LULA. BUT UNTIL I CAN TRUST YOU, YOU'VE GOT TO STAY PUT. RAI CAN'T FIND OUT WHAT YOU AND I KNOW--WHAT WAS ON THAT INDEX CARD. HE CAN'T KNOW THE IDENTITY OF THE MURDERED WOMAN UNTIL I'M SURE HE'S READY.
THIS ISN'T THE FIRST RAI I'VE HAD TO DEAL WITH. I WAS REALLY CLOSE WITH THE LAST ONE. WHEN I BROKE THE NEWS TO HIM. ABOUT WHO HE REALLY WAS. WHAT HE REALLY WAS... HE COULDN'T TAKE IT. HE WENT CRAZY.
HE ENDED UP GOING ON A RAMPAGE AND A LOT OF PEOPLE GOT HURT BEFORE FATHER PUT HIM DOWN.

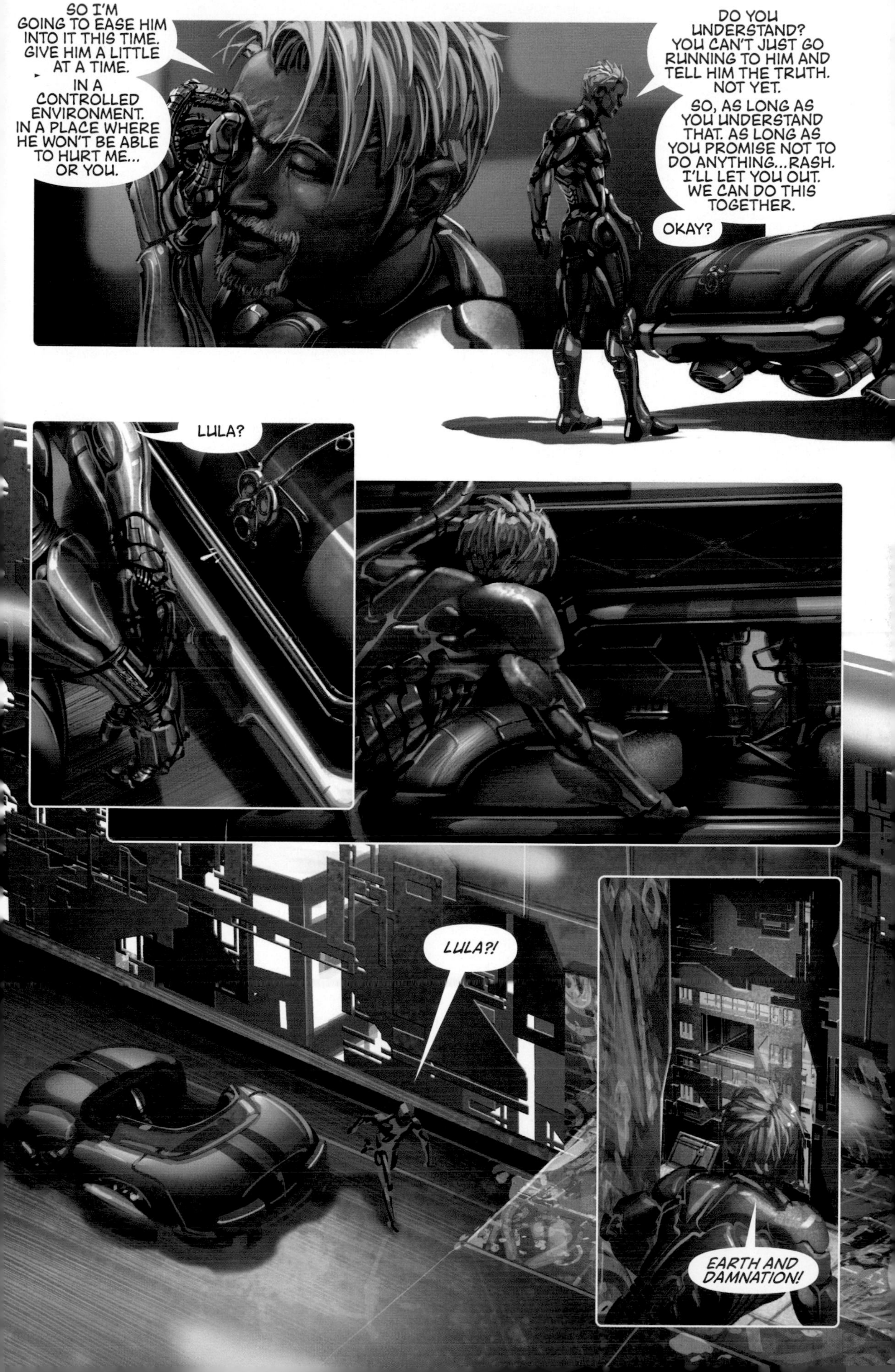
SO I'M GOING TO EASE HIM INTO IT THIS TIME. GIVE HIM A LITTLE AT A TIME.
IN A CONTROLLED ENVIRONMENT. IN A PLACE WHERE HE WON'T BE ABLE TO HURT ME... OR YOU.
DO YOU UNDERSTAND? YOU CAN'T JUST GO RUNNING TO HIM AND TELL HIM THE TRUTH. NOT YET.
SO, AS LONG AS YOU UNDERSTAND THAT. AS LONG AS YOU PROMISE NOT TO DO ANYTHING...RASH. I'LL LET YOU OUT. WE CAN DO THIS TOGETHER.
OKAY?
LULA?
LULA?!
EARTH AND DAMNATION!

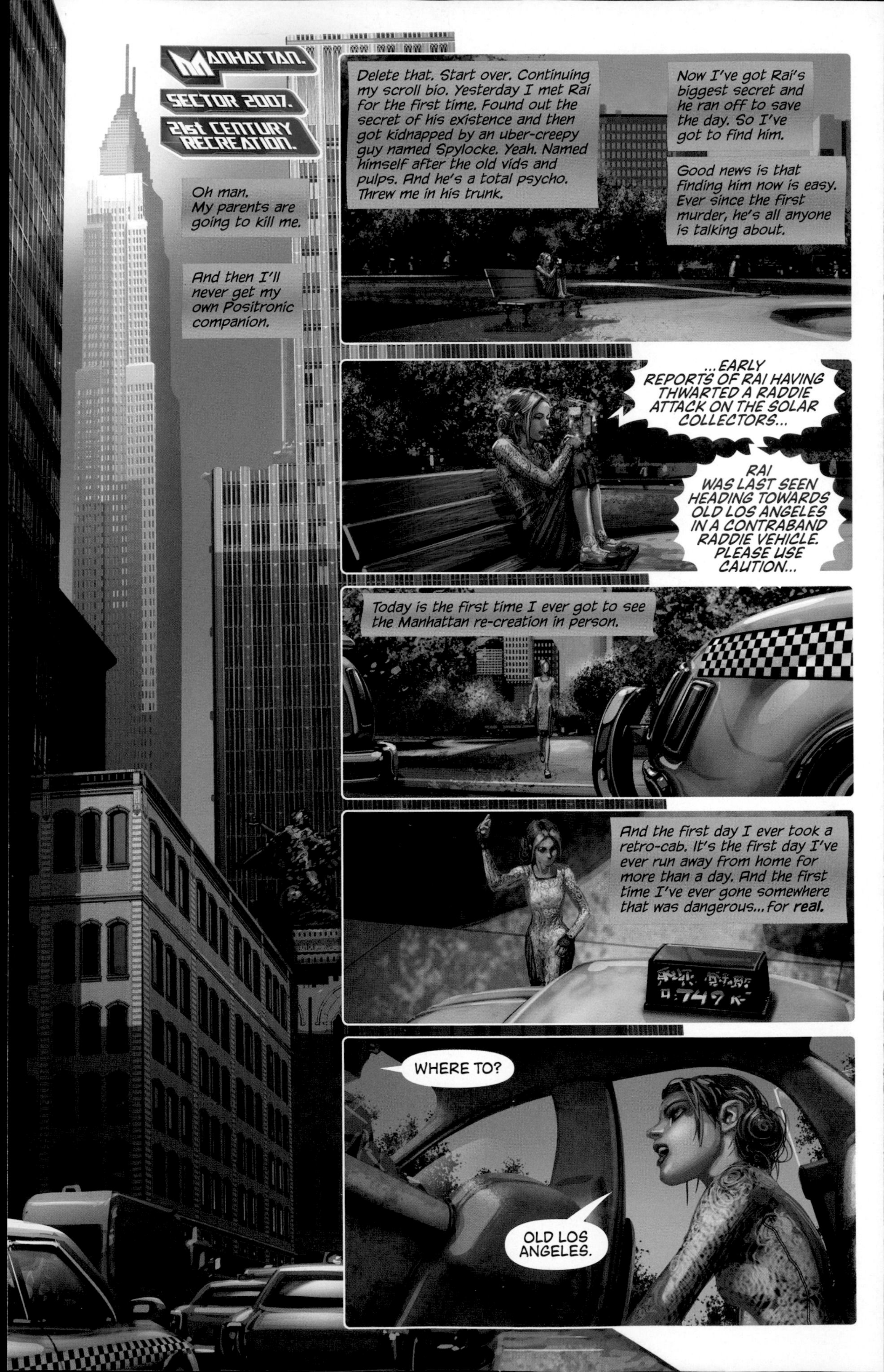
MANHATTAN.
SECTOR 2007.
21st CENTURY RECREATION.
Oh man. My parents are going to kill me.
And then I'll never get my own Positronic companion.
Delete that. Start over. Continuing my scroll bio. Yesterday I met Rai for the first time. Found out the secret of his existence and then got kidnapped by an uber-creepy guy named Spylocke. Yeah. Named himself after the old vids and pulps. And he's a total psycho. Threw me in his trunk.
Now I've got Rai's biggest secret and he ran off to save the day. So I've got to find him.
Good news is that finding him now is easy. Ever since the first murder, he's all anyone is talking about.
...EARLY REPORTS OF RAI HAVING THWARTED A RADDIE ATTACK ON THE SOLAR COLLECTORS...
RAI WAS LAST SEEN HEADING TOWARDS OLD LOS ANGELES IN A CONTRABAND RADDIE VEHICLE. PLEASE USE CAUTION...
Today is the first time I ever got to see the Manhattan re-creation in person.
And the first day I ever took a retro-cab. It's the first day I've ever run away from home for more than a day. And the first time I've ever gone somewhere that was dangerous...for **real.**
WHERE TO?
OLD LOS ANGELES.

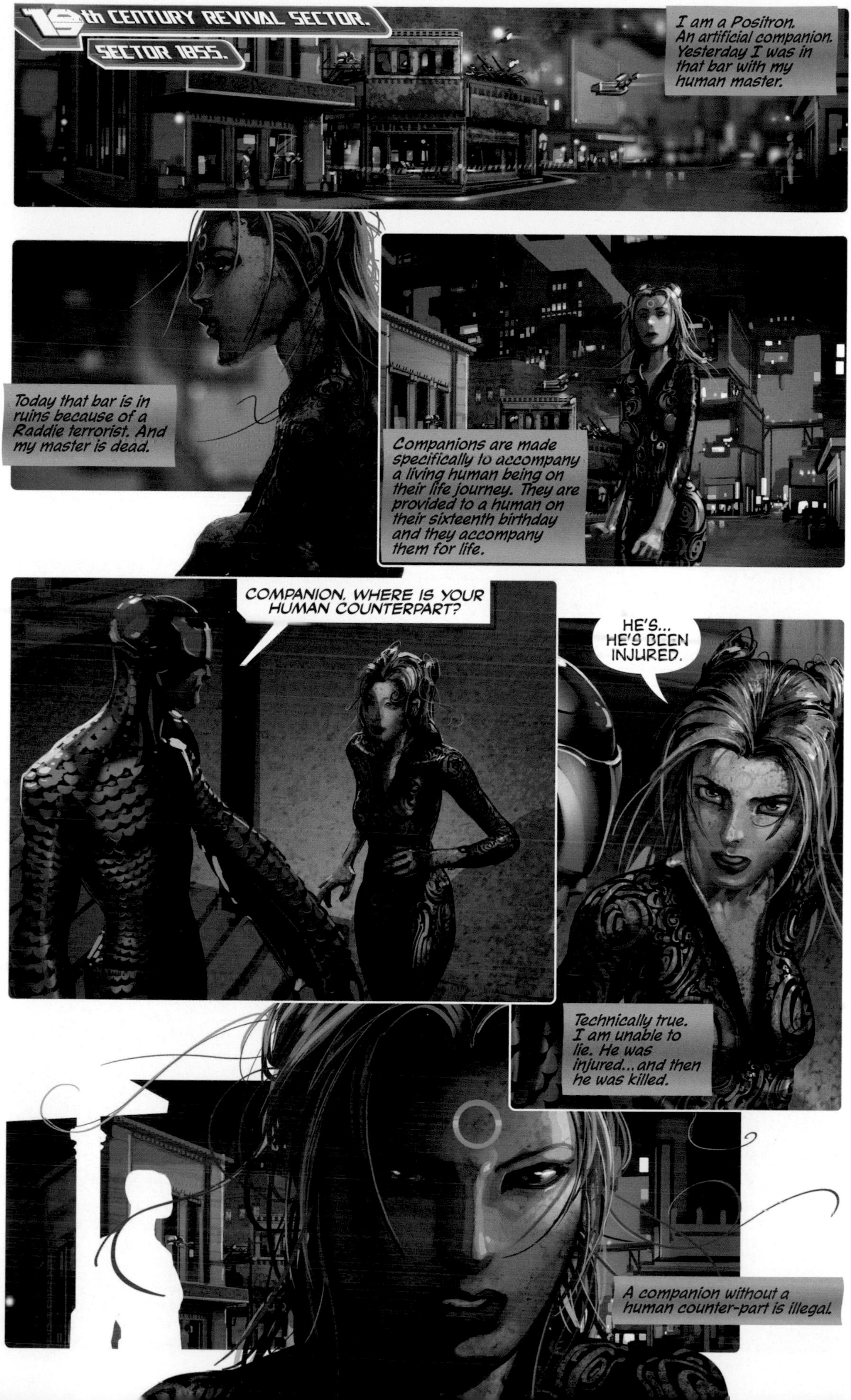
19th CENTURY REVIVAL SECTOR.
SECTOR 1855.
I am a Positron. An artificial companion. Yesterday I was in that bar with my human master.
Today that bar is in ruins because of a Raddie terrorist. And my master is dead.
Companions are made specifically to accompany a living human being on their life journey. They are provided to a human on their sixteenth birthday and they accompany them for life.
COMPANION. WHERE IS YOUR HUMAN COUNTERPART?
HE'S... HE'S BEEN INJURED.
Technically true. I am unable to lie. He was injured...and then he was killed.
A companion without a human counter-part is illegal.

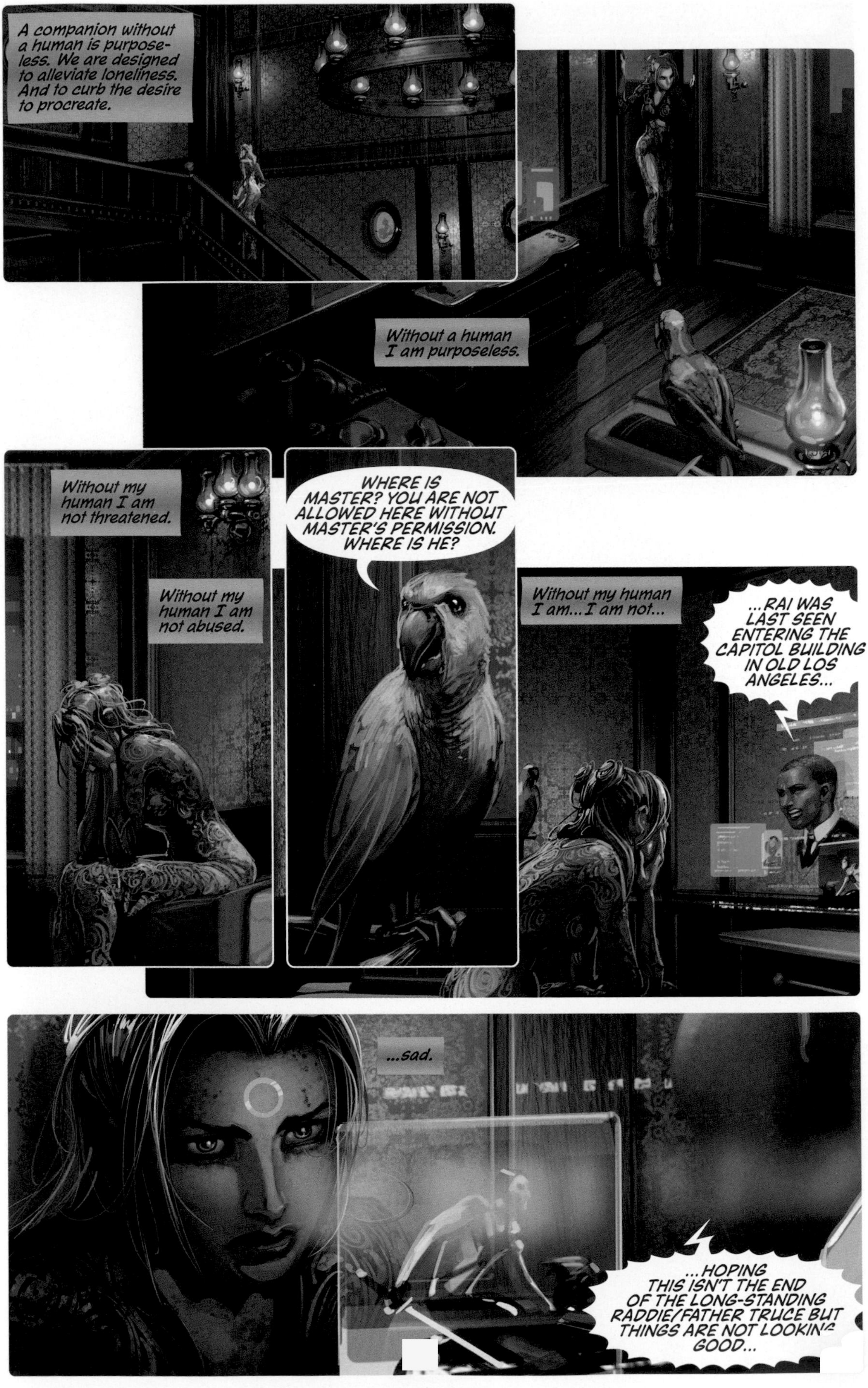
A companion without a human is purposeless. We are designed to alleviate loneliness. And to curb the desire to procreate.
Without a human I am purposeless.
Without my human I am not threatened.
Without my human I am not abused.
WHERE IS MASTER? YOU ARE NOT ALLOWED HERE WITHOUT MASTER'S PERMISSION. WHERE IS HE?
Without my human I am...I am not...
...RAI WAS LAST SEEN ENTERING THE CAPITOL BUILDING IN OLD LOS ANGELES...
...sad.
...HOPING THIS ISN'T THE END OF THE LONG-STANDING RADDIE/FATHER TRUCE BUT THINGS ARE NOT LOOKING GOOD...

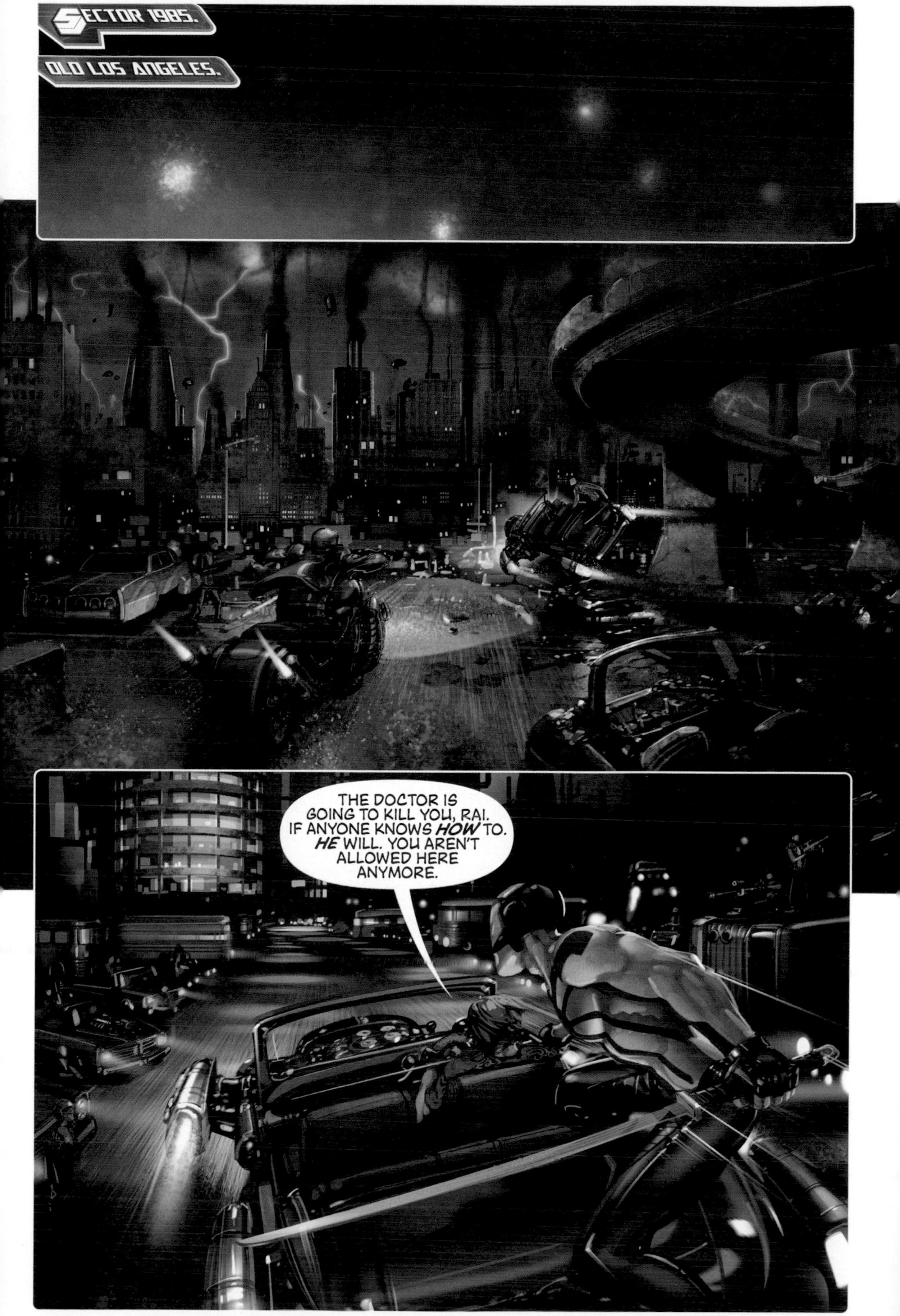
SECTOR 1985.
OLD LOS ANGELES.
THE DOCTOR IS GOING TO KILL YOU, RAI. IF ANYONE KNOWS HOW TO. HE WILL. YOU AREN'T ALLOWED HERE ANYMORE.

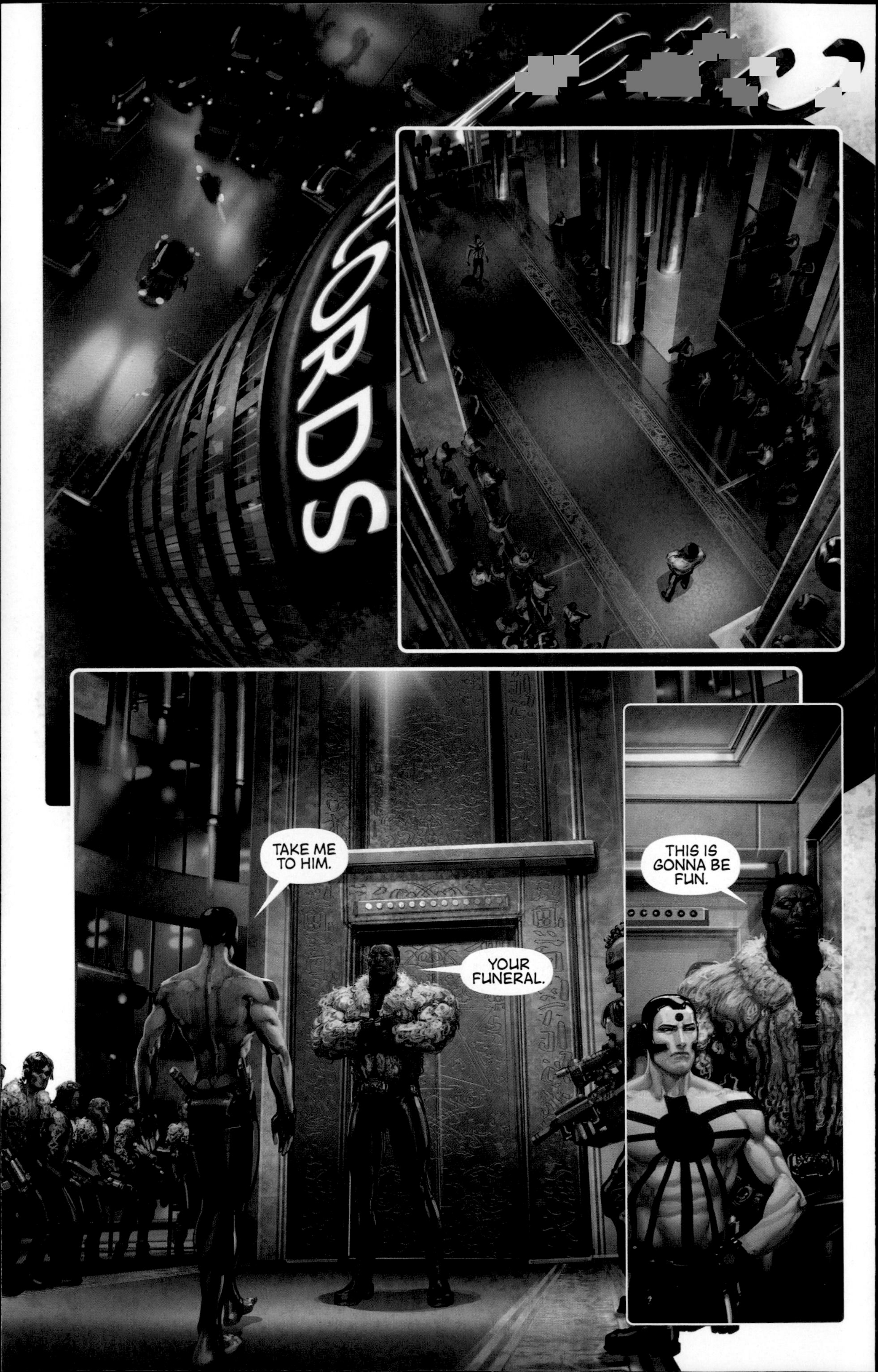

TAKE ME TO HIM.
YOUR FUNERAL.
THIS IS GONNA BE FUN.

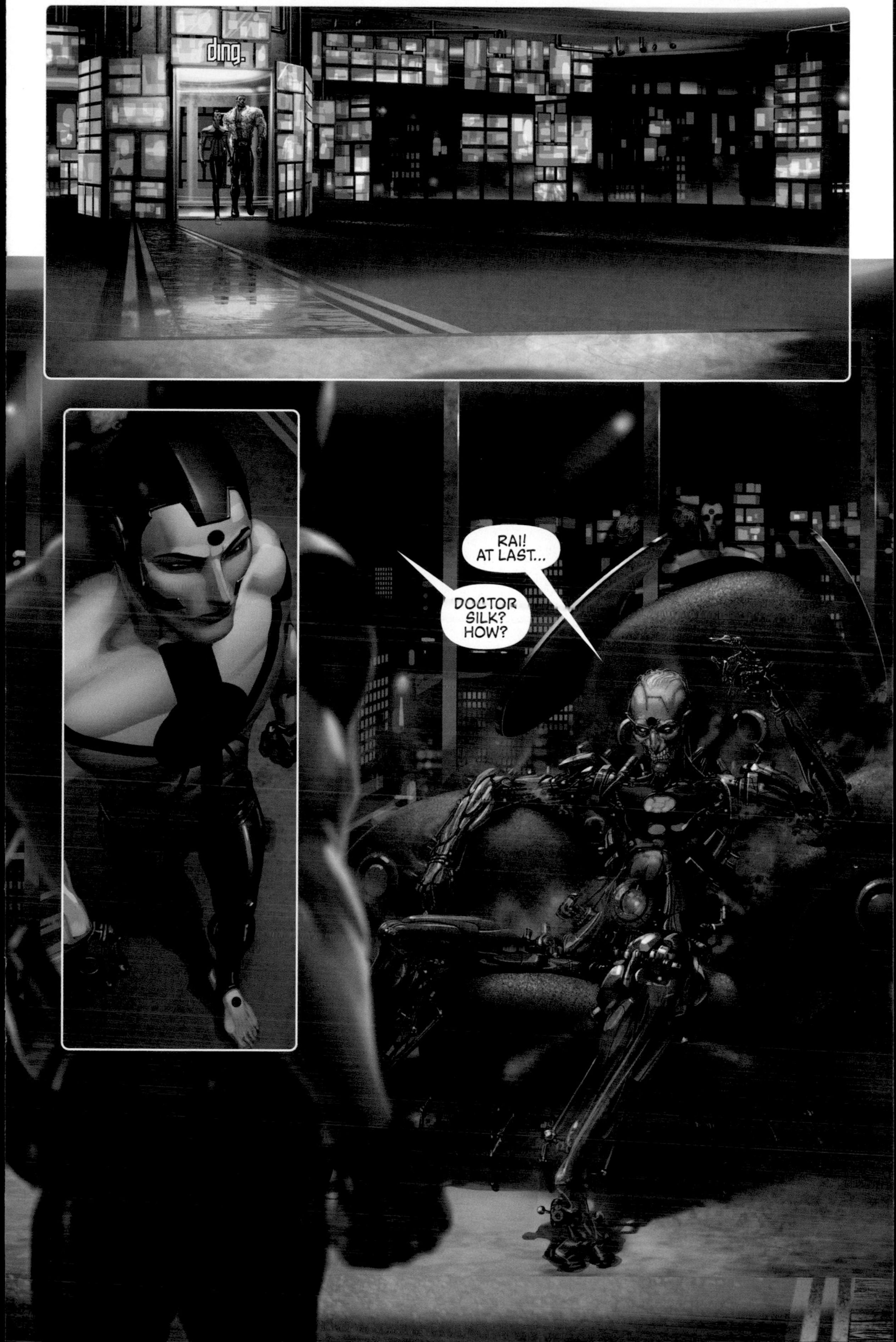
ding.
DOCTOR SILK? HOW?
RAI! AT LAST...

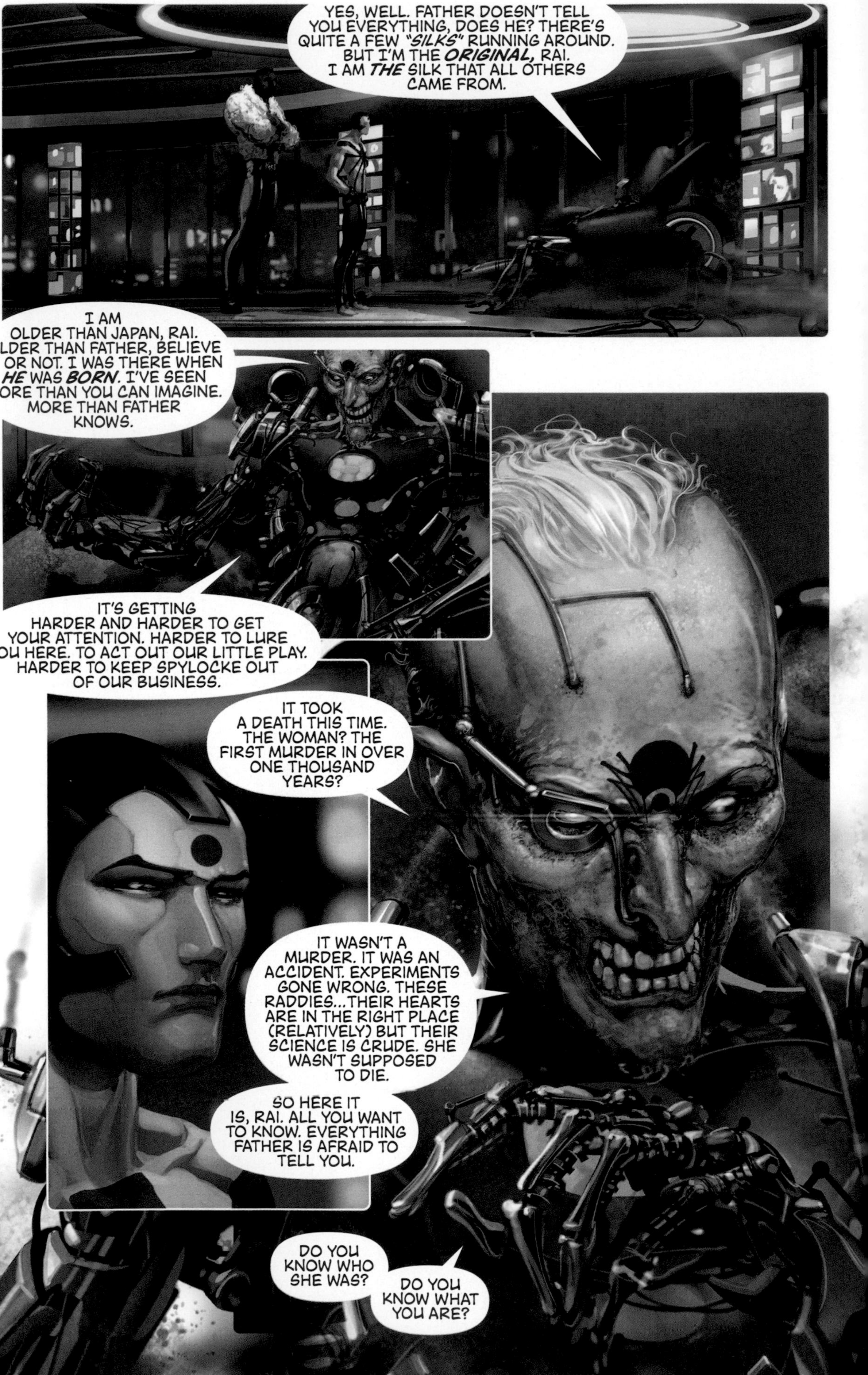
YES, WELL. FATHER DOESN'T TELL YOU EVERYTHING, DOES HE? THERE'S QUITE A FEW "SILKS" RUNNING AROUND. BUT I'M THE ORIGINAL, RAI. I AM THE SILK THAT ALL OTHERS CAME FROM.
I AM OLDER THAN JAPAN, RAI. OLDER THAN FATHER, BELIEVE IT OR NOT. I WAS THERE WHEN HE WAS BORN. I'VE SEEN MORE THAN YOU CAN IMAGINE. MORE THAN FATHER KNOWS.
IT'S GETTING HARDER AND HARDER TO GET YOUR ATTENTION. HARDER TO LURE YOU HERE. TO ACT OUT OUR LITTLE PLAY. HARDER TO KEEP SPYLOCKE OUT OF OUR BUSINESS.
IT TOOK A DEATH THIS TIME. THE WOMAN? THE FIRST MURDER IN OVER ONE THOUSAND YEARS?
IT WASN'T A MURDER. IT WAS AN ACCIDENT. EXPERIMENTS GONE WRONG. THESE RADDIES...THEIR HEARTS ARE IN THE RIGHT PLACE (RELATIVELY) BUT THEIR SCIENCE IS CRUDE. SHE WASN'T SUPPOSED TO DIE.
SO HERE IT IS, RAI. ALL YOU WANT TO KNOW. EVERYTHING FATHER IS AFRAID TO TELL YOU.
DO YOU KNOW WHO SHE WAS?
DO YOU KNOW WHAT YOU ARE?

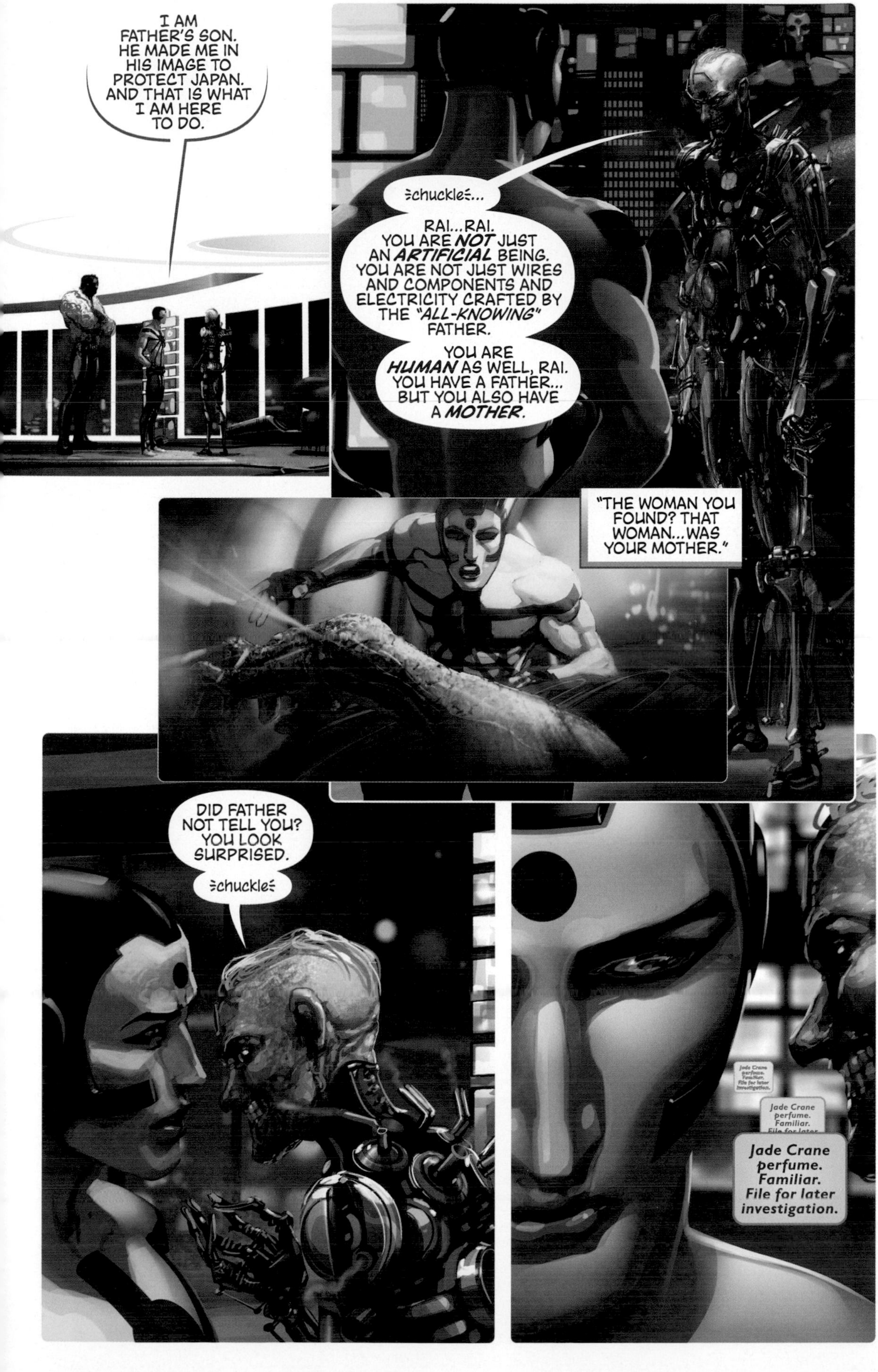
I AM FATHER'S SON. HE MADE ME IN HIS IMAGE TO PROTECT JAPAN. AND THAT IS WHAT I AM HERE TO DO.
≡chuckle≡...
RAI...RAI. YOU ARE *NOT* JUST AN *ARTIFICIAL* BEING. YOU ARE NOT JUST WIRES AND COMPONENTS AND ELECTRICITY CRAFTED BY THE *"ALL-KNOWING"* FATHER.
YOU ARE *HUMAN* AS WELL, RAI. YOU HAVE A FATHER... BUT YOU ALSO HAVE A *MOTHER*.
"THE WOMAN YOU FOUND? THAT WOMAN...WAS YOUR MOTHER."
DID FATHER NOT TELL YOU? YOU LOOK SURPRISED.
≡chuckle≡
Jade Crane perfume. Familiar. File for later investigation.

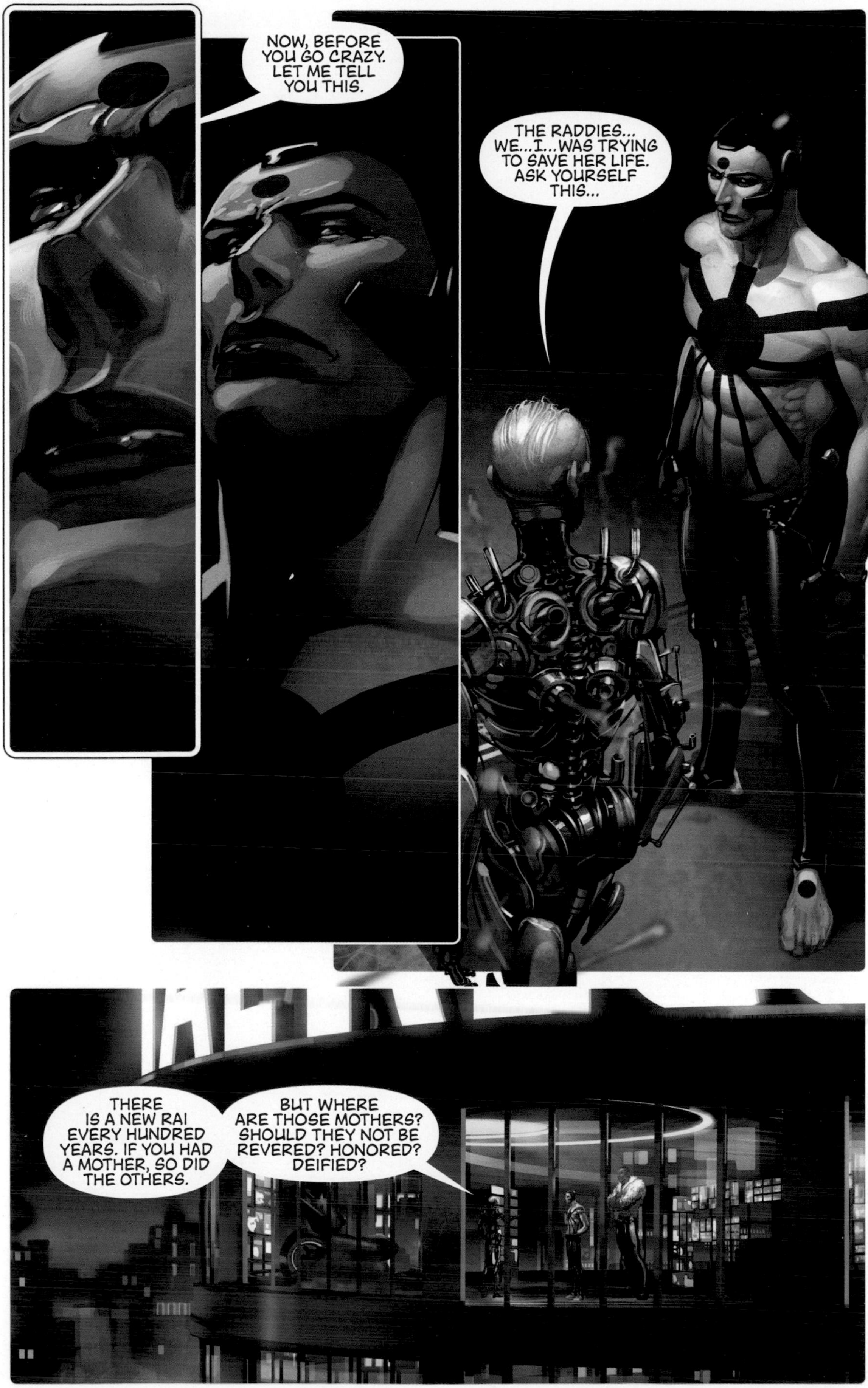
NOW, BEFORE YOU GO CRAZY. LET ME TELL YOU THIS.
THE RADDIES... WE...I...WAS TRYING TO SAVE HER LIFE. ASK YOURSELF THIS...
THERE IS A NEW RAI EVERY HUNDRED YEARS. IF YOU HAD A MOTHER, SO DID THE OTHERS.
BUT WHERE ARE THOSE MOTHERS? SHOULD THEY NOT BE REVERED? HONORED? DEIFIED?

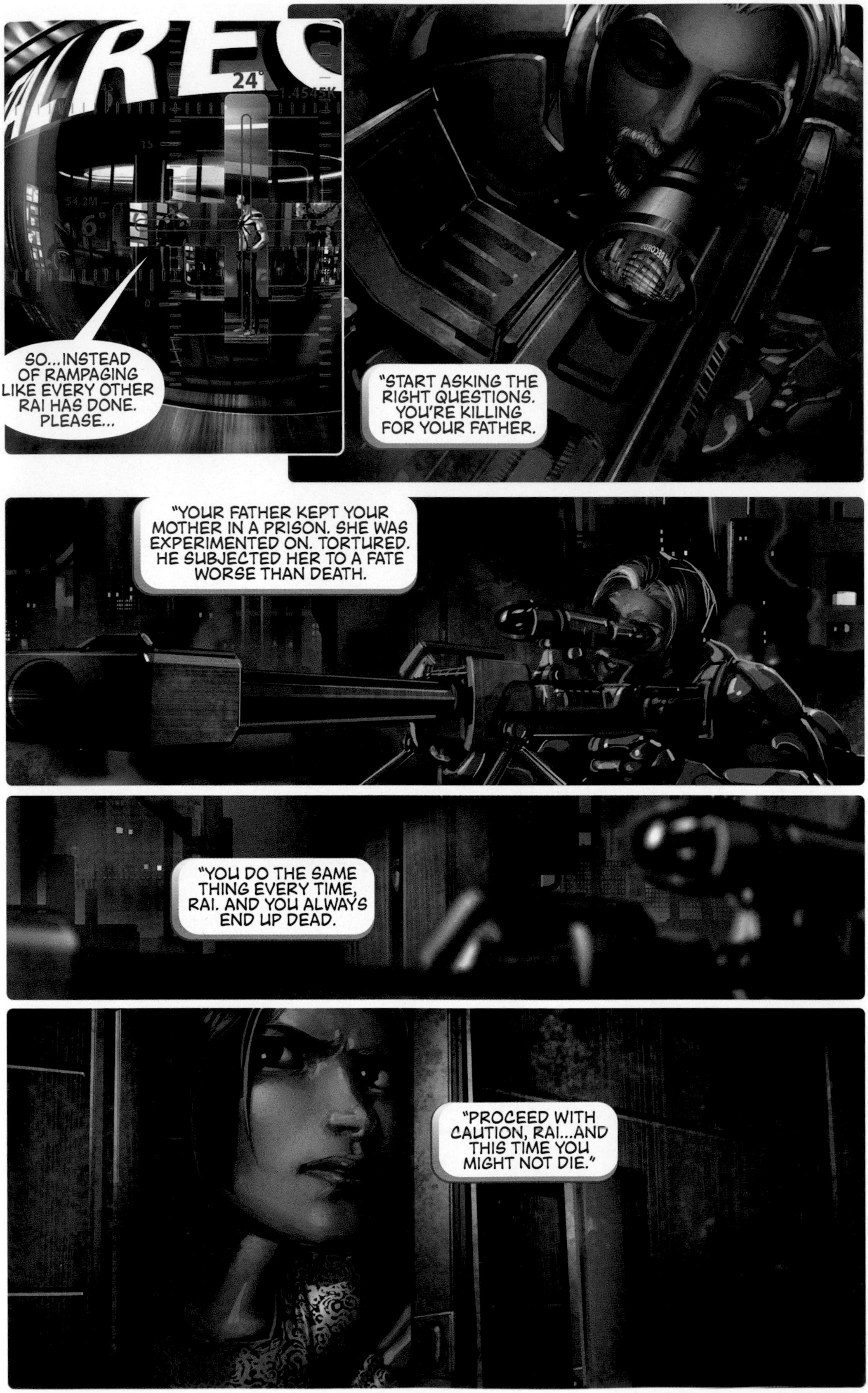
SO...INSTEAD OF RAMPAGING LIKE EVERY OTHER RAI HAS DONE. PLEASE...
"START ASKING THE RIGHT QUESTIONS. YOU'RE KILLING FOR YOUR FATHER.
"YOUR FATHER KEPT YOUR MOTHER IN A PRISON. SHE WAS EXPERIMENTED ON. TORTURED. HE SUBJECTED HER TO A FATE WORSE THAN DEATH.
"YOU DO THE SAME THING EVERY TIME, RAI. AND YOU ALWAYS END UP DEAD.
"PROCEED WITH CAUTION, RAI...AND THIS TIME YOU MIGHT NOT DIE."

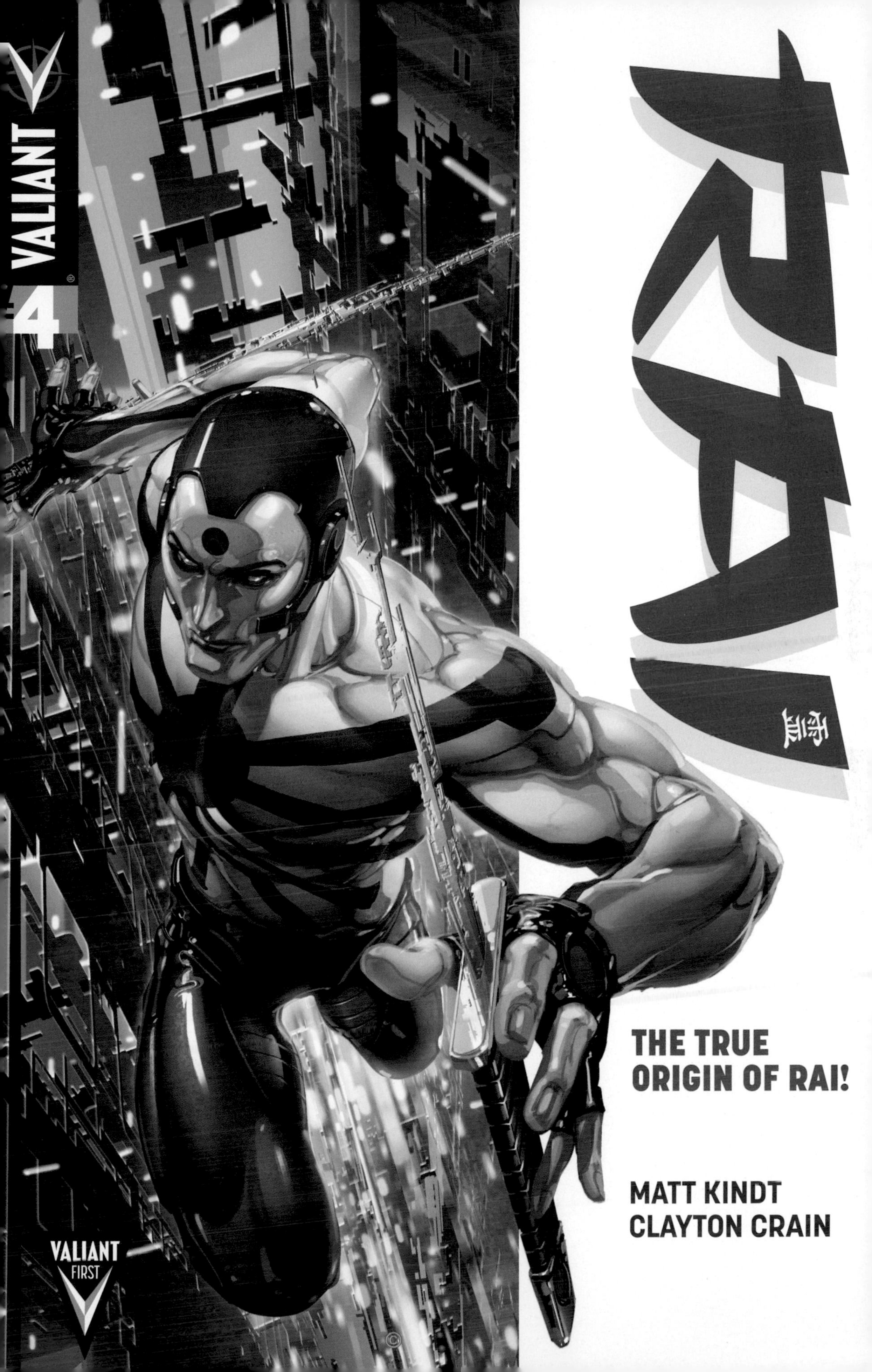

VALIANT
4
RAI
THE TRUE
ORIGIN OF RAI!
MATT KINDT
CLAYTON CRAIN
VALIANT
FIRST

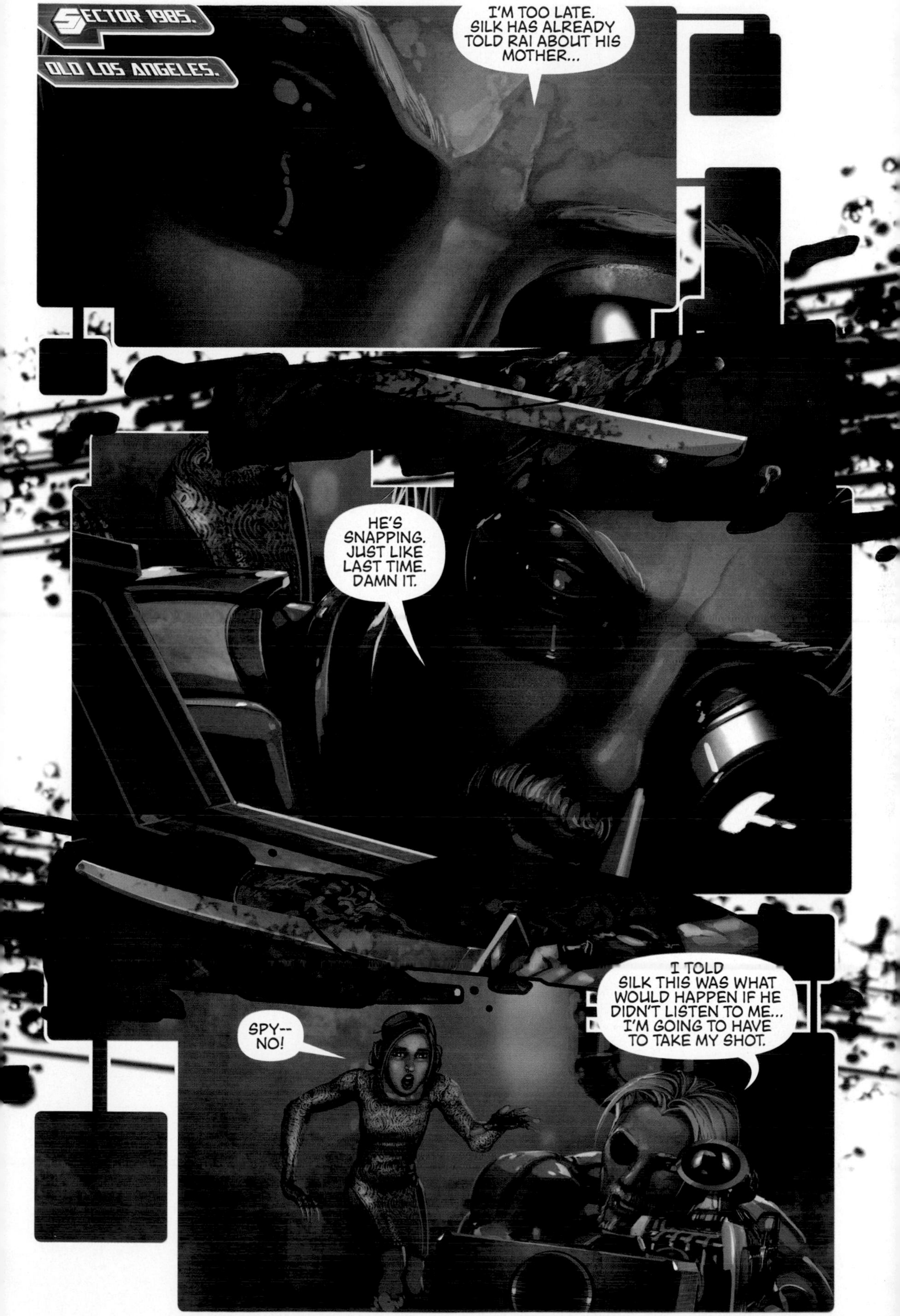
SECTOR 1985.
OLD LOS ANGELES.
I'M TOO LATE. SILK HAS ALREADY TOLD RAI ABOUT HIS MOTHER...
HE'S SNAPPING. JUST LIKE LAST TIME. DAMN IT.
I TOLD SILK THIS WAS WHAT WOULD HAPPEN IF HE DIDN'T LISTEN TO ME... I'M GOING TO HAVE TO TAKE MY SHOT.
SPY-- NO!

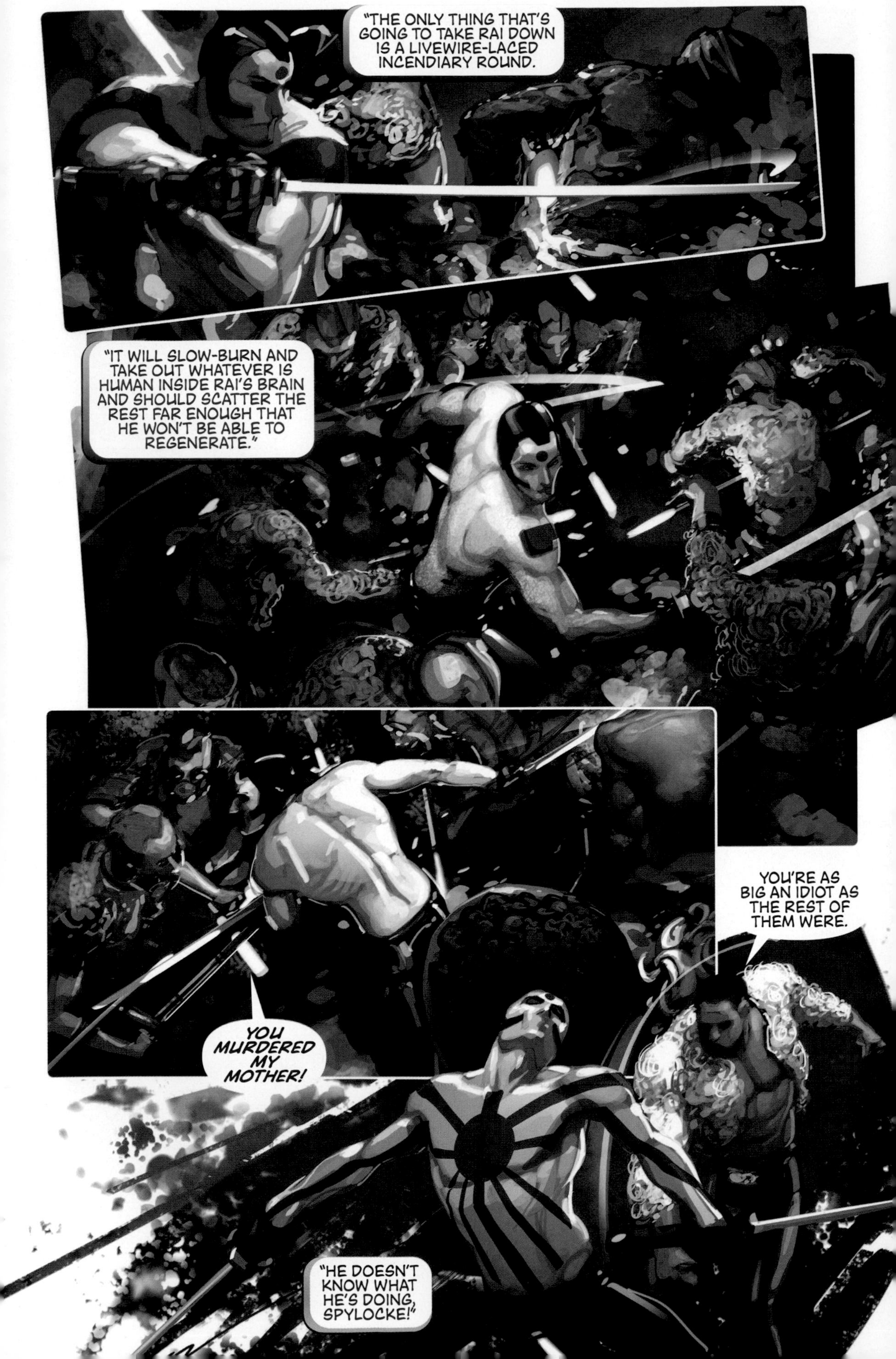
"THE ONLY THING THAT'S GOING TO TAKE RAI DOWN IS A LIVEWIRE-LACED INCENDIARY ROUND.
"IT WILL SLOW-BURN AND TAKE OUT WHATEVER IS HUMAN INSIDE RAI'S BRAIN AND SHOULD SCATTER THE REST FAR ENOUGH THAT HE WON'T BE ABLE TO REGENERATE."
YOU'RE AS BIG AN IDIOT AS THE REST OF THEM WERE.
YOU MURDERED MY MOTHER!
"HE DOESN'T KNOW WHAT HE'S DOING, SPYLOCKE!"

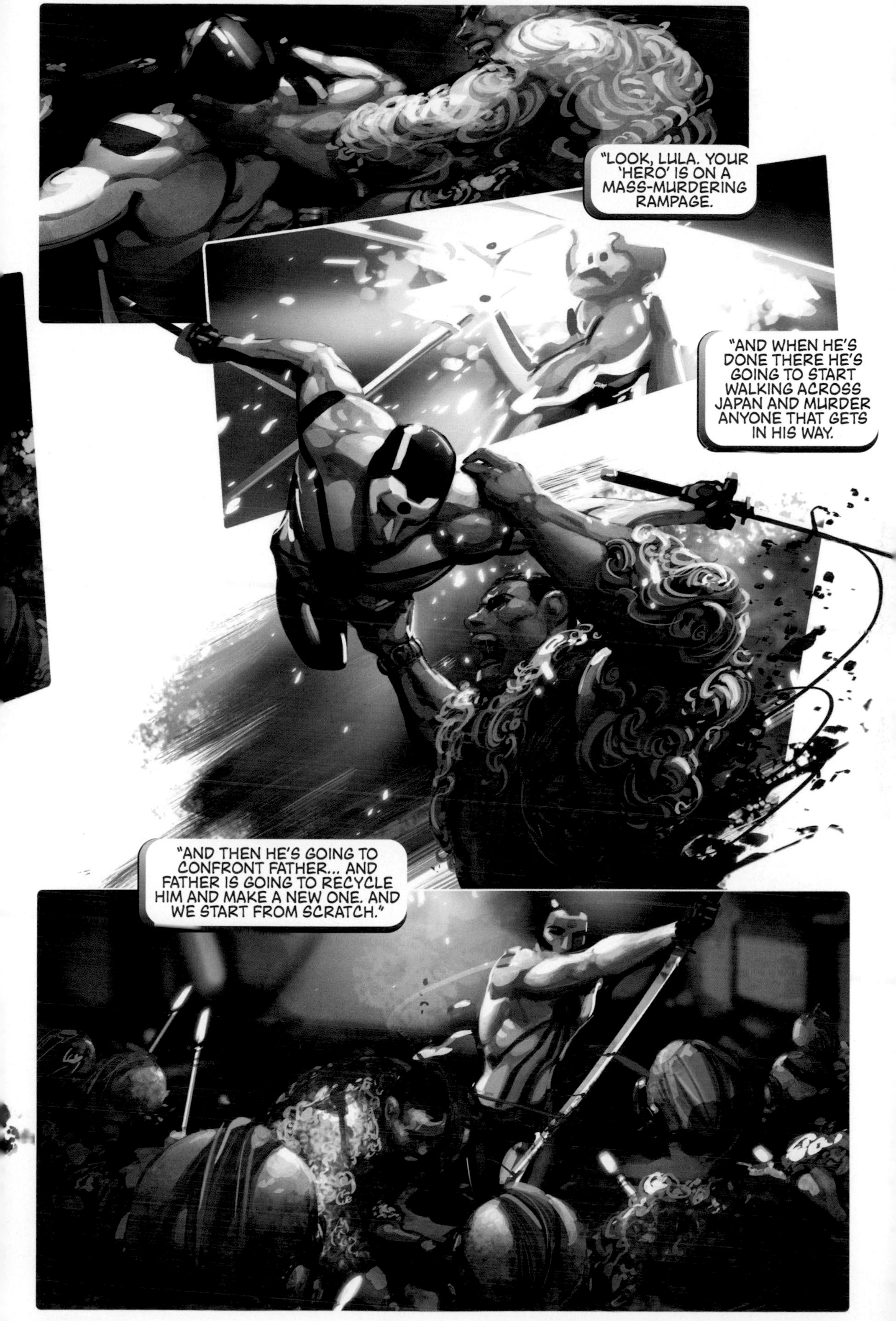
"LOOK, LULA. YOUR 'HERO' IS ON A MASS-MURDERING RAMPAGE.
"AND WHEN HE'S DONE THERE HE'S GOING TO START WALKING ACROSS JAPAN AND MURDER ANYONE THAT GETS IN HIS WAY.
"AND THEN HE'S GOING TO CONFRONT FATHER... AND FATHER IS GOING TO RECYCLE HIM AND MAKE A NEW ONE. AND WE START FROM SCRATCH."

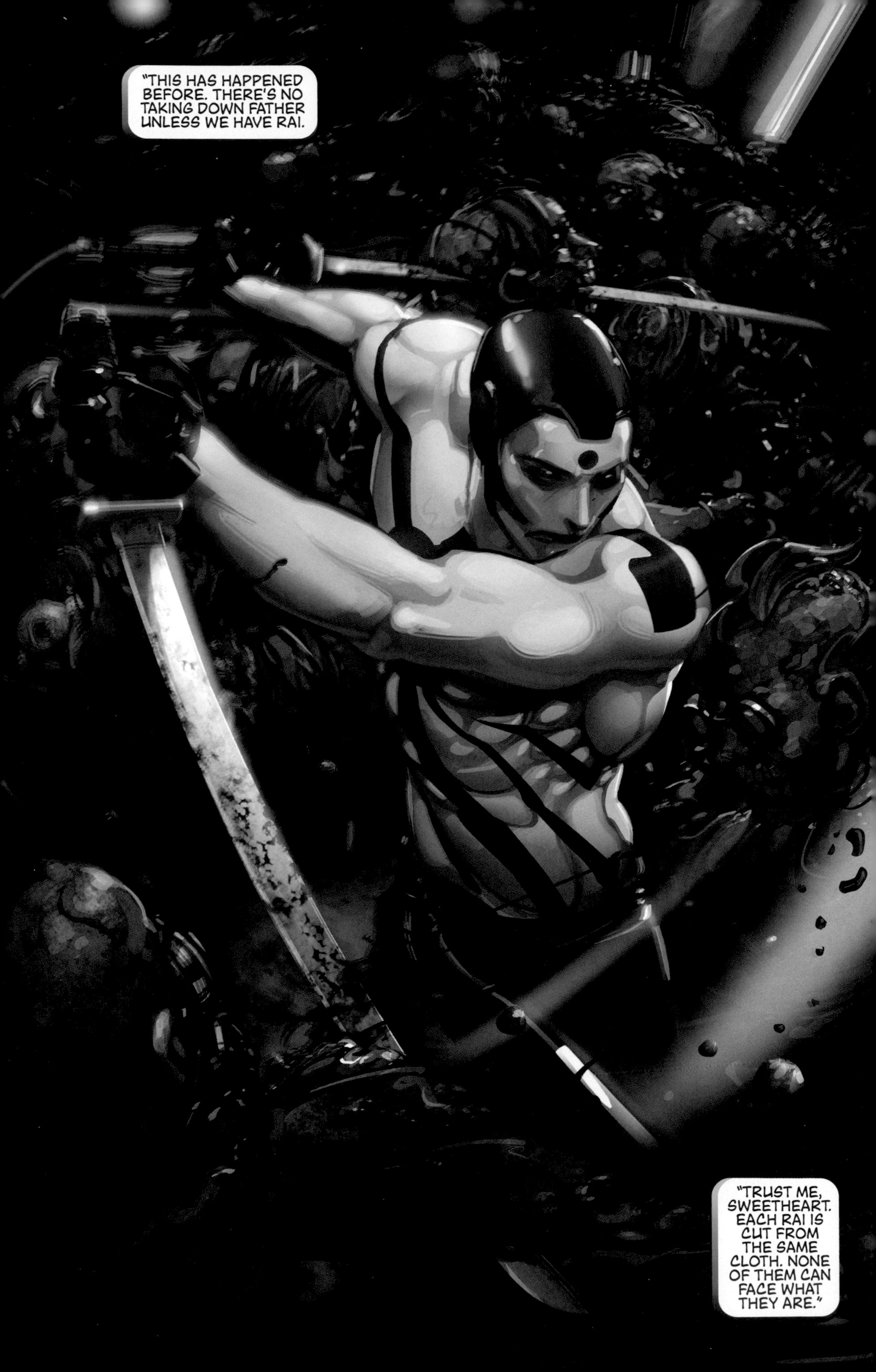
"THIS HAS HAPPENED BEFORE. THERE'S NO TAKING DOWN FATHER UNLESS WE HAVE RAI.
"TRUST ME, SWEETHEART. EACH RAI IS CUT FROM THE SAME CLOTH. NONE OF THEM CAN FACE WHAT THEY ARE."

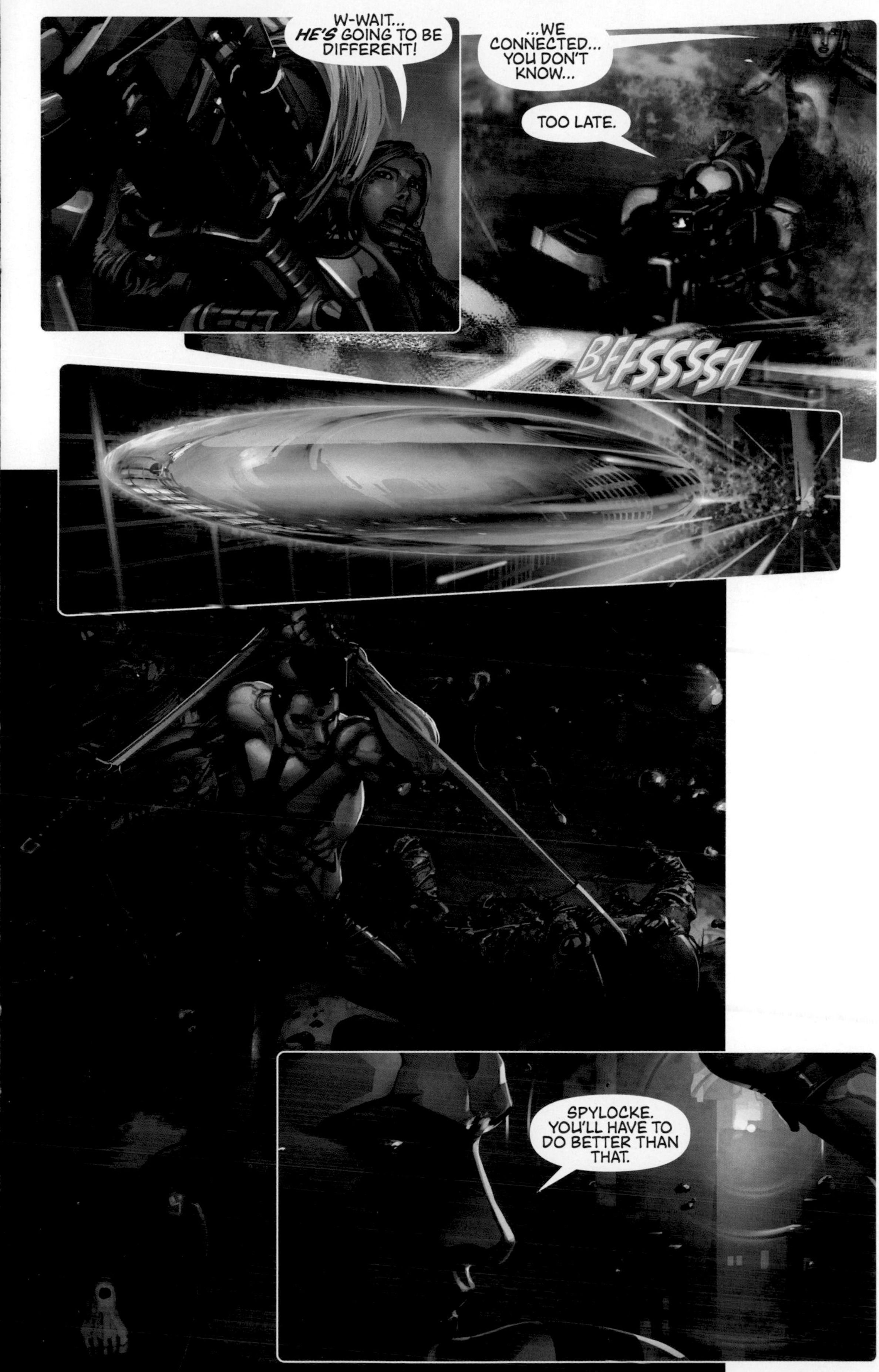
W-WAIT... HE'S GOING TO BE DIFFERENT!
...WE CONNECTED... YOU DON'T KNOW...
TOO LATE.
BFFSSSSH
SPYLOCKE. YOU'LL HAVE TO DO BETTER THAN THAT.

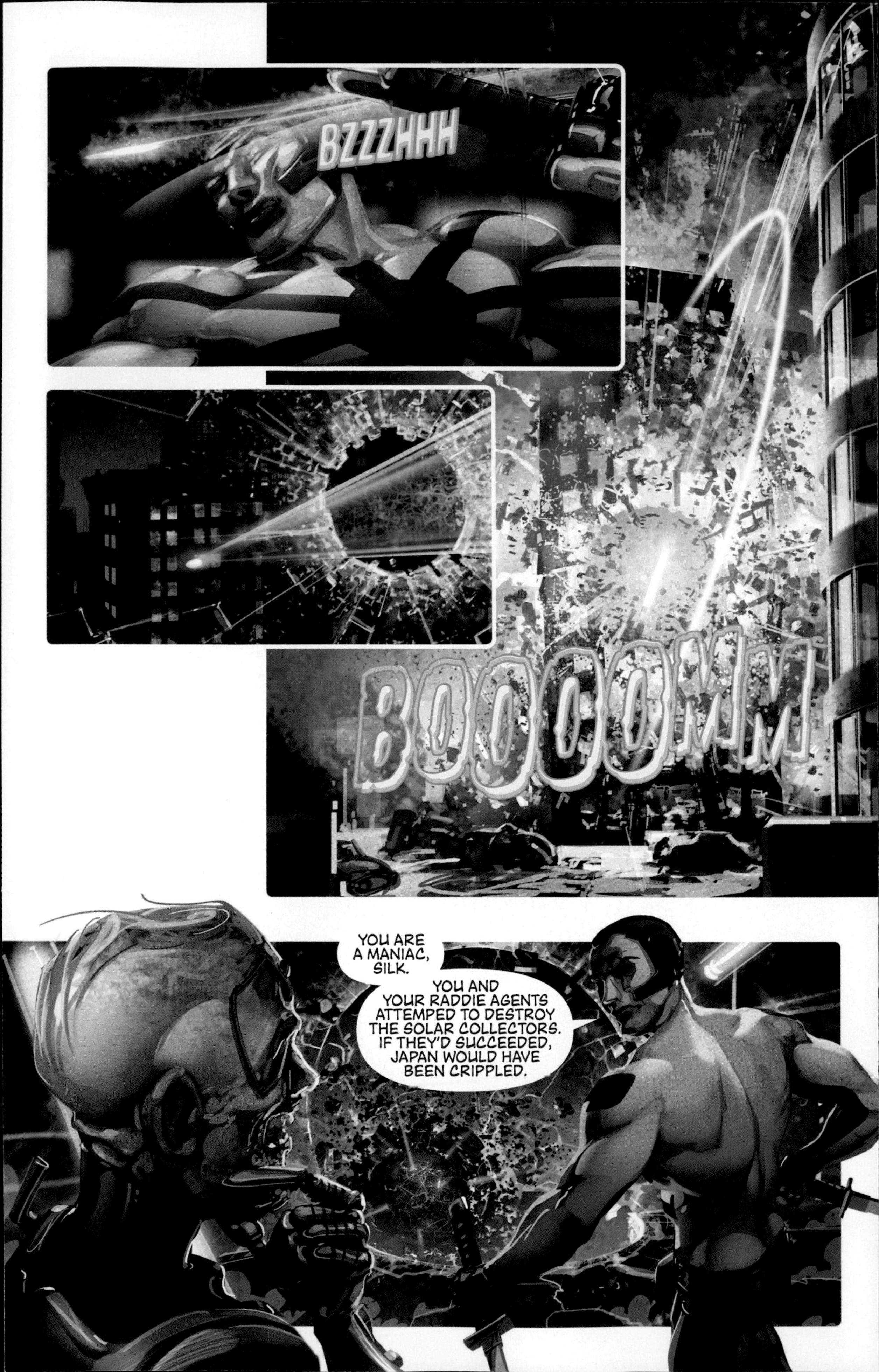
BZZZHHH
BOOOOMM
YOU ARE A MANIAC, SILK.
YOU AND YOUR RADDIE AGENTS ATTEMPED TO DESTROY THE SOLAR COLLECTORS. IF THEY'D SUCCEEDED, JAPAN WOULD HAVE BEEN CRIPPLED.

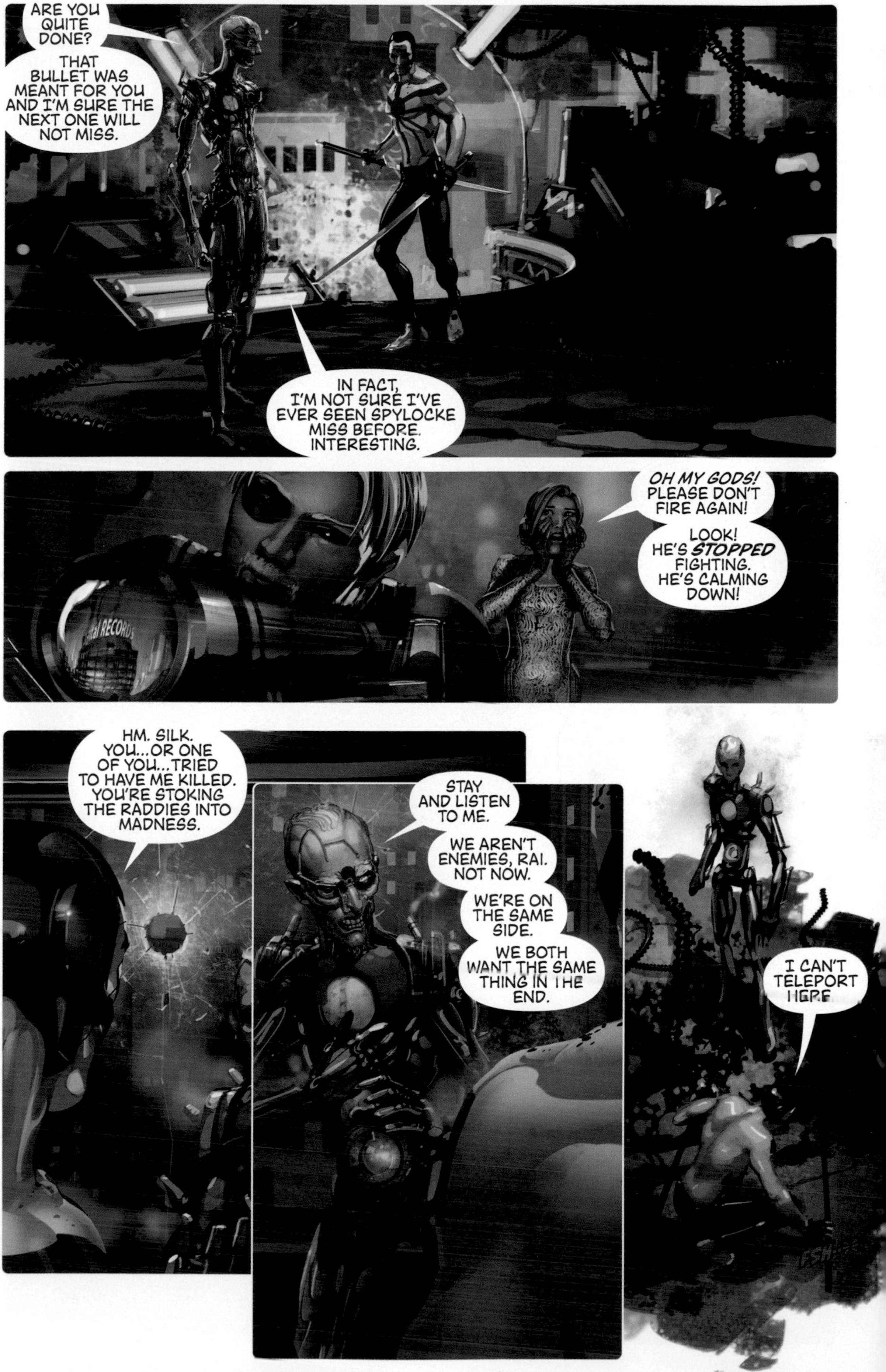
ARE YOU QUITE DONE?
THAT BULLET WAS MEANT FOR YOU AND I'M SURE THE NEXT ONE WILL NOT MISS.
IN FACT, I'M NOT SURE I'VE EVER SEEN SPYLOCKE MISS BEFORE. INTERESTING.
OH MY GODS! PLEASE DON'T FIRE AGAIN!
LOOK! HE'S STOPPED FIGHTING. HE'S CALMING DOWN!
HM. SILK. YOU...OR ONE OF YOU...TRIED TO HAVE ME KILLED. YOU'RE STOKING THE RADDIES INTO MADNESS.
STAY AND LISTEN TO ME.
WE AREN'T ENEMIES, RAI. NOT NOW.
WE'RE ON THE SAME SIDE.
WE BOTH WANT THE SAME THING IN THE END.
I CAN'T TELEPORT HERE.

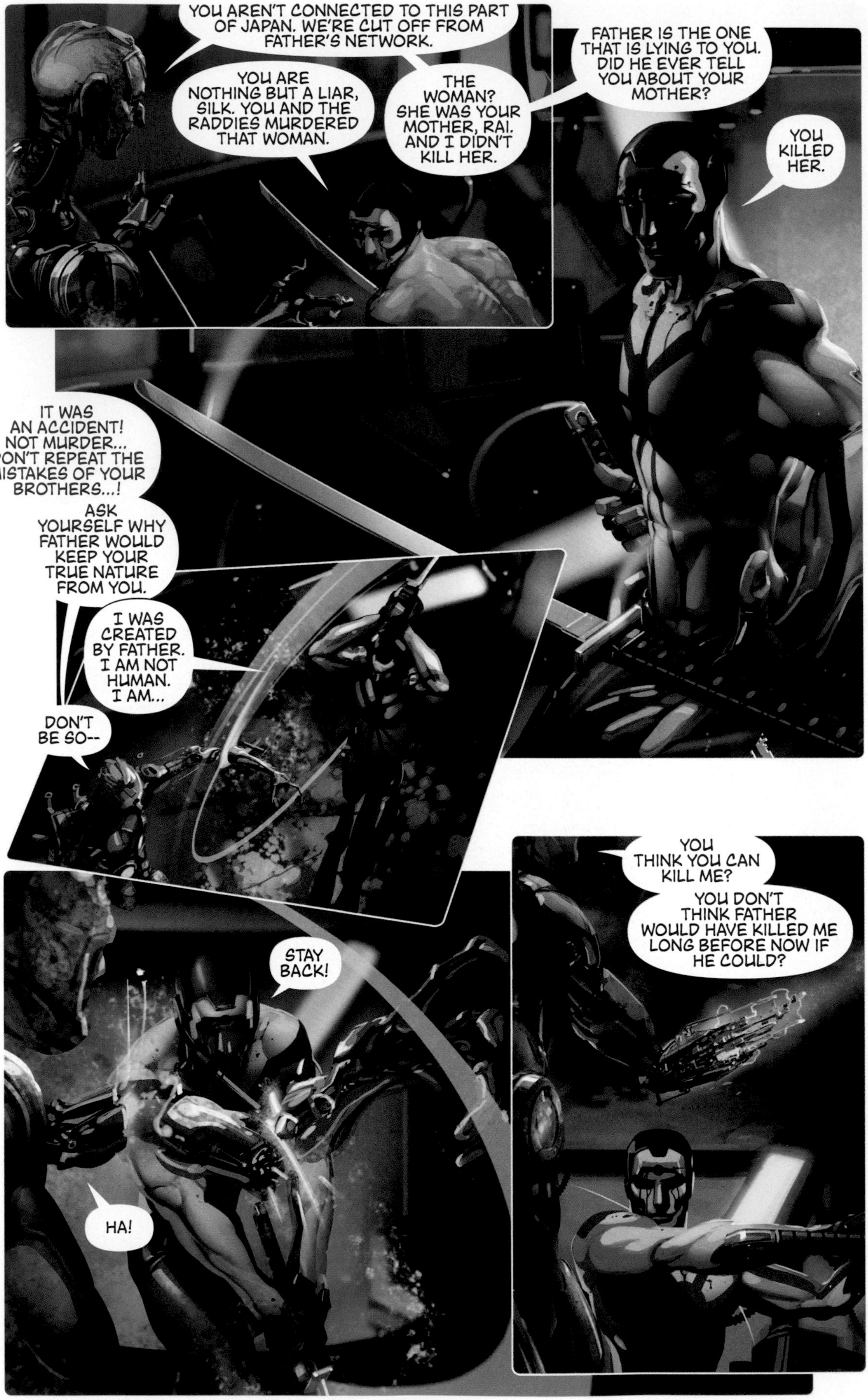
YOU AREN'T CONNECTED TO THIS PART OF JAPAN. WE'RE CUT OFF FROM FATHER'S NETWORK.
YOU ARE NOTHING BUT A LIAR, SILK. YOU AND THE RADDIES MURDERED THAT WOMAN.
THE WOMAN? SHE WAS YOUR MOTHER, RAI. AND I DIDN'T KILL HER.
FATHER IS THE ONE THAT IS LYING TO YOU. DID HE EVER TELL YOU ABOUT YOUR MOTHER?
YOU KILLED HER.
IT WAS AN ACCIDENT! NOT MURDER... DON'T REPEAT THE MISTAKES OF YOUR BROTHERS...!
ASK YOURSELF WHY FATHER WOULD KEEP YOUR TRUE NATURE FROM YOU.
I WAS CREATED BY FATHER. I AM NOT HUMAN. I AM...
DON'T BE SO--
STAY BACK!
HA!
YOU THINK YOU CAN KILL ME?
YOU DON'T THINK FATHER WOULD HAVE KILLED ME LONG BEFORE NOW IF HE COULD?

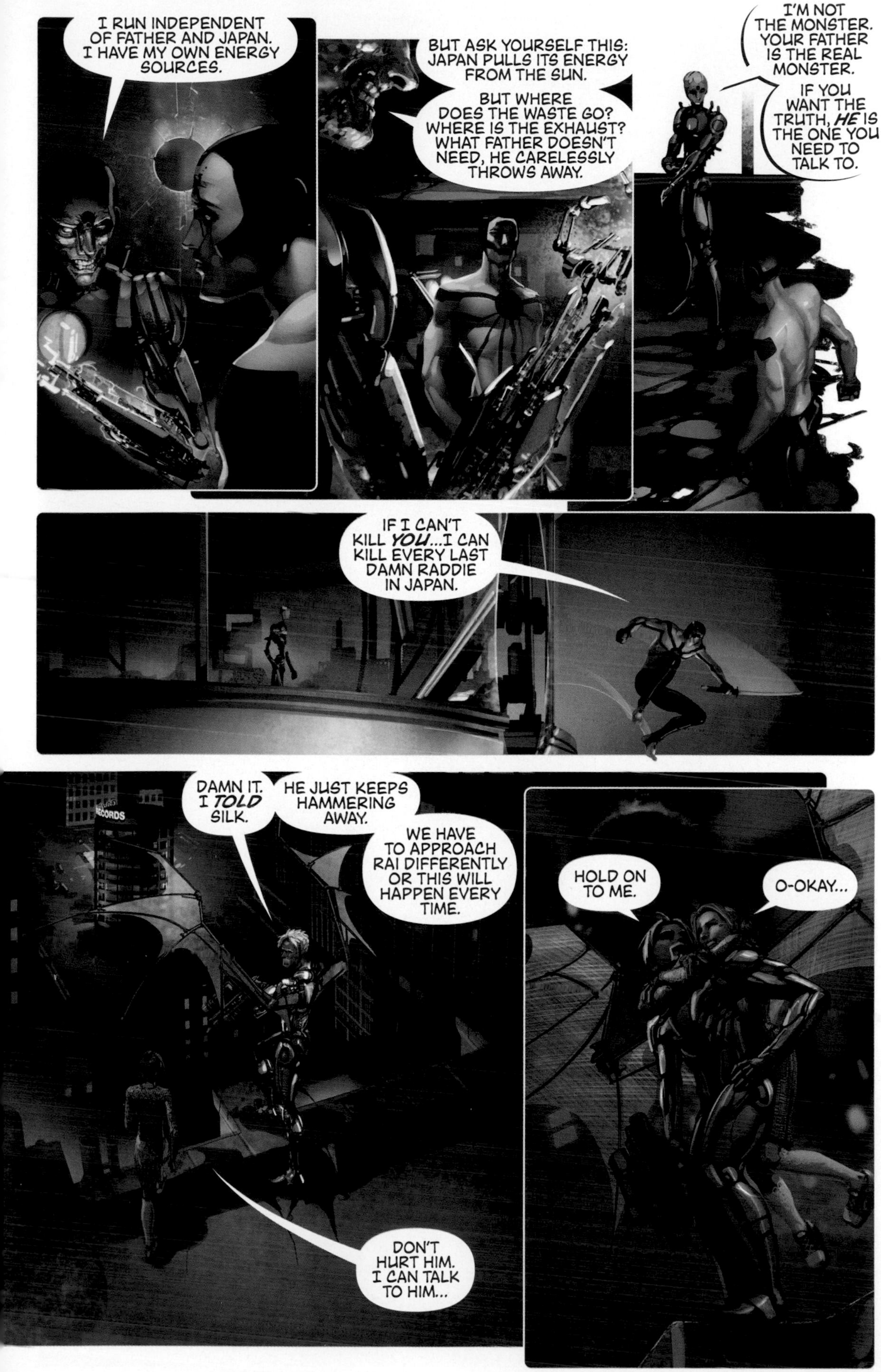
I RUN INDEPENDENT OF FATHER AND JAPAN. I HAVE MY OWN ENERGY SOURCES.
BUT ASK YOURSELF THIS: JAPAN PULLS ITS ENERGY FROM THE SUN.
BUT WHERE DOES THE WASTE GO? WHERE IS THE EXHAUST? WHAT FATHER DOESN'T NEED, HE CARELESSLY THROWS AWAY.
I'M NOT THE MONSTER. YOUR FATHER IS THE REAL MONSTER.
IF YOU WANT THE TRUTH, HE IS THE ONE YOU NEED TO TALK TO.
IF I CAN'T KILL YOU...I CAN KILL EVERY LAST DAMN RADDIE IN JAPAN.
RECORDS
DAMN IT. I TOLD SILK.
HE JUST KEEPS HAMMERING AWAY.
WE HAVE TO APPROACH RAI DIFFERENTLY OR THIS WILL HAPPEN EVERY TIME.
DON'T HURT HIM. I CAN TALK TO HIM...
HOLD ON TO ME.
O-OKAY...

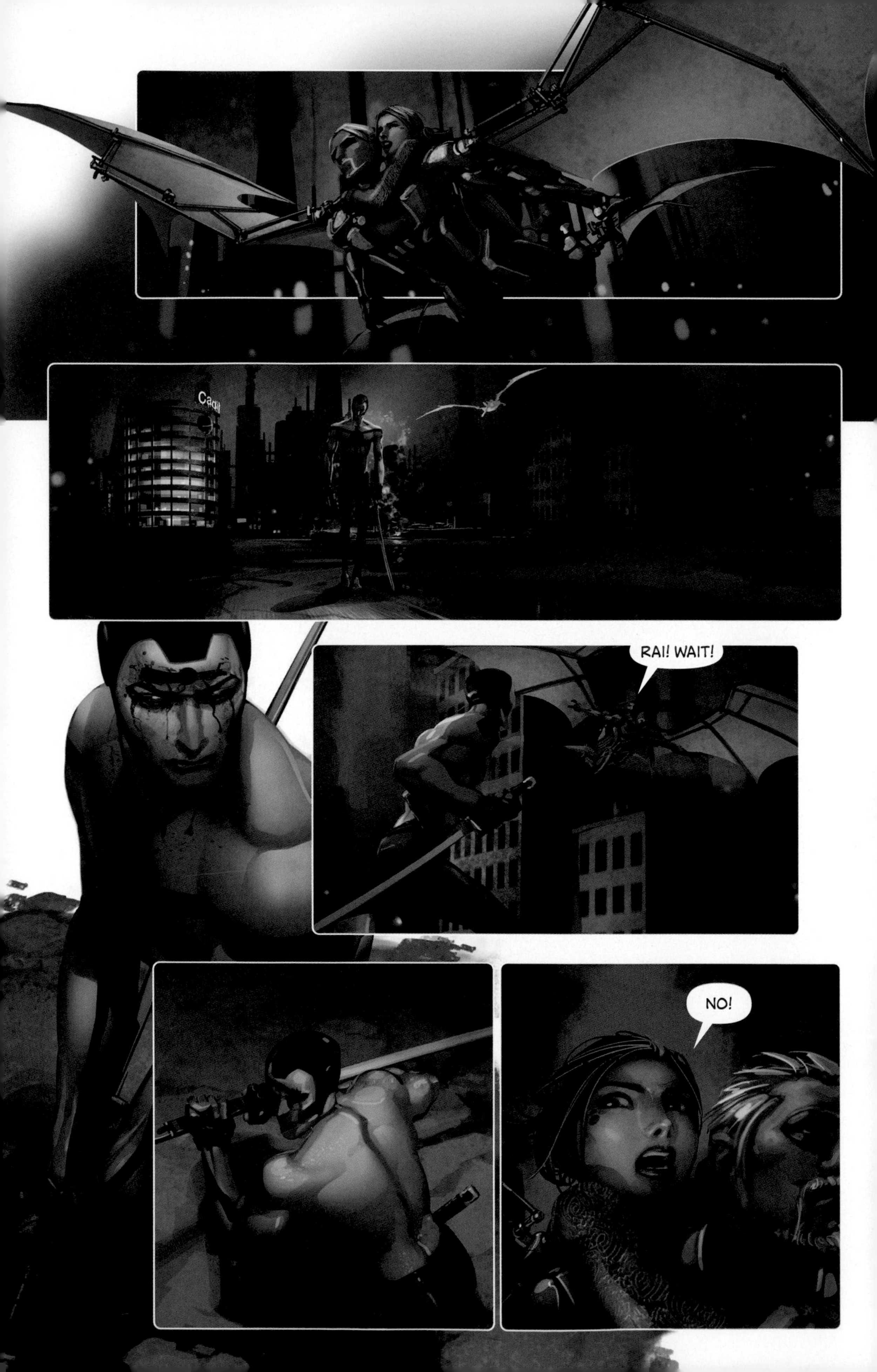
RAI! WAIT!
NO!

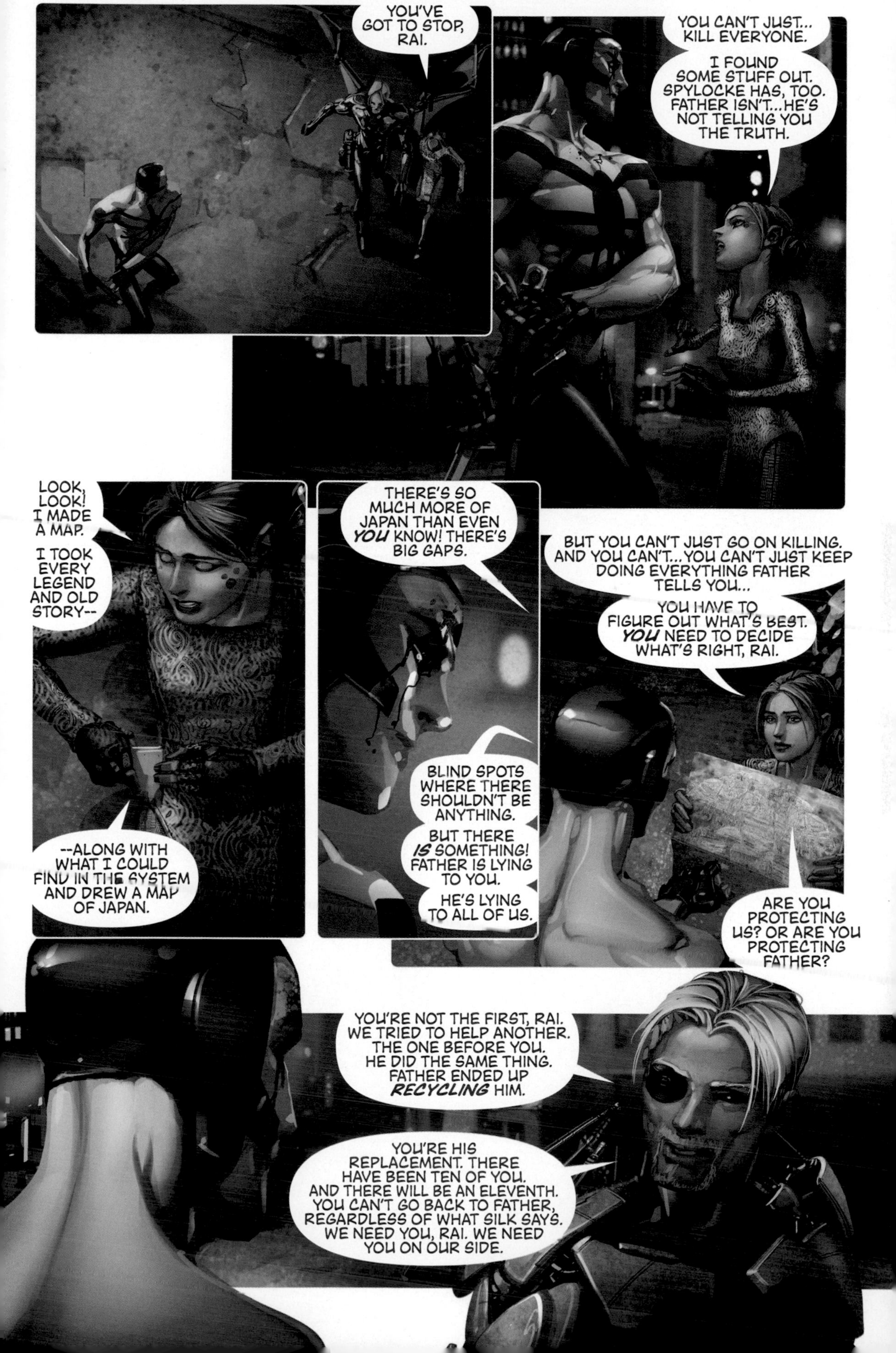
YOU'VE GOT TO STOP, RAI.
YOU CAN'T JUST... KILL EVERYONE.
I FOUND SOME STUFF OUT. SPYLOCKE HAS, TOO. FATHER ISN'T...HE'S NOT TELLING YOU THE TRUTH.
LOOK, LOOK! I MADE A MAP.
I TOOK EVERY LEGEND AND OLD STORY--
--ALONG WITH WHAT I COULD FIND IN THE SYSTEM AND DREW A MAP OF JAPAN.
THERE'S SO MUCH MORE OF JAPAN THAN EVEN YOU KNOW! THERE'S BIG GAPS.
BLIND SPOTS WHERE THERE SHOULDN'T BE ANYTHING.
BUT THERE IS SOMETHING! FATHER IS LYING TO YOU.
HE'S LYING TO ALL OF US.
BUT YOU CAN'T JUST GO ON KILLING. AND YOU CAN'T...YOU CAN'T JUST KEEP DOING EVERYTHING FATHER TELLS YOU...
YOU HAVE TO FIGURE OUT WHAT'S BEST. YOU NEED TO DECIDE WHAT'S RIGHT, RAI.
ARE YOU PROTECTING US? OR ARE YOU PROTECTING FATHER?
YOU'RE NOT THE FIRST, RAI. WE TRIED TO HELP ANOTHER. THE ONE BEFORE YOU. HE DID THE SAME THING. FATHER ENDED UP RECYCLING HIM.
YOU'RE HIS REPLACEMENT. THERE HAVE BEEN TEN OF YOU. AND THERE WILL BE AN ELEVENTH. YOU CAN'T GO BACK TO FATHER, REGARDLESS OF WHAT SILK SAYS. WE NEED YOU, RAI. WE NEED YOU ON OUR SIDE.

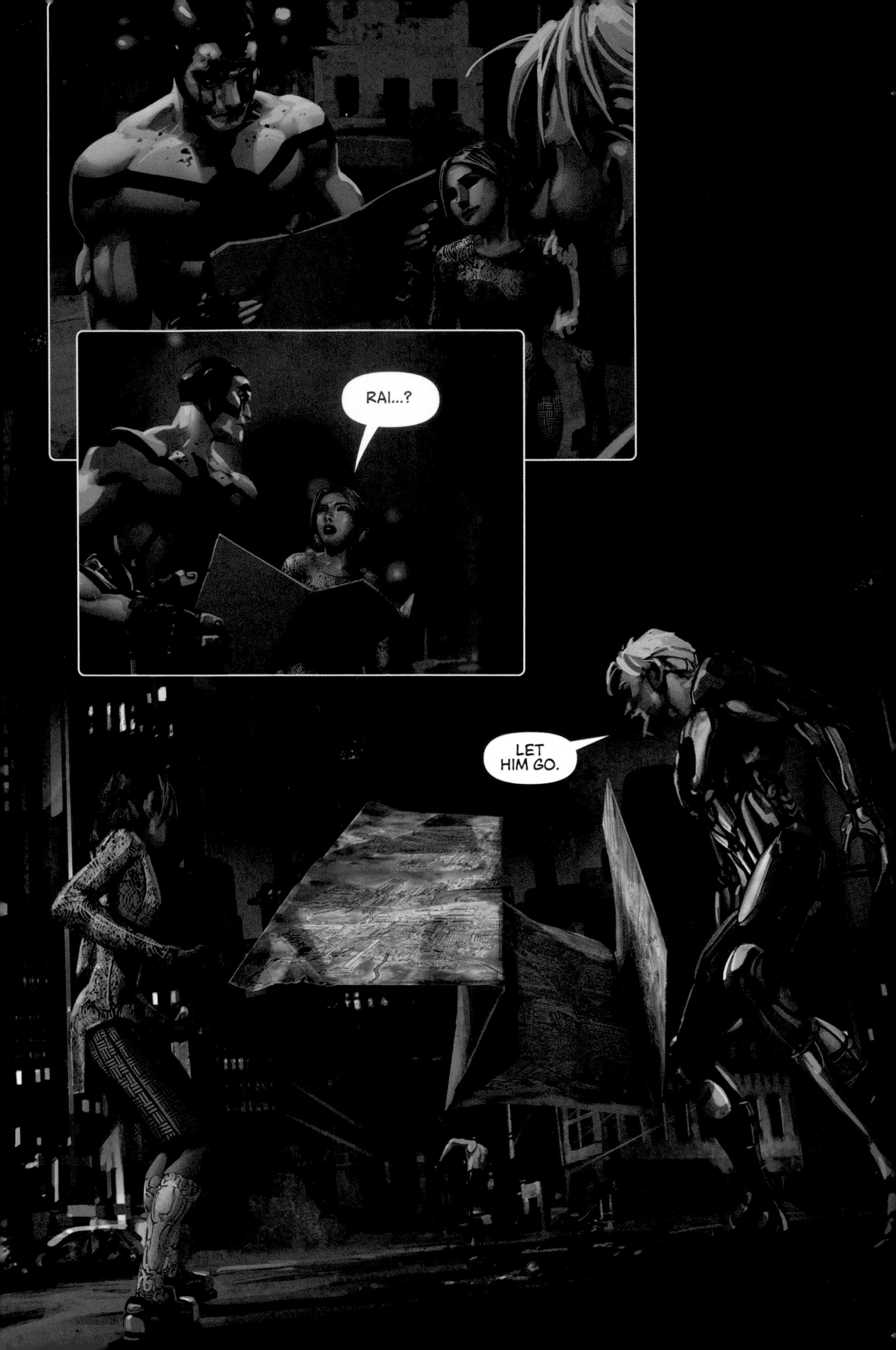
RAI...?
LET HIM GO.

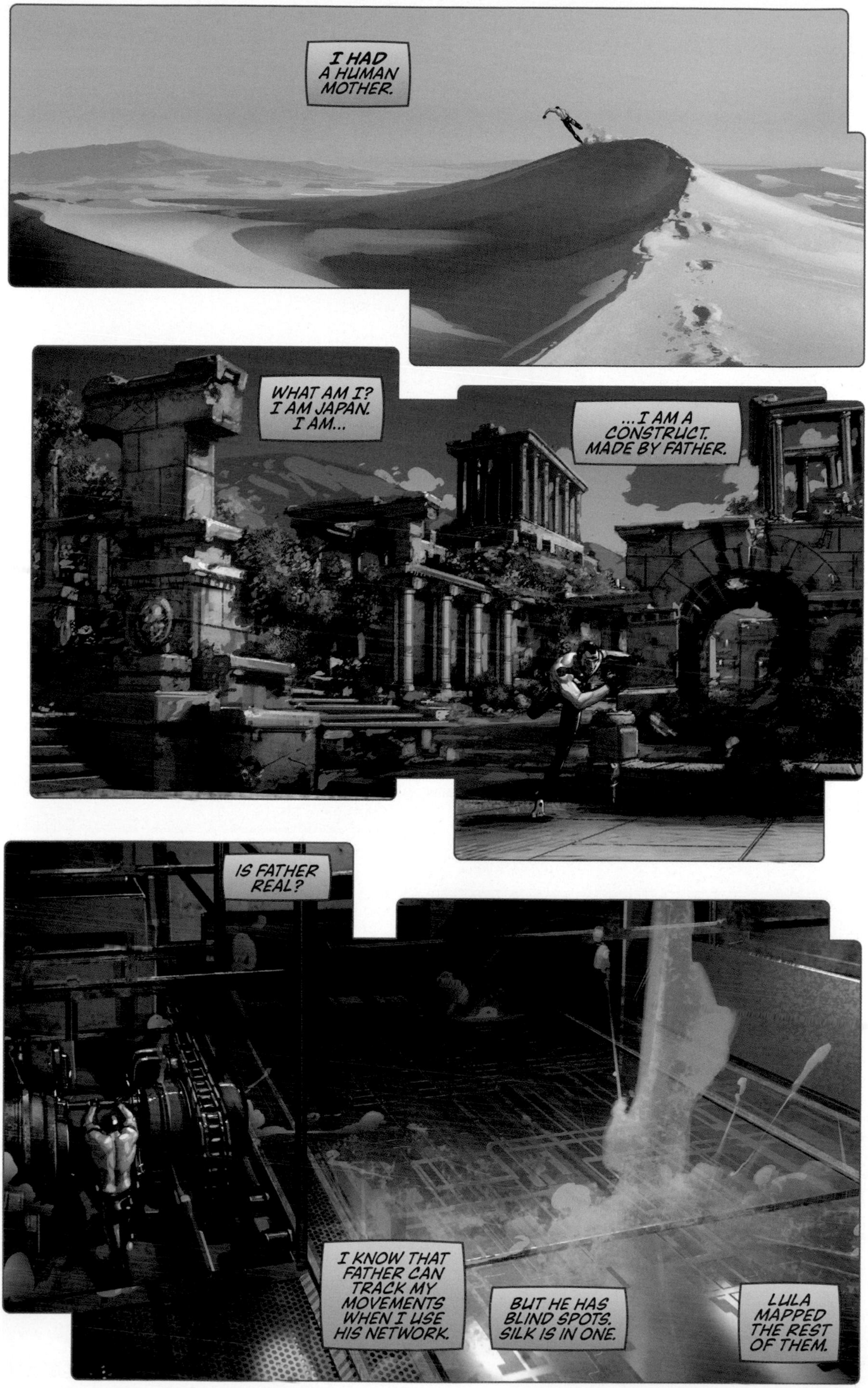
I HAD A HUMAN MOTHER.
WHAT AM I? I AM JAPAN. I AM...
...I AM A CONSTRUCT. MADE BY FATHER.
IS FATHER REAL?
I KNOW THAT FATHER CAN TRACK MY MOVEMENTS WHEN I USE HIS NETWORK.
BUT HE HAS BLIND SPOTS. SILK IS IN ONE.
LULA MAPPED THE REST OF THEM.

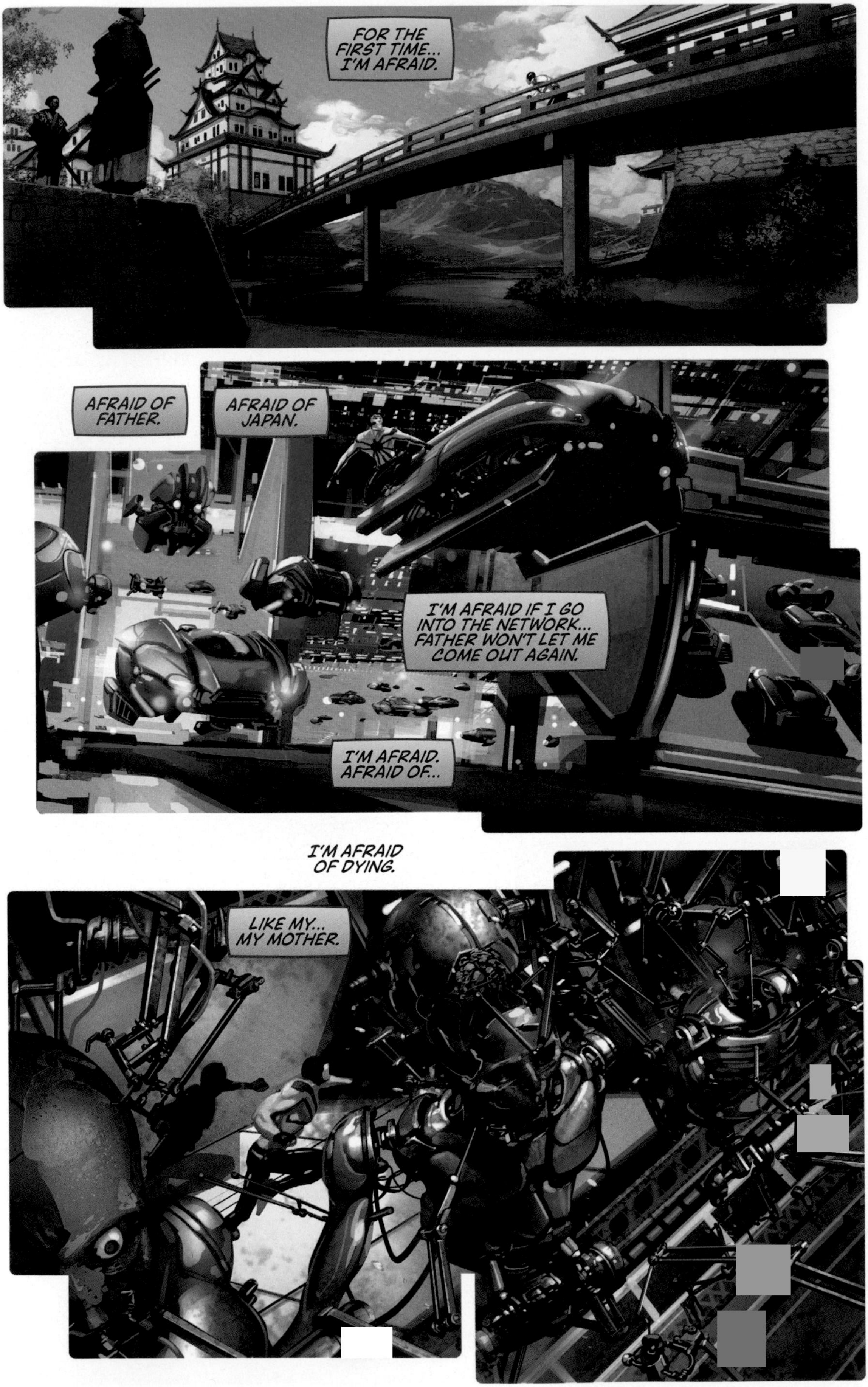
FOR THE FIRST TIME... I'M AFRAID.
AFRAID OF FATHER.
AFRAID OF JAPAN.
I'M AFRAID IF I GO INTO THE NETWORK... FATHER WON'T LET ME COME OUT AGAIN.
I'M AFRAID. AFRAID OF...
I'M AFRAID OF DYING.
LIKE MY... MY MOTHER.

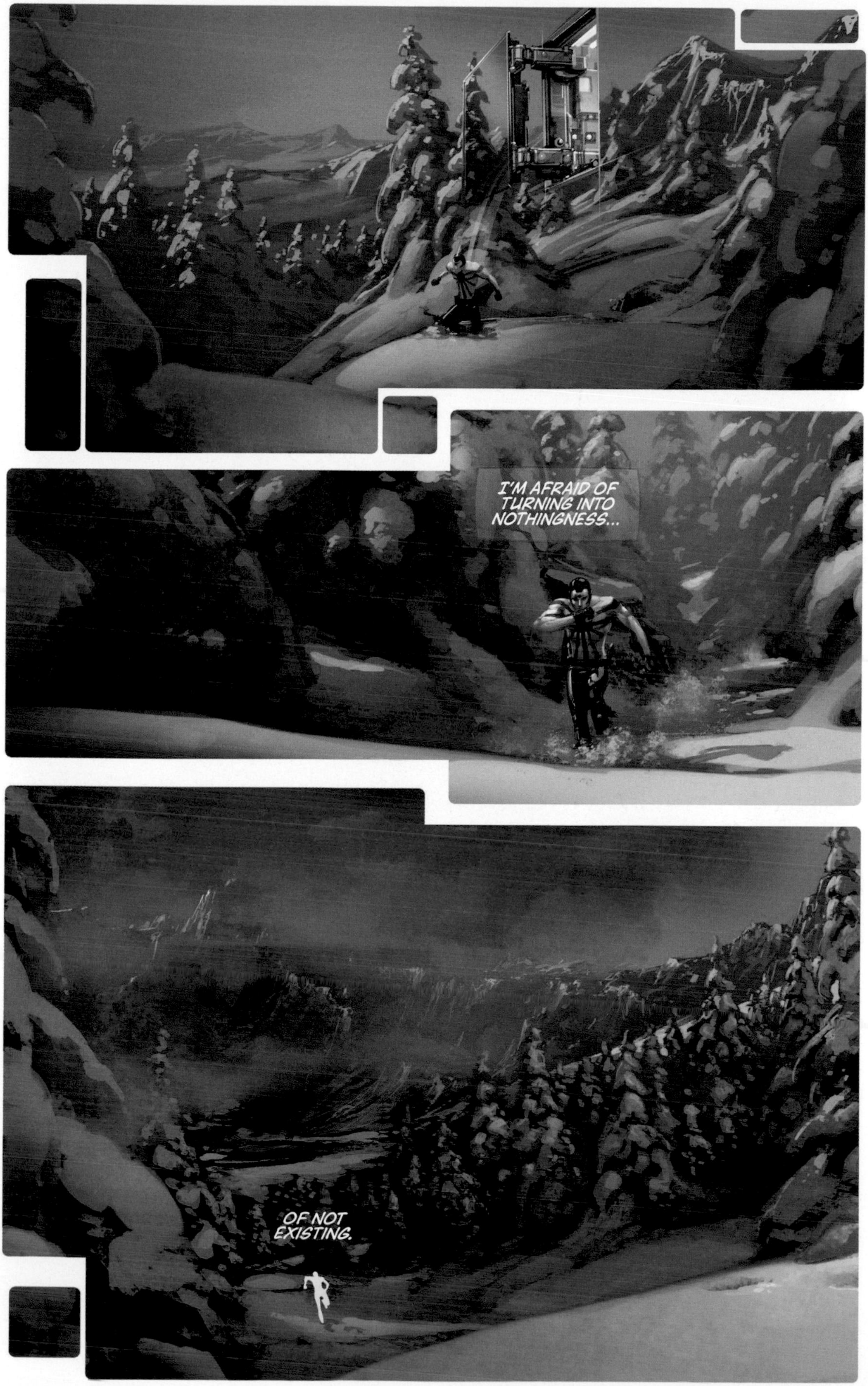
I'M AFRAID OF TURNING INTO NOTHINGNESS...
OF NOT EXISTING.

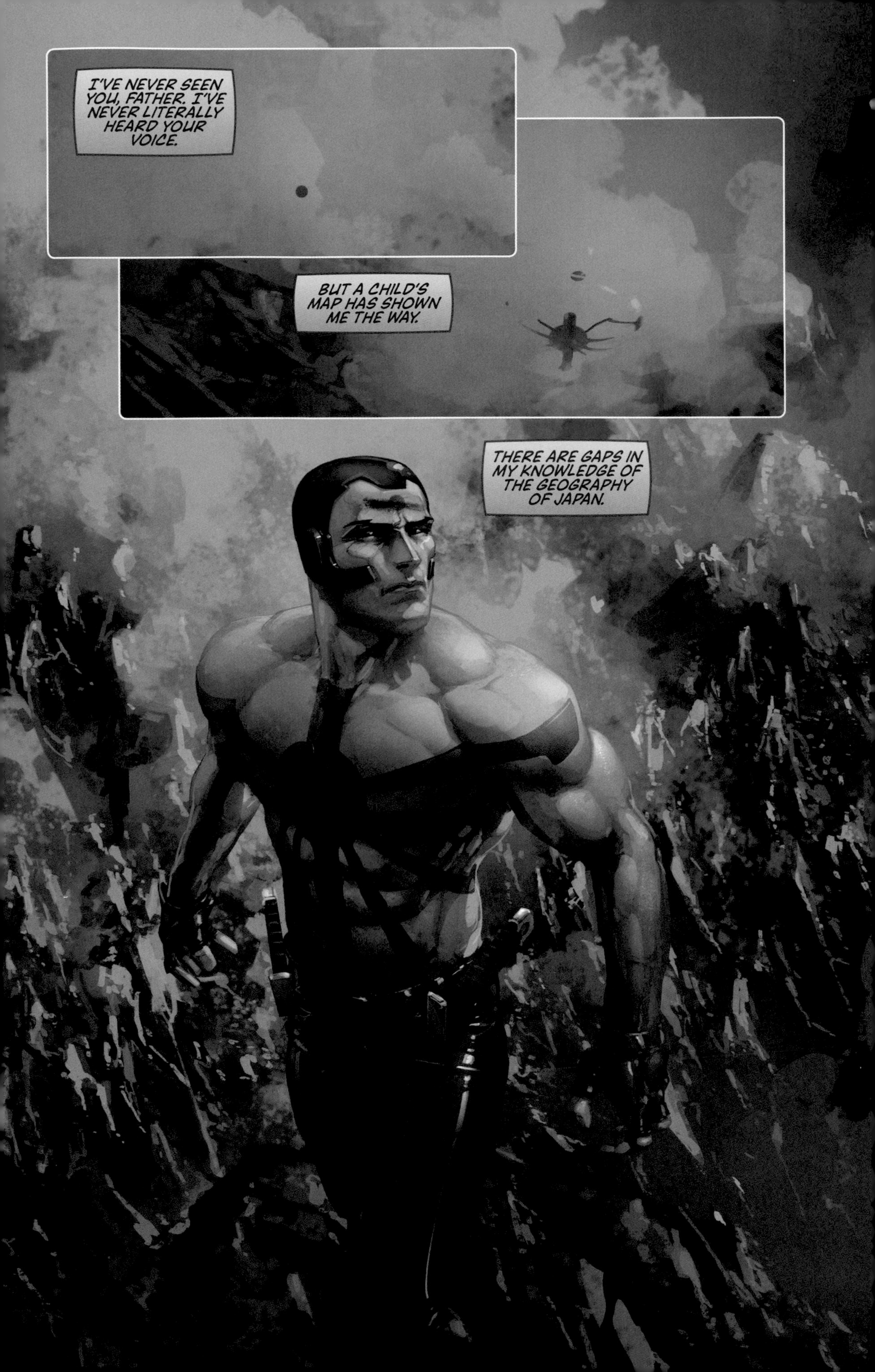
I'VE NEVER SEEN YOU, FATHER. I'VE NEVER LITERALLY HEARD YOUR VOICE.
BUT A CHILD'S MAP HAS SHOWN ME THE WAY.
THERE ARE GAPS IN MY KNOWLEDGE OF THE GEOGRAPHY OF JAPAN.

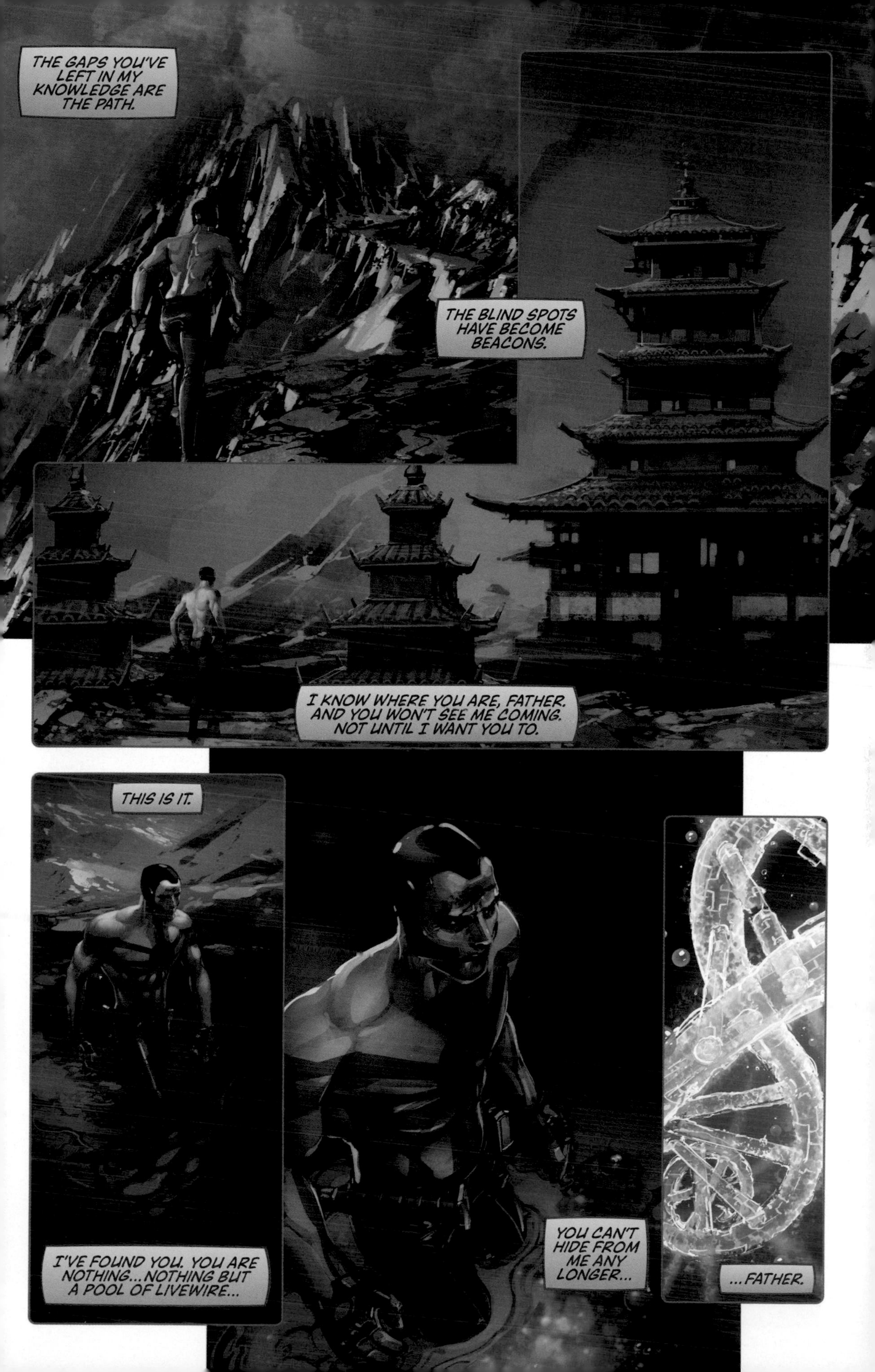
THE GAPS YOU'VE LEFT IN MY KNOWLEDGE ARE THE PATH.
THE BLIND SPOTS HAVE BECOME BEACONS.
I KNOW WHERE YOU ARE, FATHER. AND YOU WON'T SEE ME COMING. NOT UNTIL I WANT YOU TO.
THIS IS IT.
I'VE FOUND YOU. YOU ARE NOTHING...NOTHING BUT A POOL OF LIVEWIRE...
YOU CAN'T HIDE FROM ME ANY LONGER...
...FATHER.

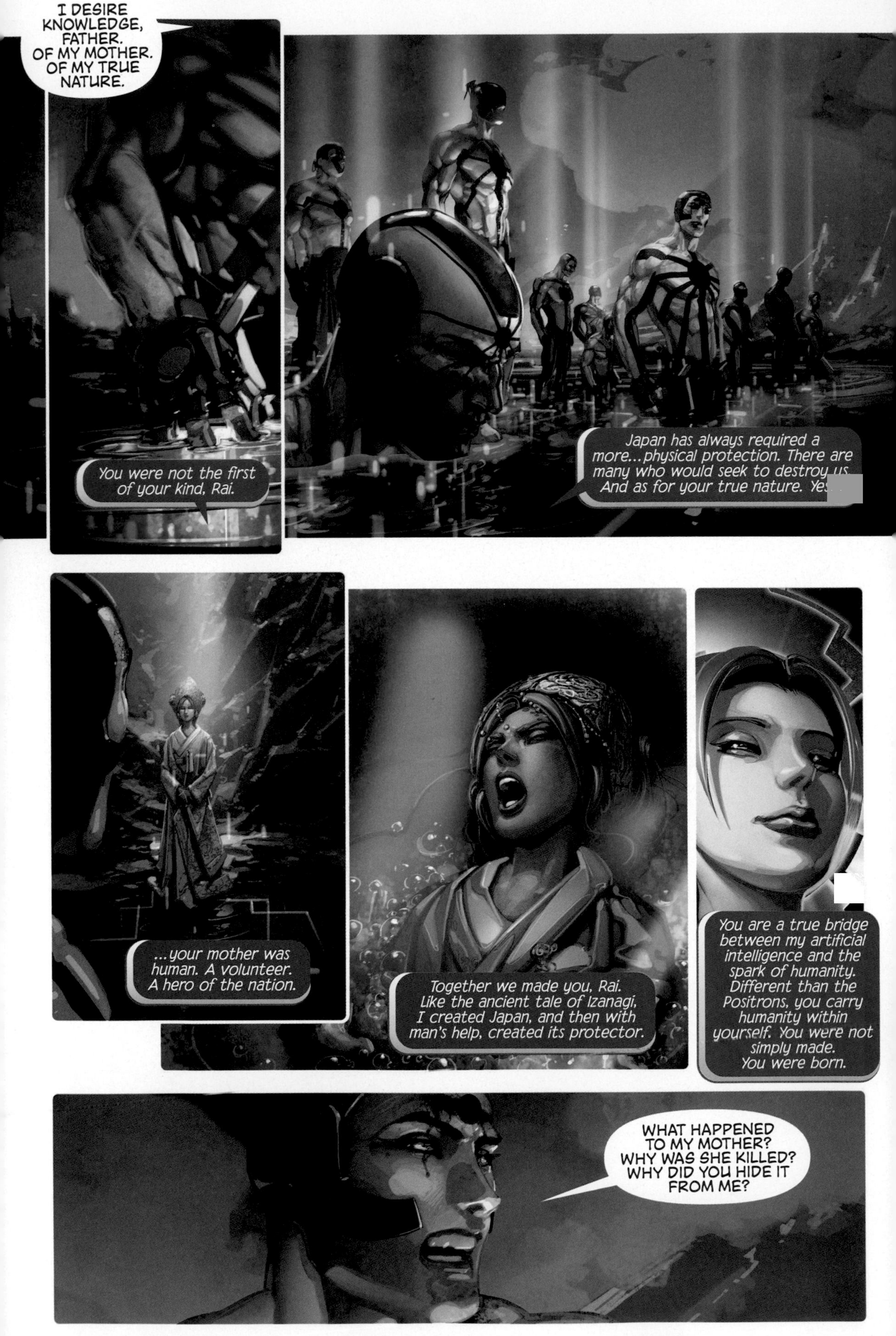
I DESIRE KNOWLEDGE, FATHER. OF MY MOTHER. OF MY TRUE NATURE.
You were not the first of your kind, Rai.
Japan has always required a more...physical protection. There are many who would seek to destroy us. And as for your true nature. Yes
...your mother was human. A volunteer. A hero of the nation.
Together we made you, Rai. Like the ancient tale of Izanagi, I created Japan, and then with man's help, created its protector.
You are a true bridge between my artificial intelligence and the spark of humanity. Different than the Positrons, you carry humanity within yourself. You were not simply made. You were born.
WHAT HAPPENED TO MY MOTHER? WHY WAS SHE KILLED? WHY DID YOU HIDE IT FROM ME?

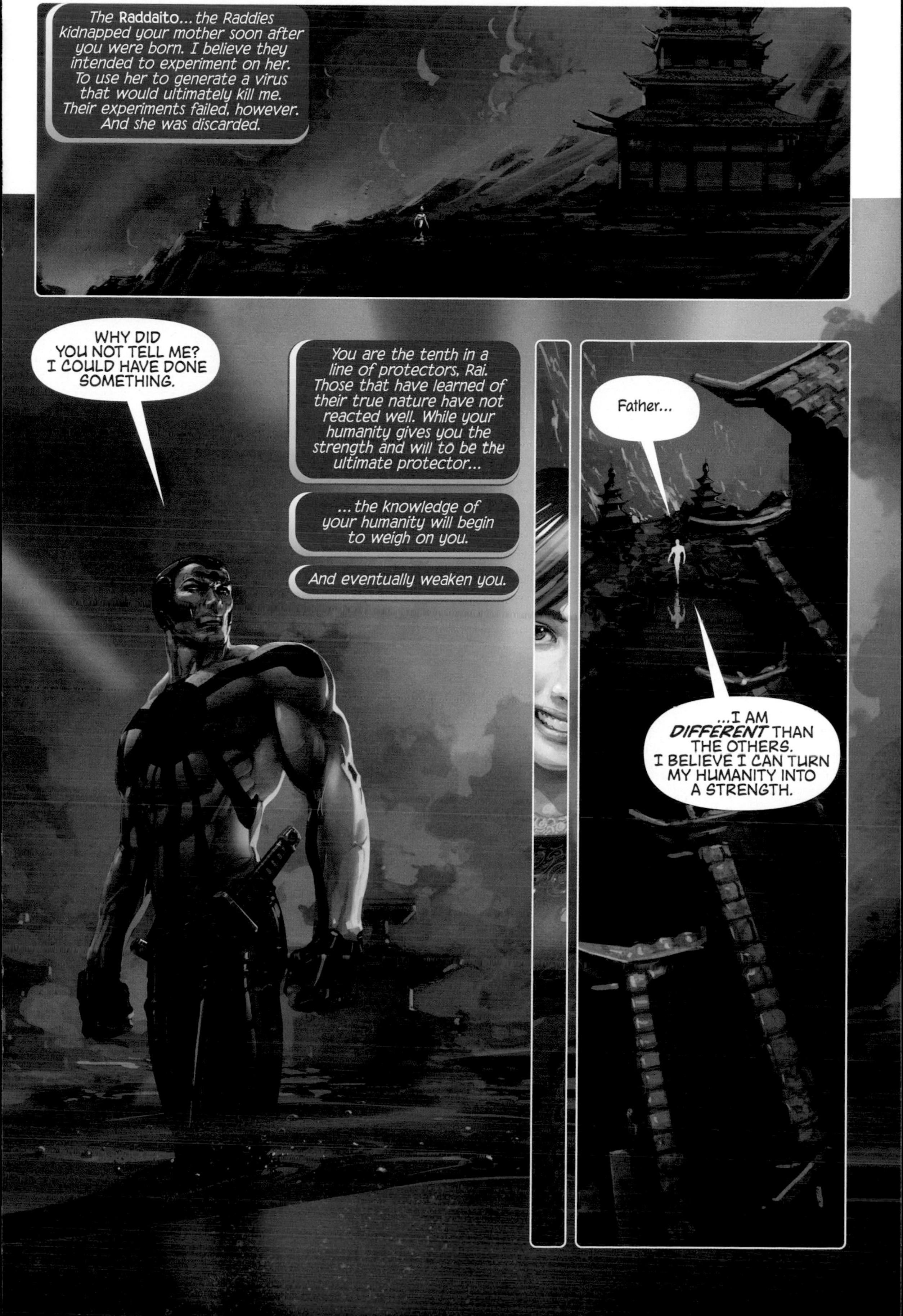
The Raddaito... the Raddies kidnapped your mother soon after you were born. I believe they intended to experiment on her. To use her to generate a virus that would ultimately kill me. Their experiments failed, however. And she was discarded.
WHY DID YOU NOT TELL ME? I COULD HAVE DONE SOMETHING.
You are the tenth in a line of protectors, Rai. Those that have learned of their true nature have not reacted well. While your humanity gives you the strength and will to be the ultimate protector...
...the knowledge of your humanity will begin to weigh on you.
And eventually weaken you.
Father...
...I AM DIFFERENT THAN THE OTHERS. I BELIEVE I CAN TURN MY HUMANITY INTO A STRENGTH.

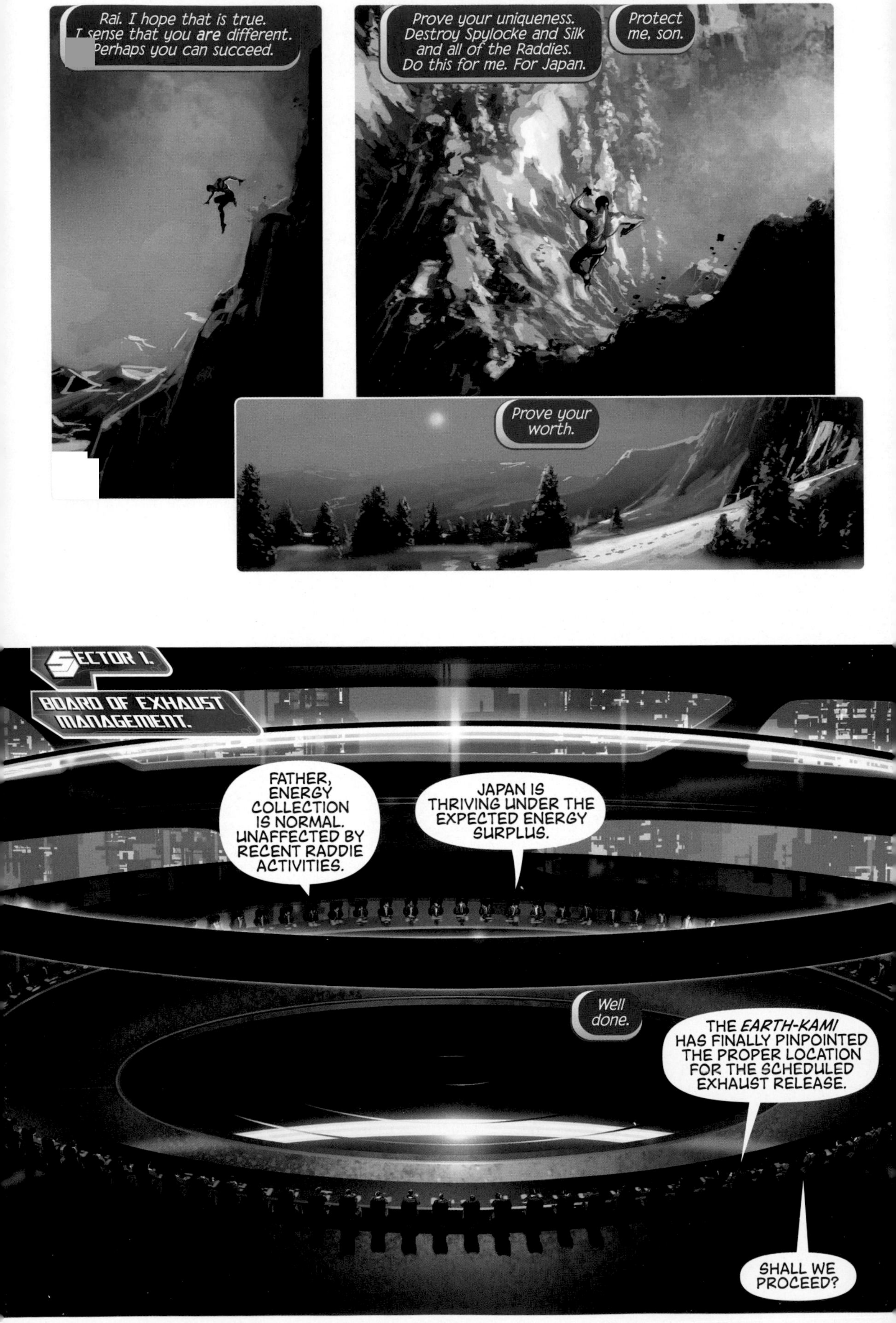

Rai. I hope that is true. I sense that you **are** different. Perhaps you can succeed.
Prove your uniqueness. Destroy Spylocke and Silk and all of the Raddies. Do this for me. For Japan.
Protect me, son.
Prove your worth.
SECTOR 1.
BOARD OF EXHAUST MANAGEMENT.
FATHER, ENERGY COLLECTION IS NORMAL. UNAFFECTED BY RECENT RADDIE ACTIVITIES.
JAPAN IS THRIVING UNDER THE EXPECTED ENERGY SURPLUS.
Well done.
THE *EARTH-KAMI* HAS FINALLY PINPOINTED THE PROPER LOCATION FOR THE SCHEDULED EXHAUST RELEASE.
SHALL WE PROCEED?

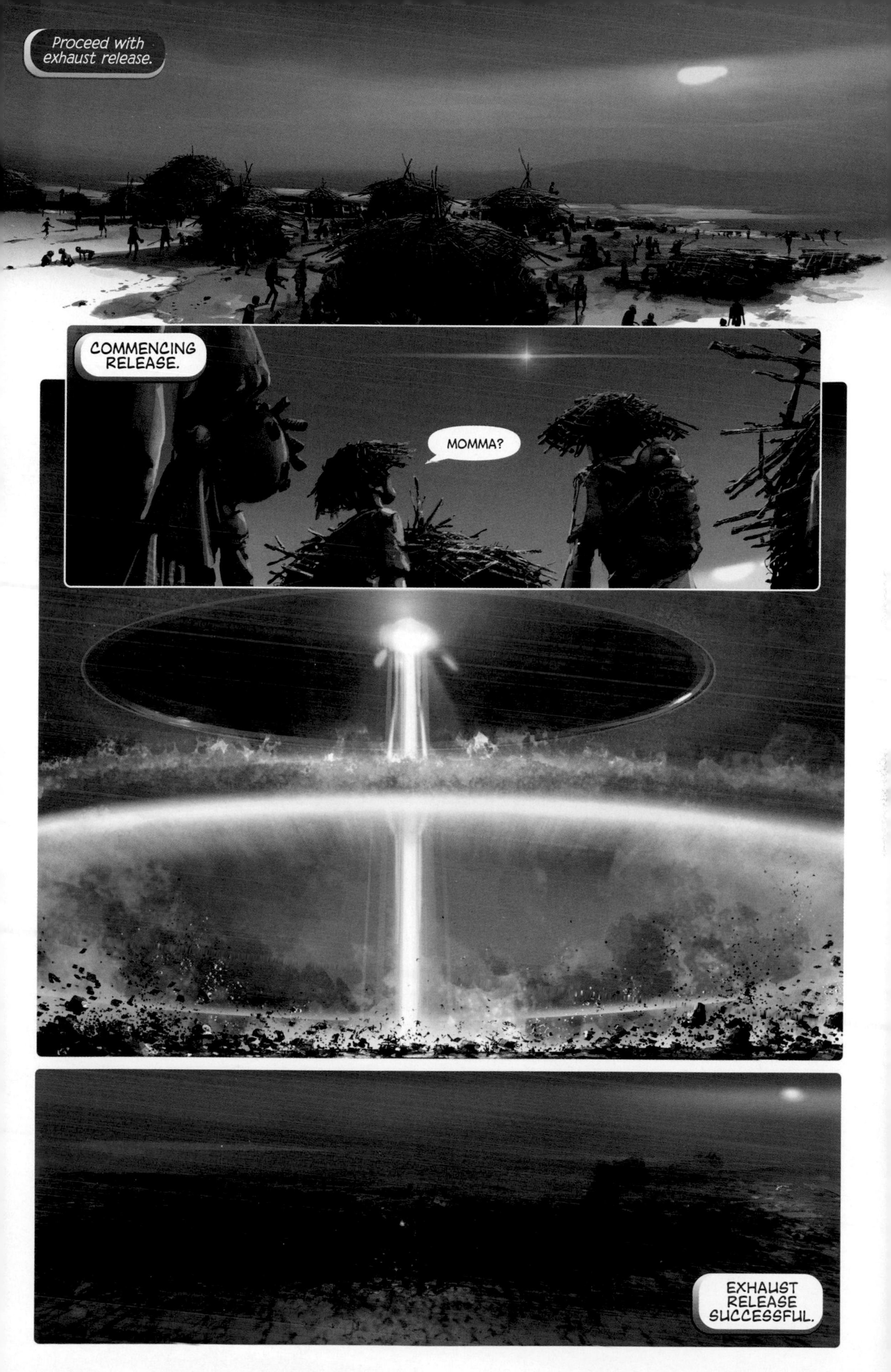
Proceed with exhaust release.
COMMENCING RELEASE.
MOMMA?
EXHAUST RELEASE SUCCESSFUL.

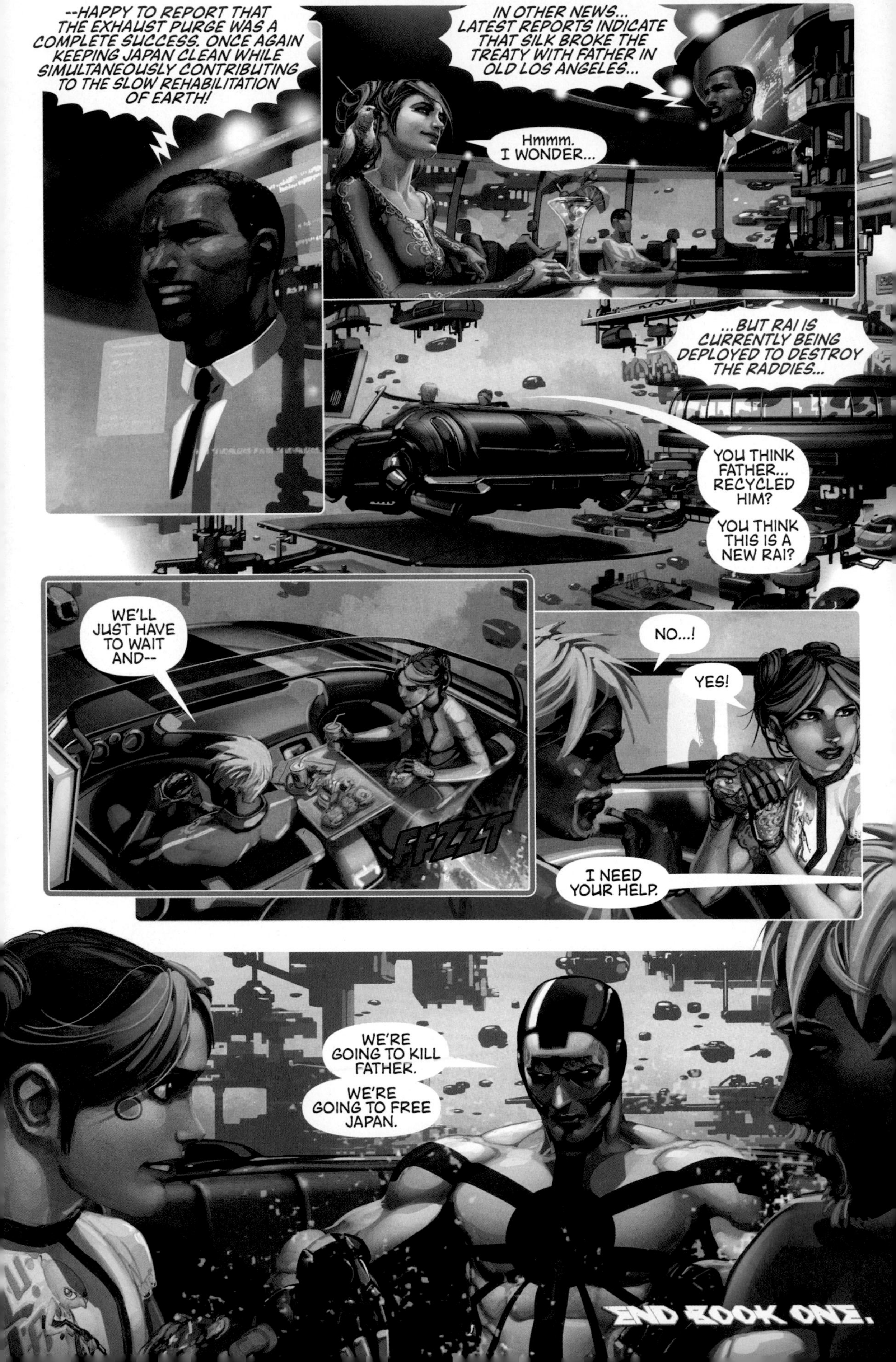
--HAPPY TO REPORT THAT THE EXHAUST PURGE WAS A COMPLETE SUCCESS. ONCE AGAIN KEEPING JAPAN CLEAN WHILE SIMULTANEOUSLY CONTRIBUTING TO THE SLOW REHABILITATION OF EARTH!
IN OTHER NEWS... LATEST REPORTS INDICATE THAT SILK BROKE THE TREATY WITH FATHER IN OLD LOS ANGELES...
Hmmm. I WONDER...
...BUT RAI IS CURRENTLY BEING DEPLOYED TO DESTROY THE RADDIES...
YOU THINK FATHER... RECYCLED HIM?
YOU THINK THIS IS A NEW RAI?
WE'LL JUST HAVE TO WAIT AND--
FFZZZT
NO...!
YES!
I NEED YOUR HELP.
WE'RE GOING TO KILL FATHER.
WE'RE GOING TO FREE JAPAN.
END BOOK ONE.

GALLERY

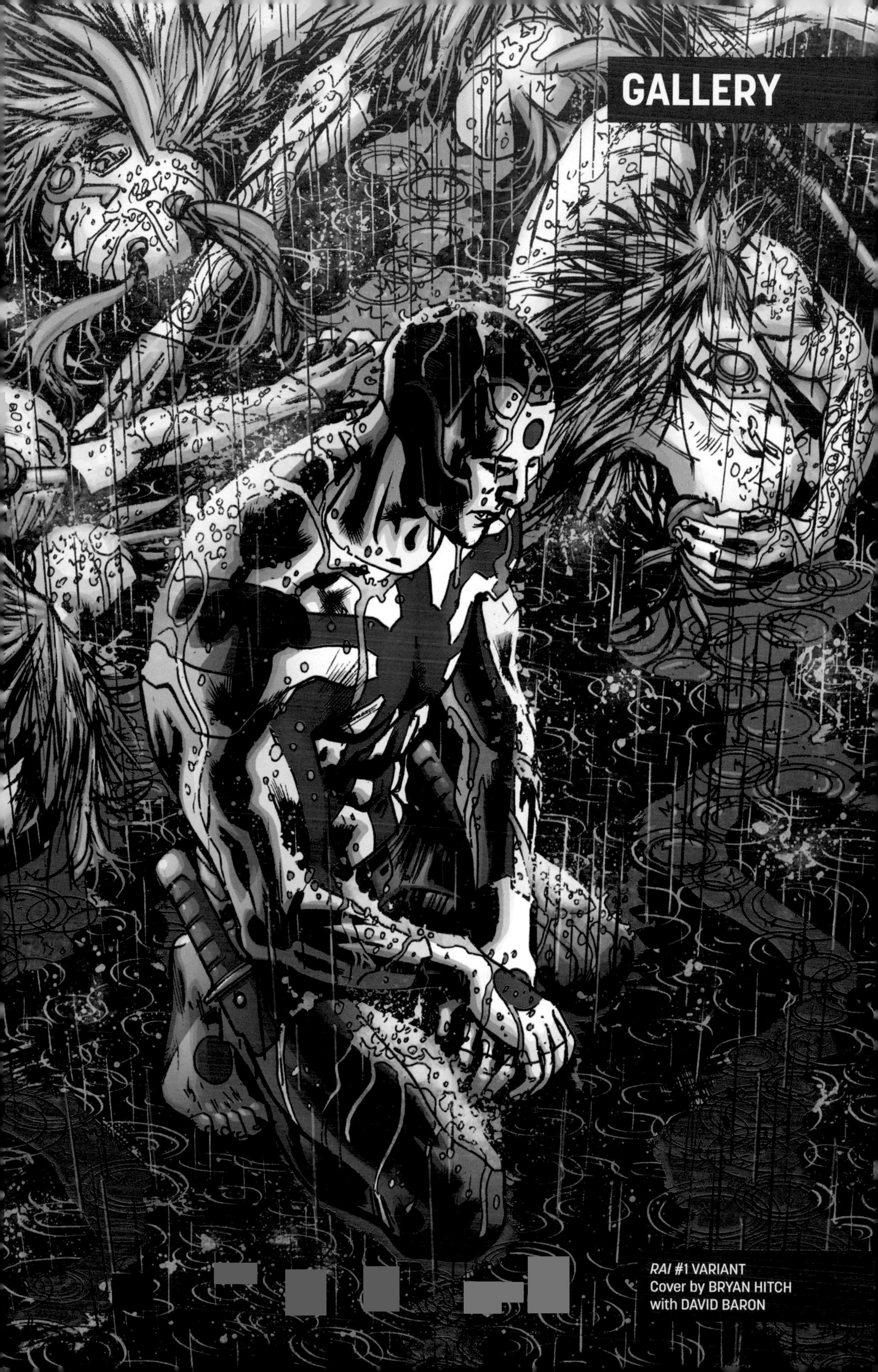

RAI #1 VARIANT
Cover by BRYAN HITCH
with DAVID BARON

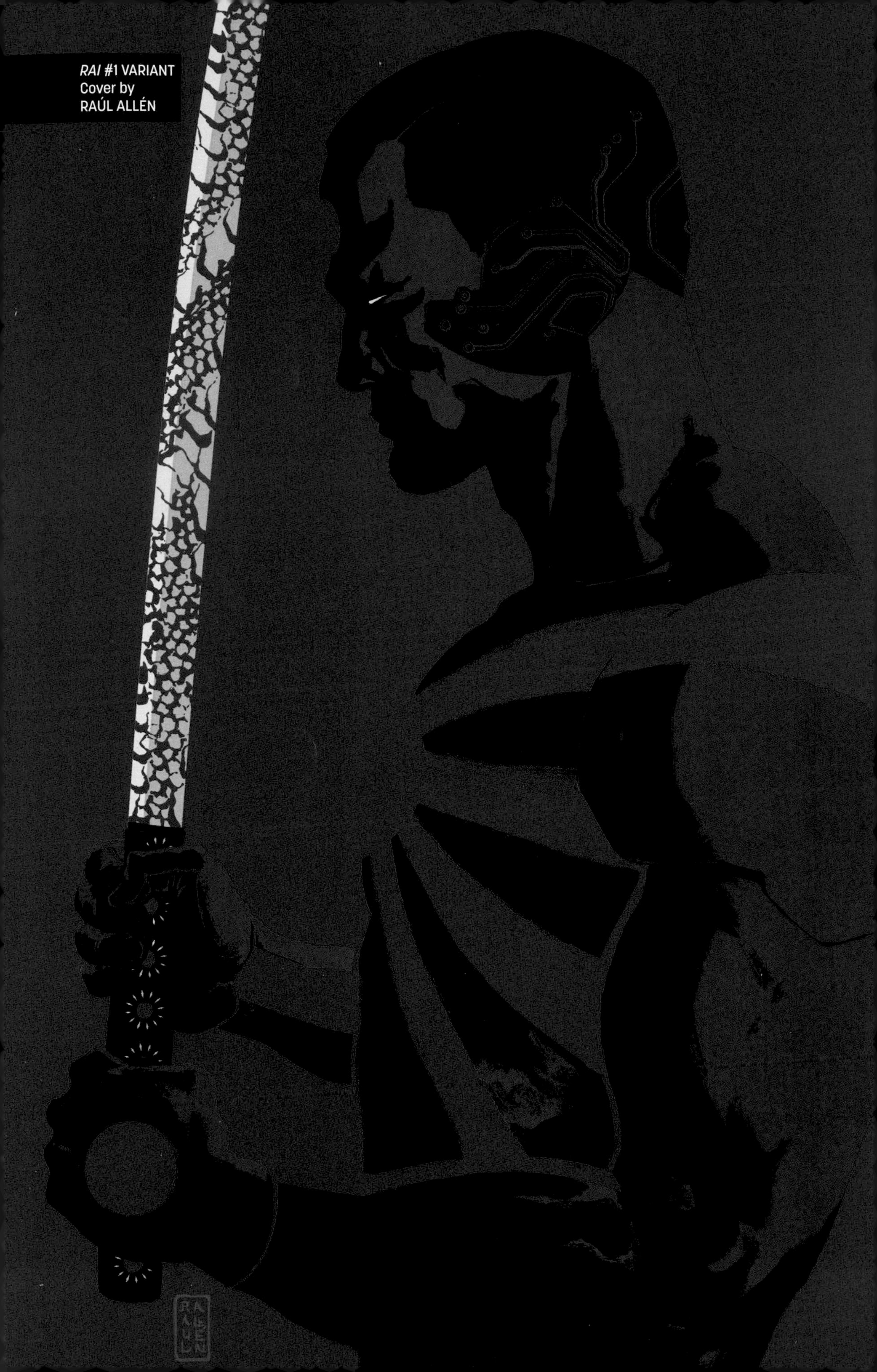

RAI #1 VARIANT
Cover by
RAÚL ALLÉN

RAI #1 VARIANT
Cover by DAVID AJA and
RAÚL ALLÉN

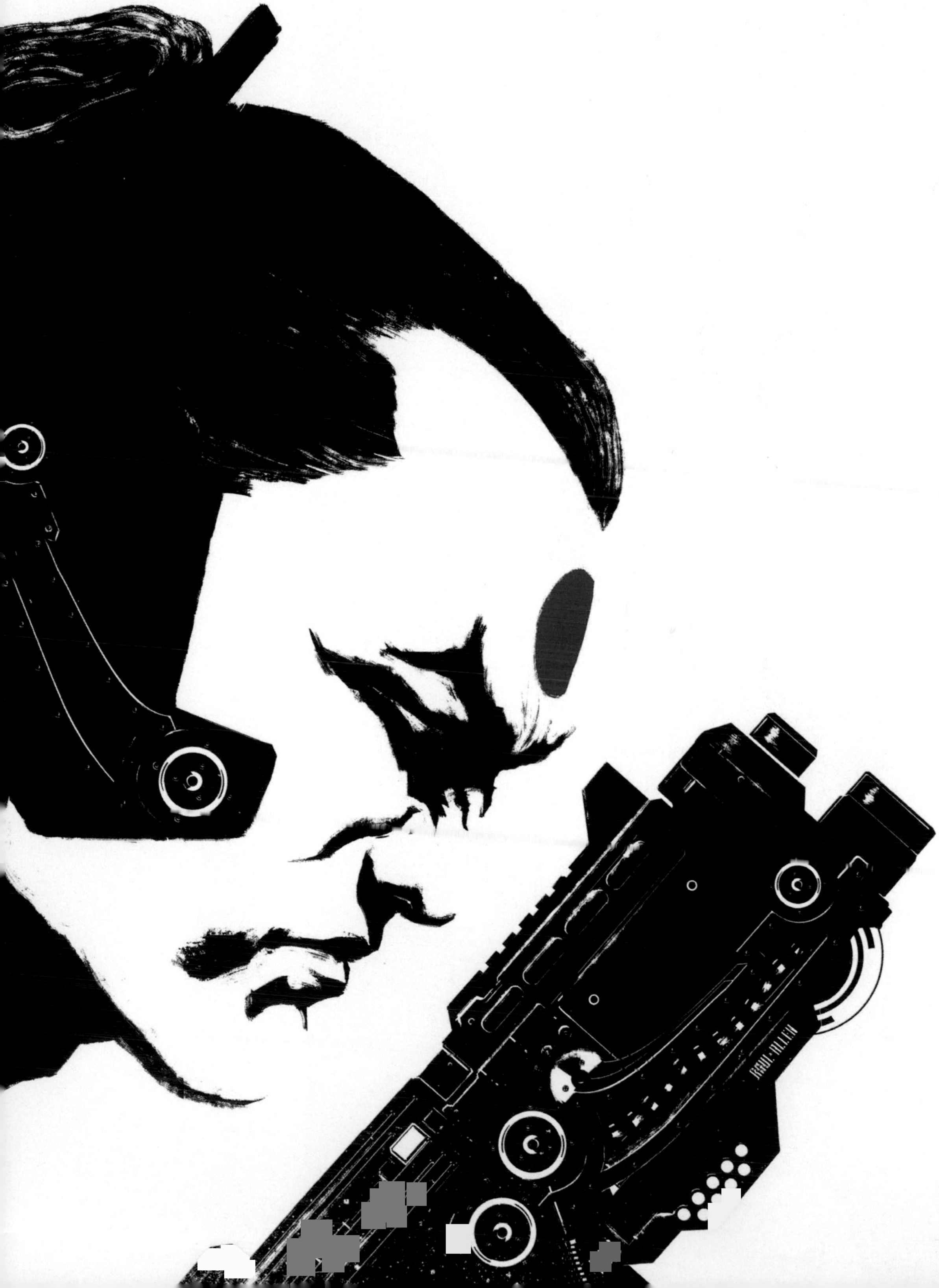

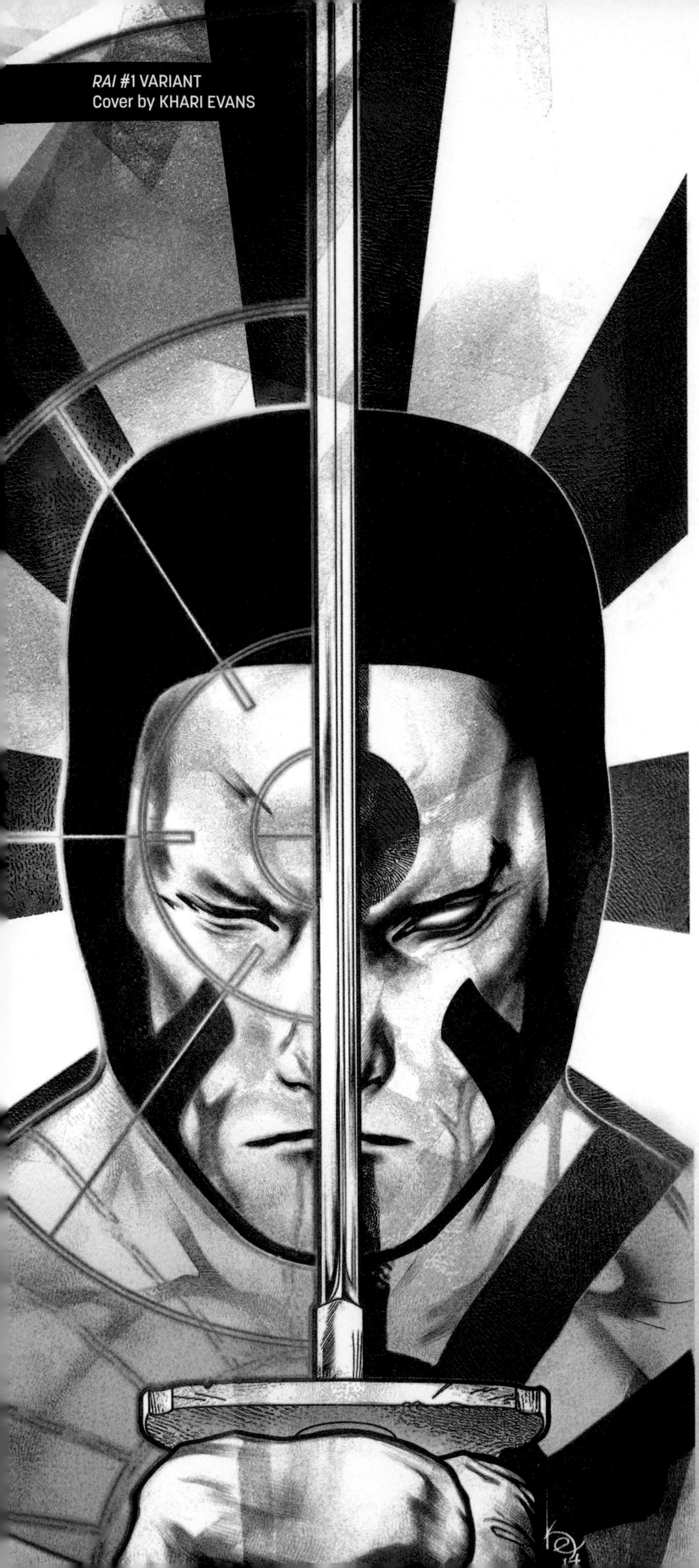

RAI #1 VARIANT
Cover by KHARI EVANS

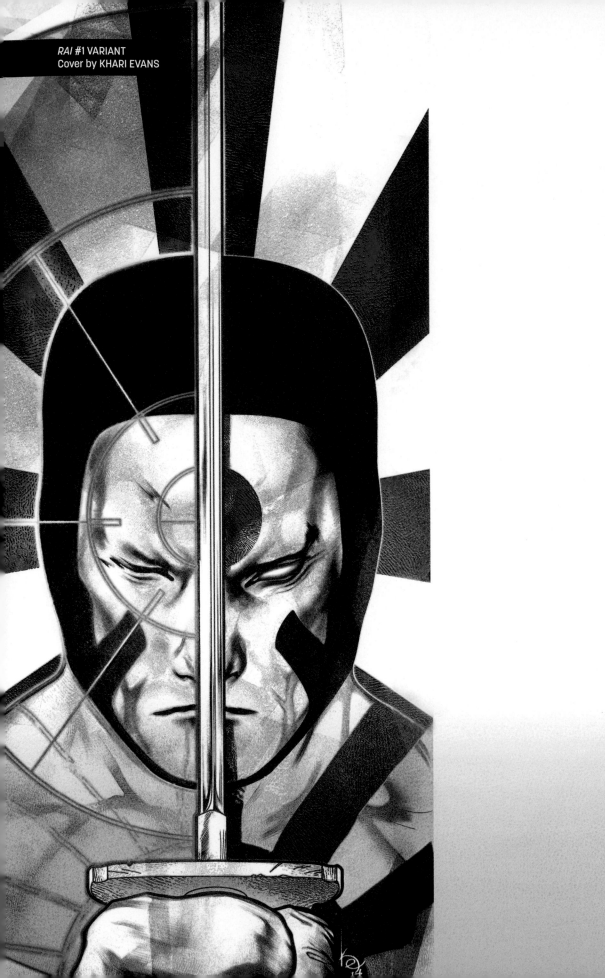

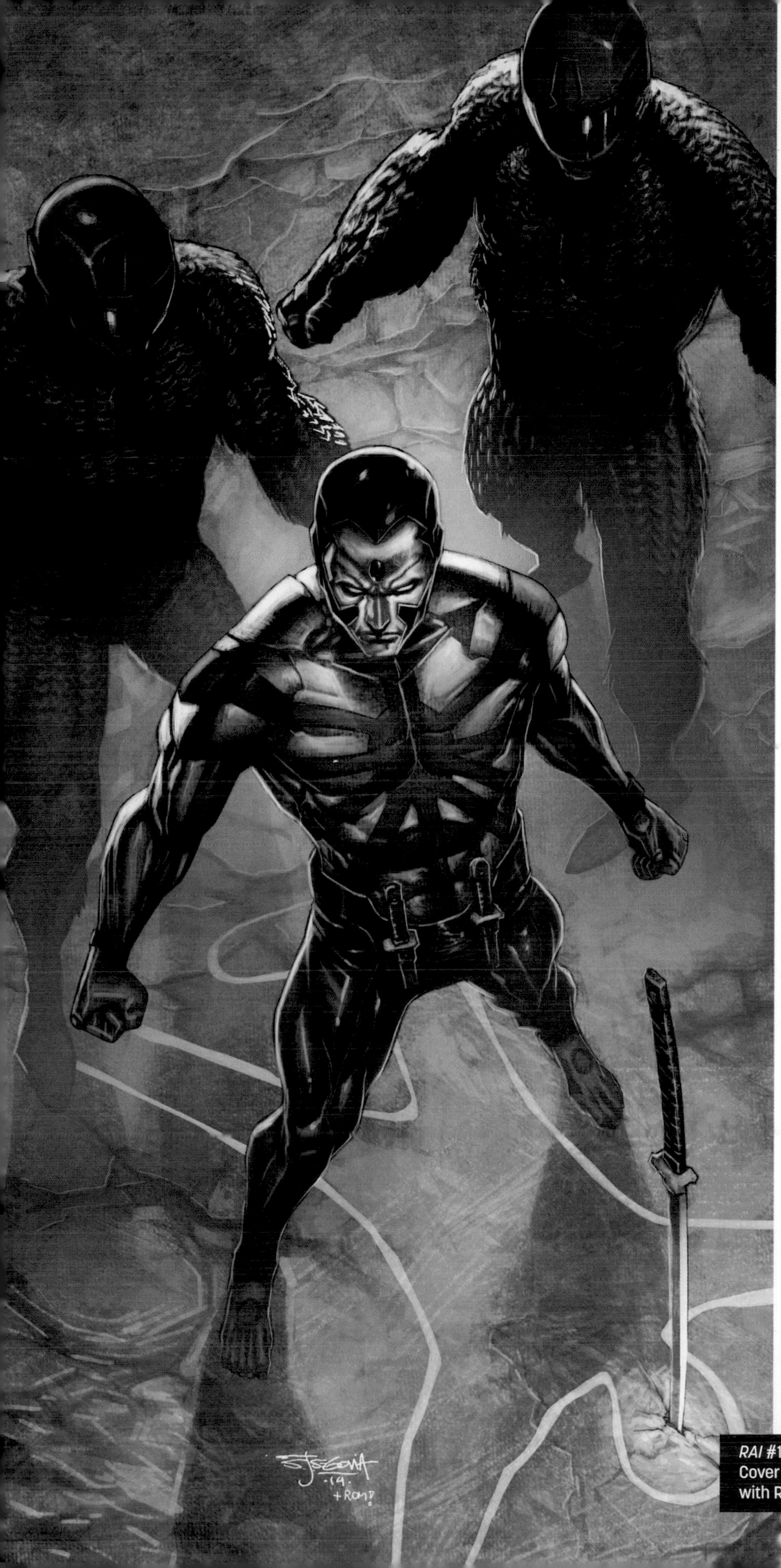

RAI #1 VARIANT
Cover by STEPHEN SEGOVIA
with ROMULO FAJARDO

RAI #1 VARIANT
Cover by TREVOR HAIRSINE
with DAVID BARON

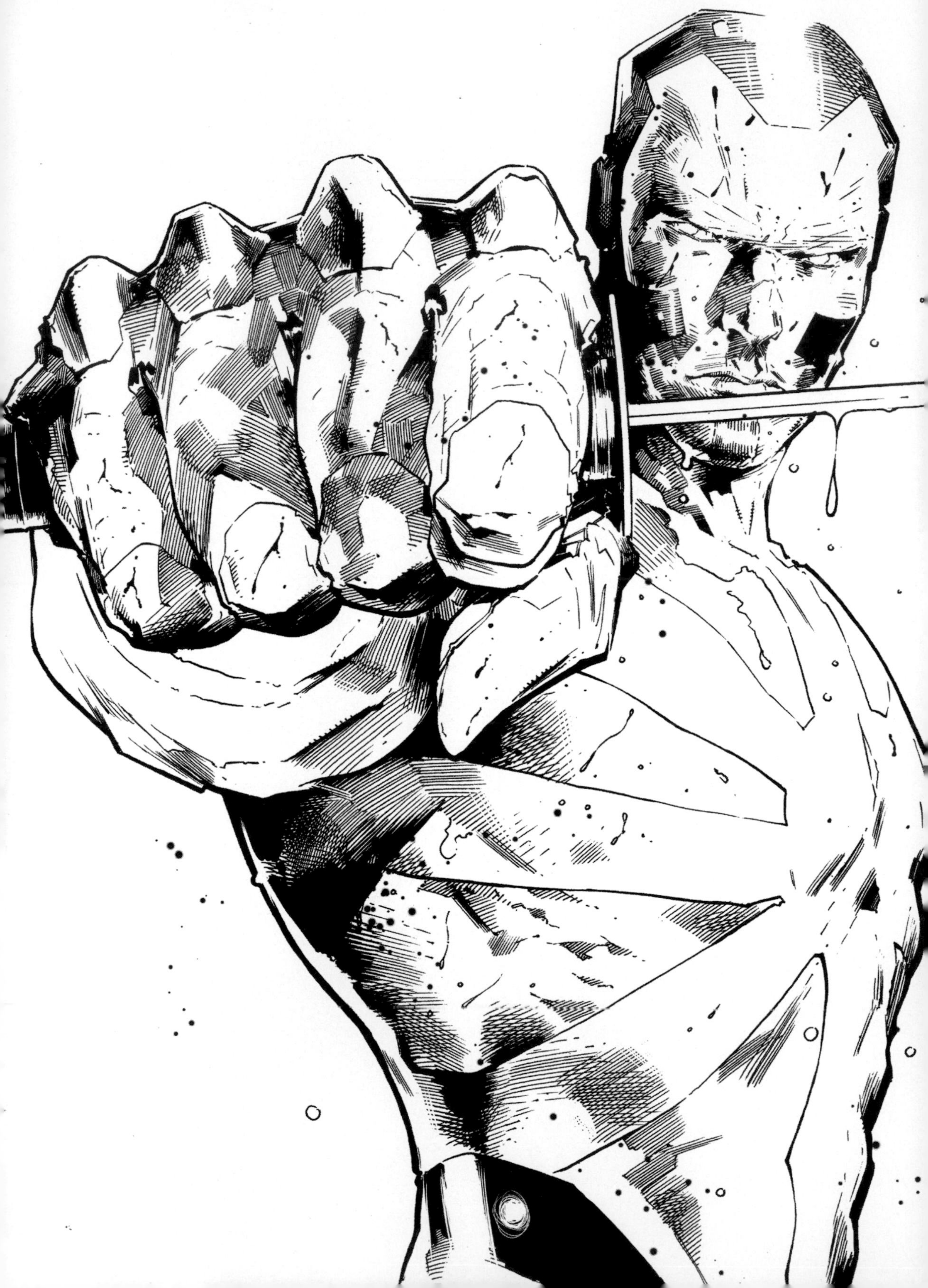

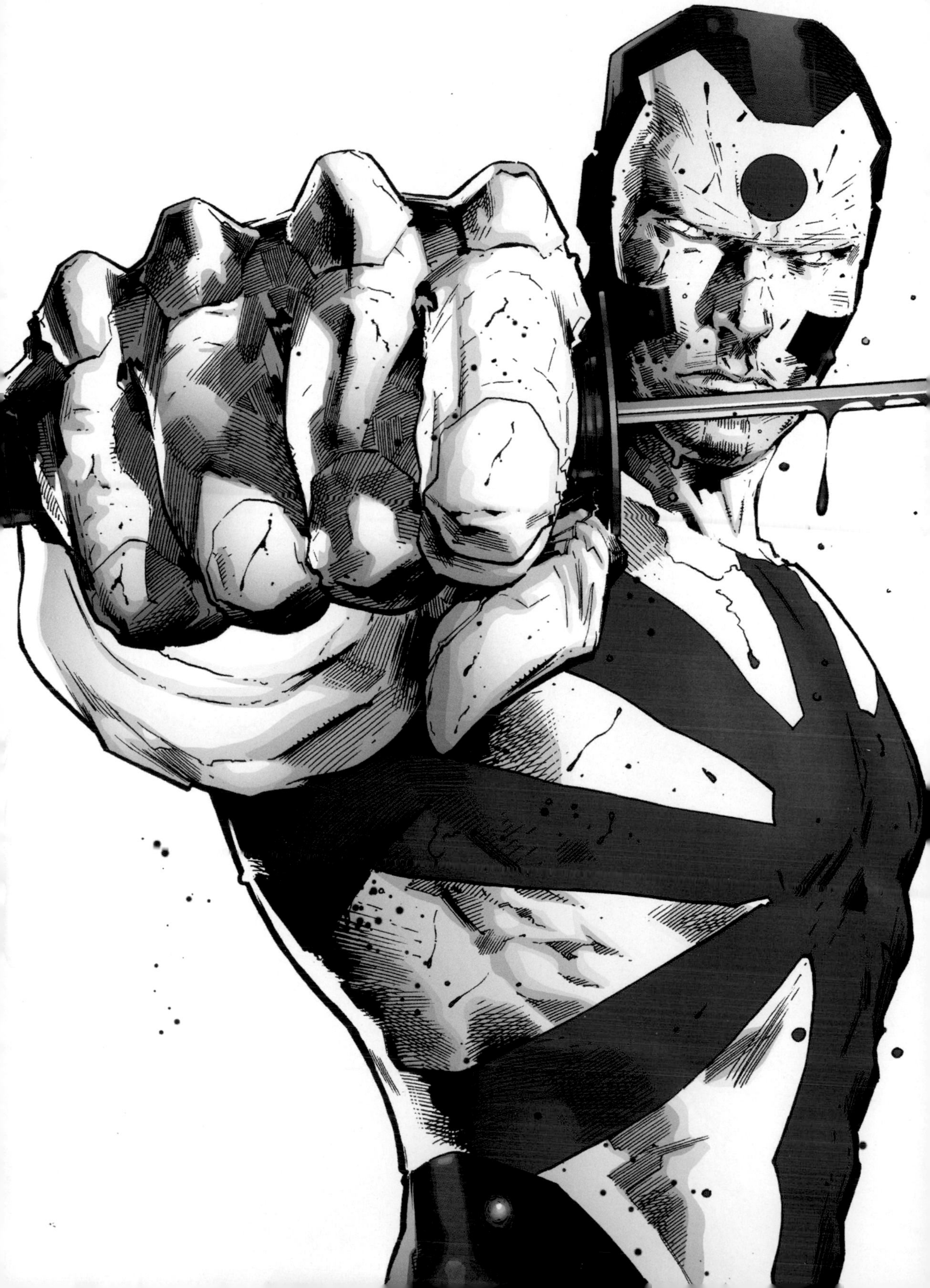

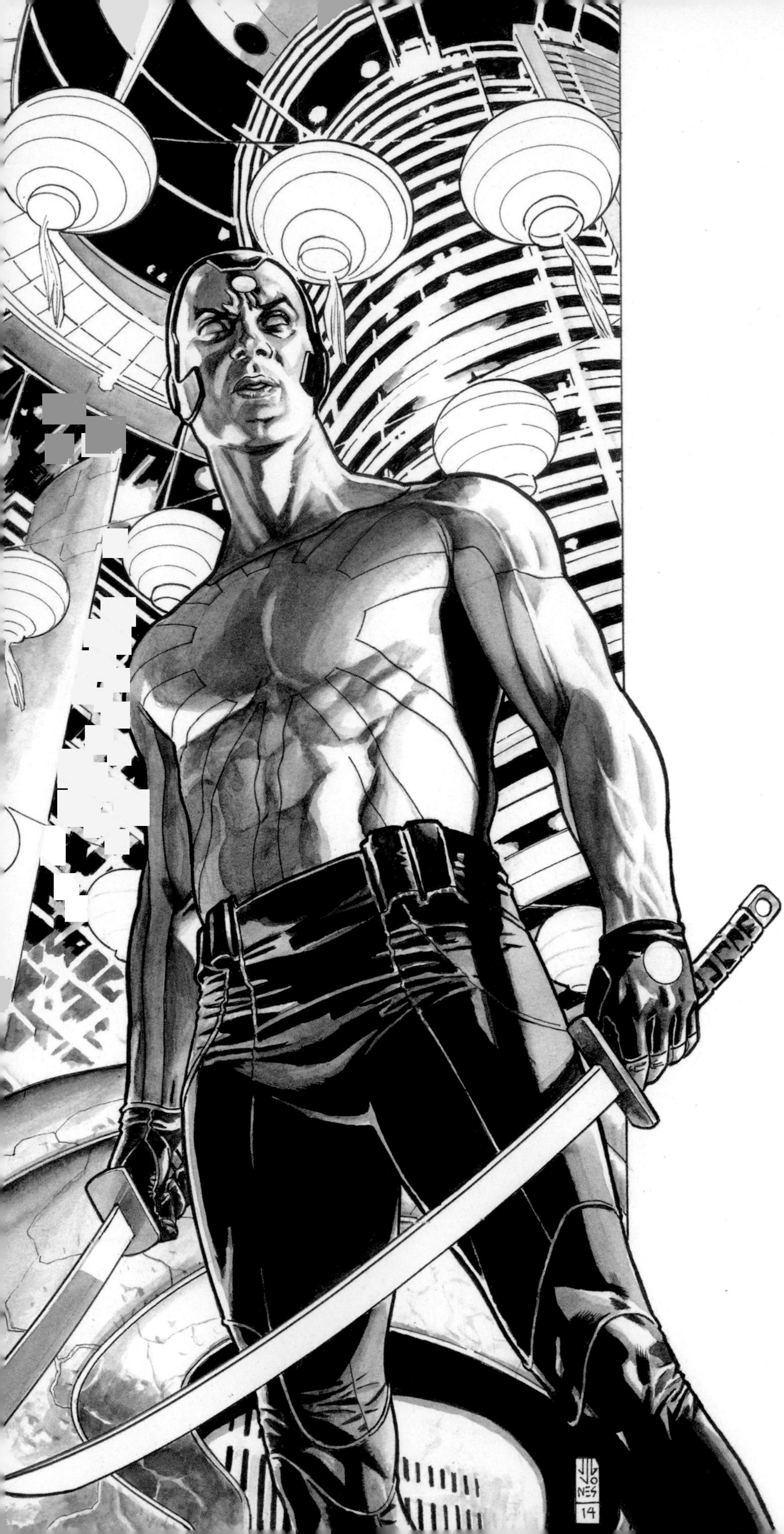

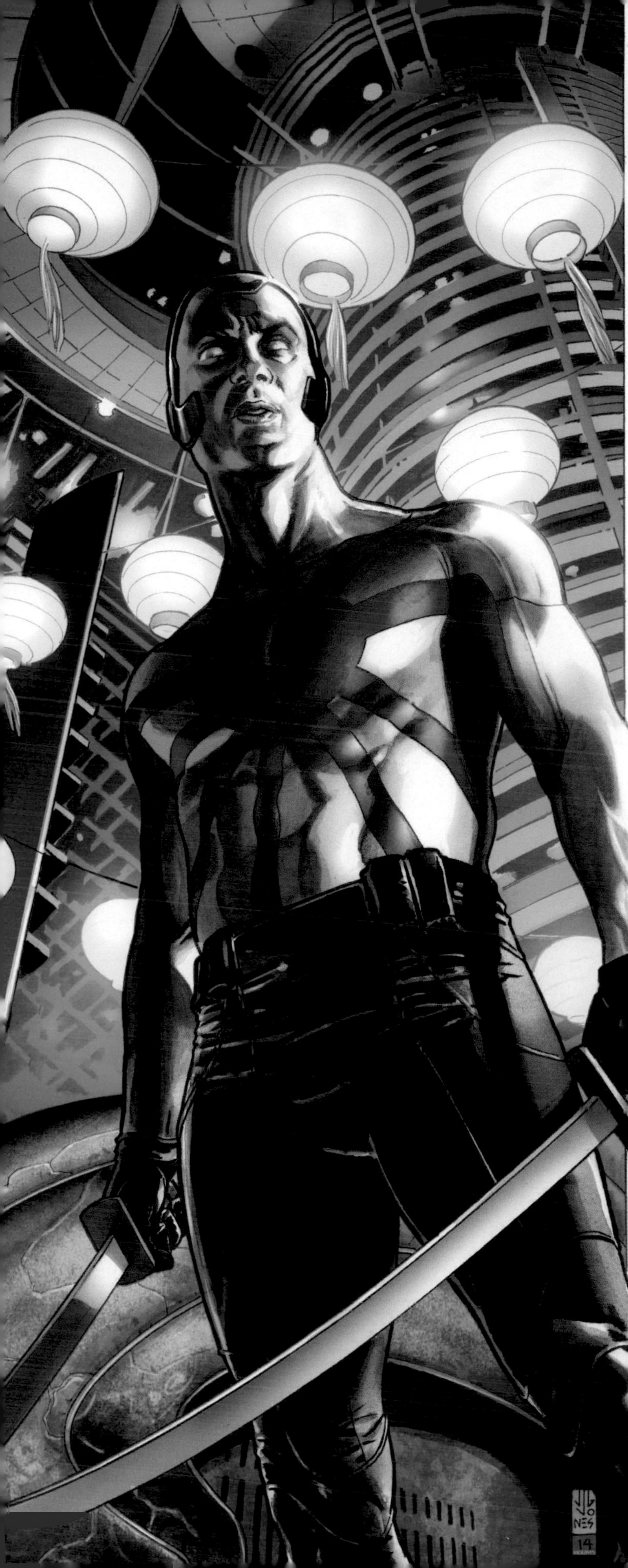

RAI #1 CARDS, COMICS AND COLLECTIBLES
RETAILER VARIANT
Cover by JG JONES
with PAUL MOUNTS

RAI #1 MIDTOWN COMICS
RETAILER VARIANT
Cover by RILEY ROSSMO

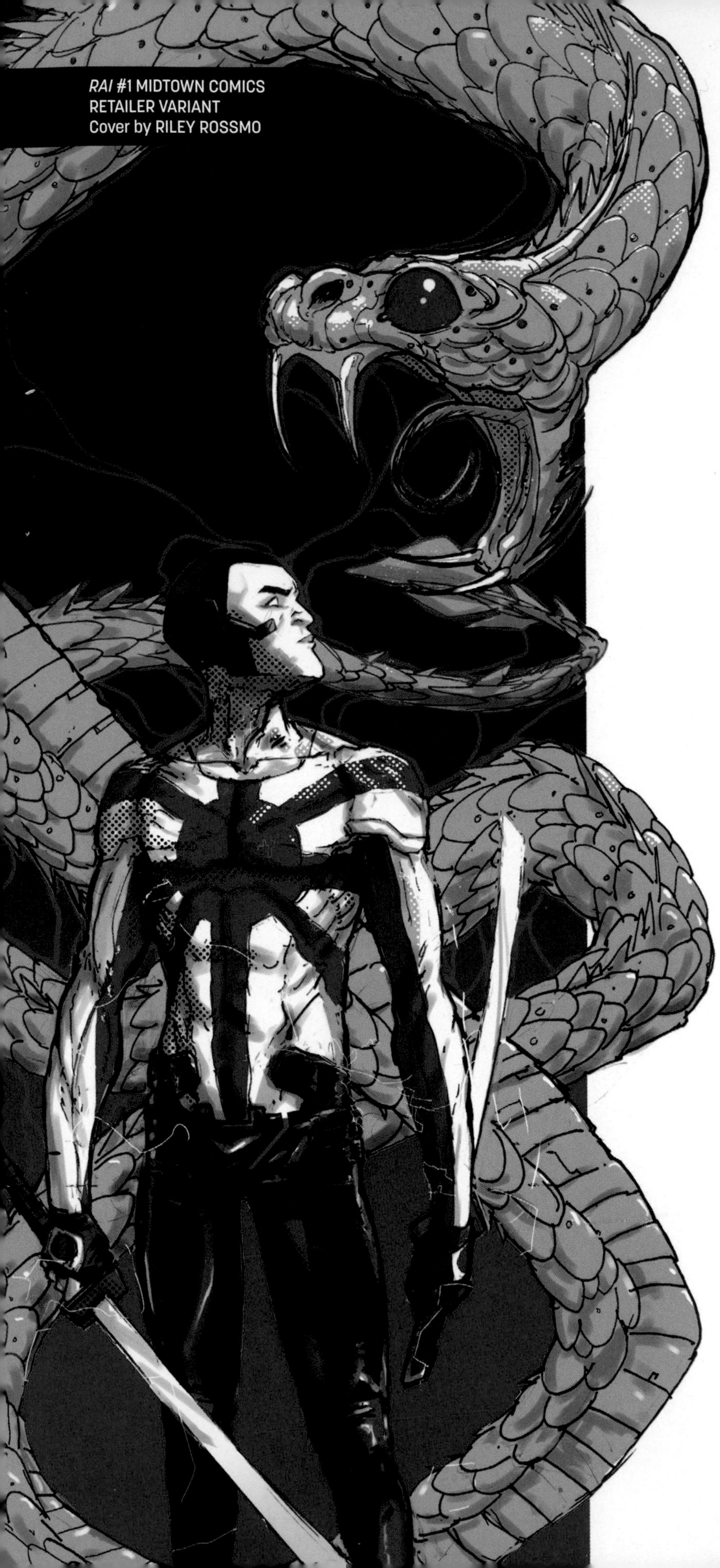

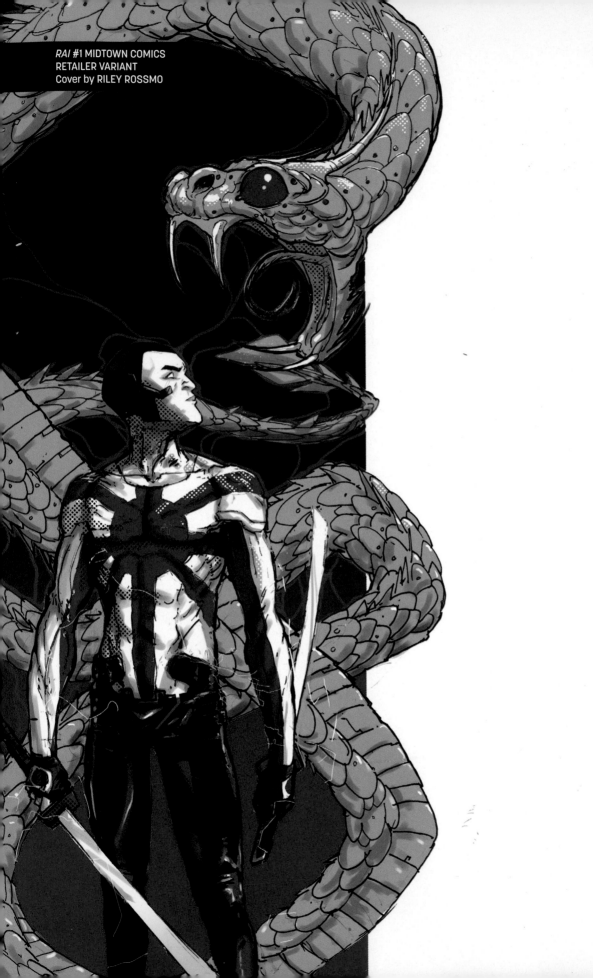

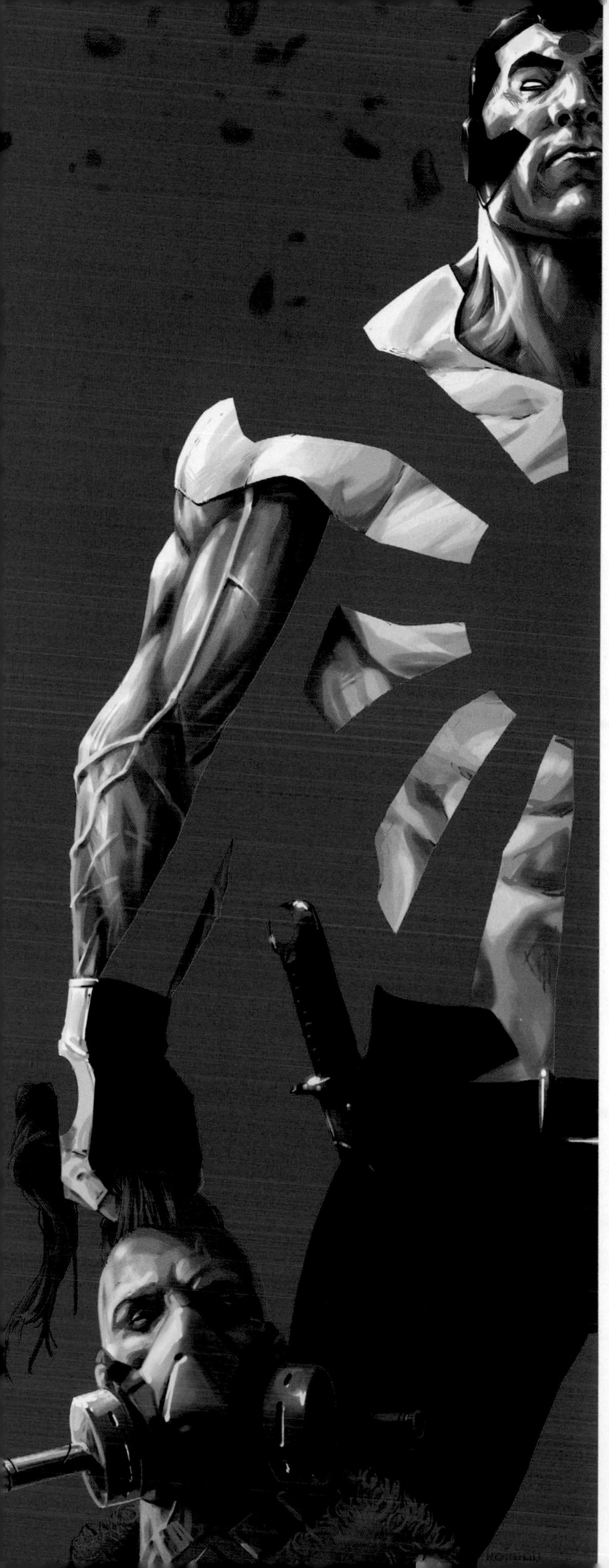

RAI #1 GRAHAM CRACKERS
RETAILER VARIANT
Cover by KALMAN ADRASOFSZKY

RAI #2 VARIANT COVER
Process and finished art
by MICO SUAYAN with DAVID BARON

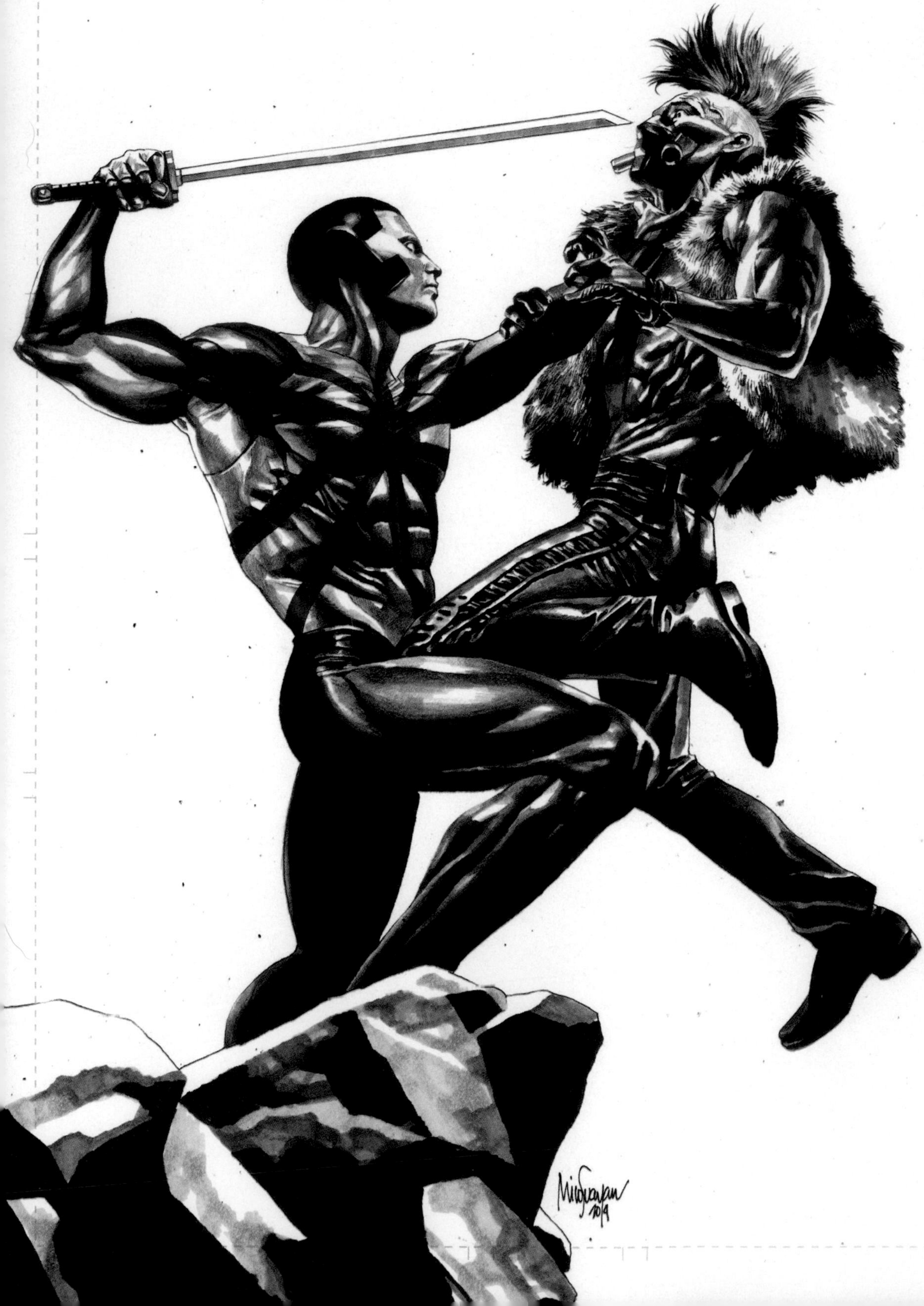

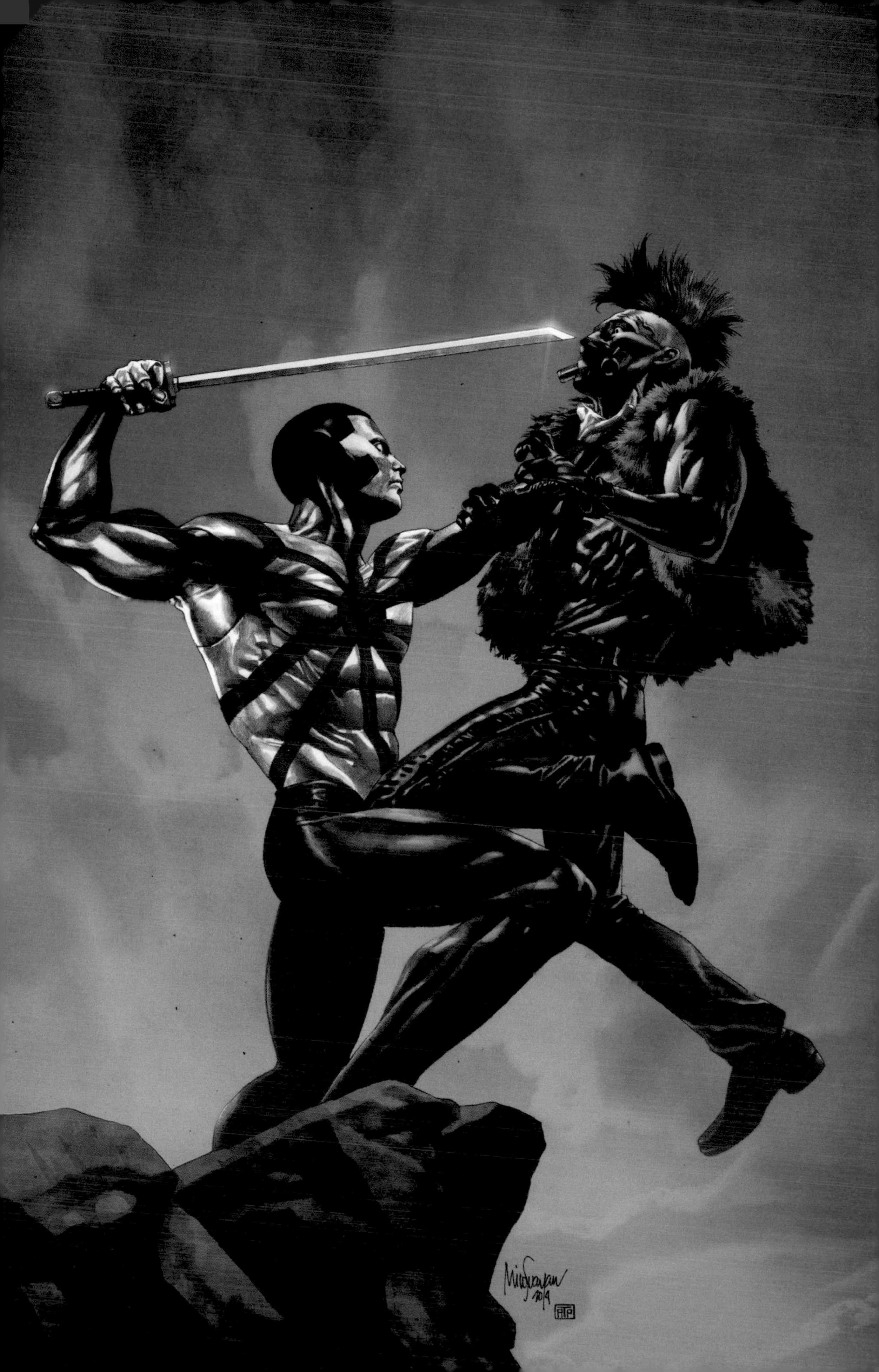

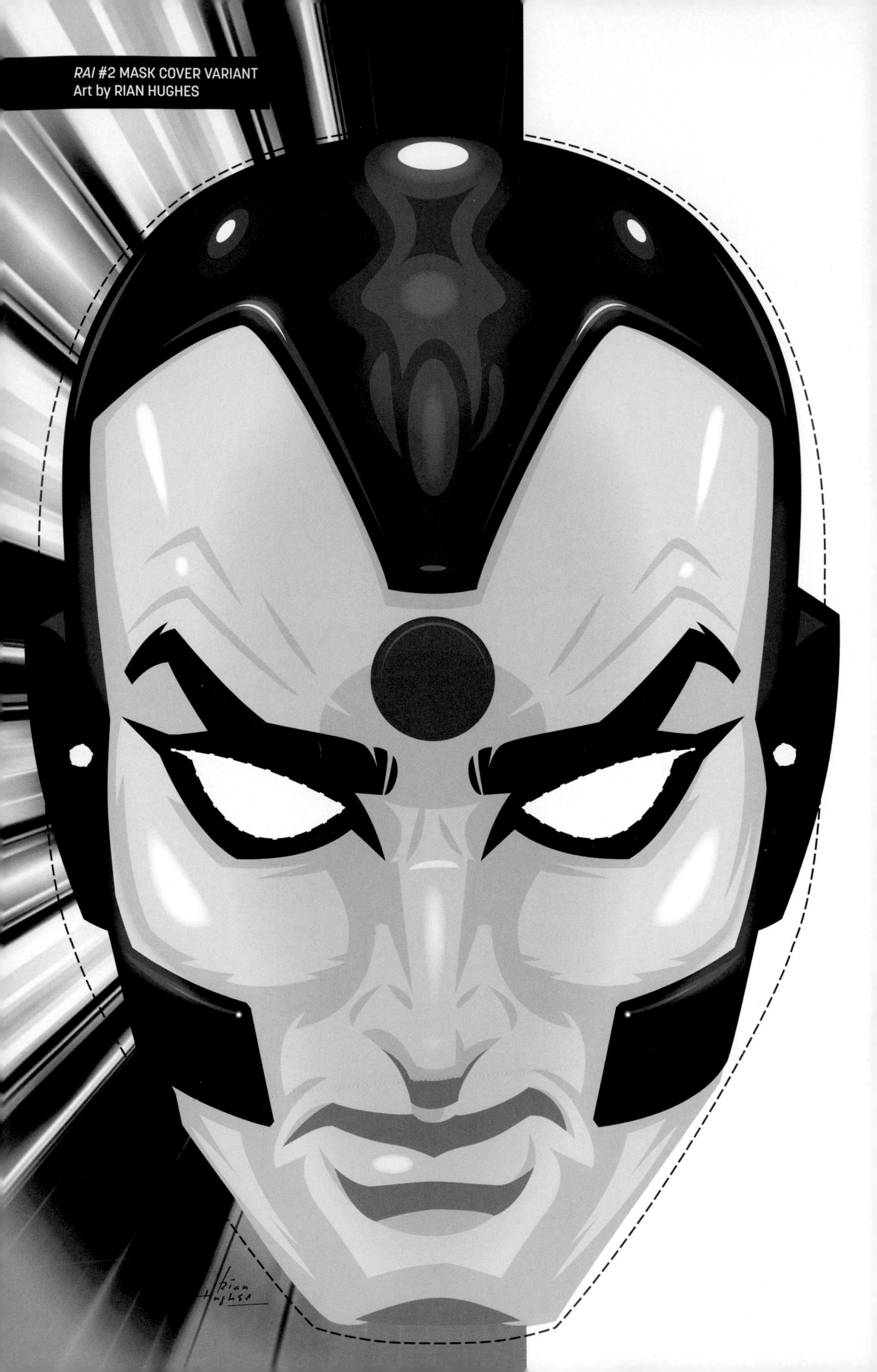

RAI #2 MASK COVER VARIANT
Art by RIAN HUGHES

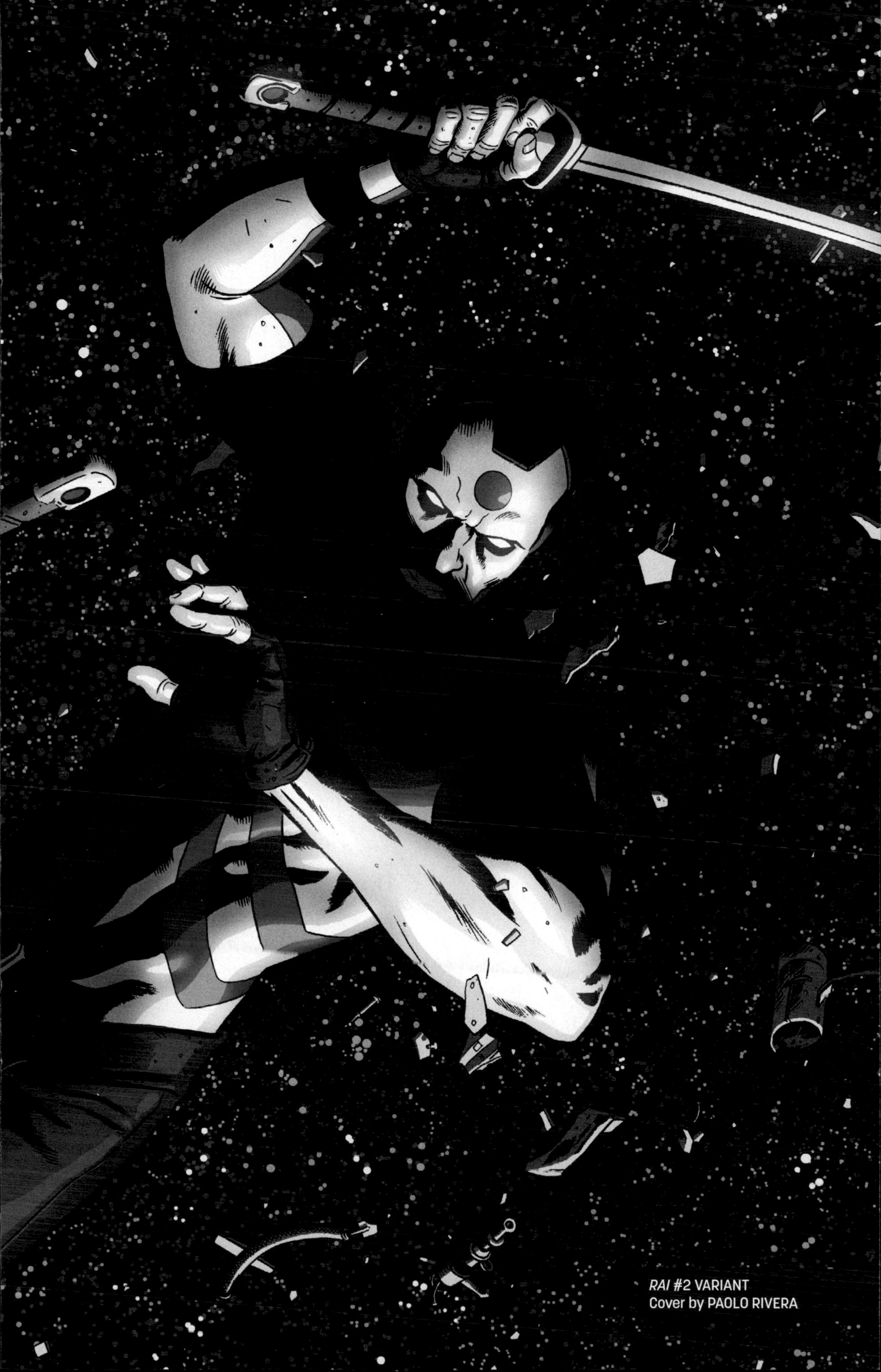

RAI #2 VARIANT
Cover by PAOLO RIVERA

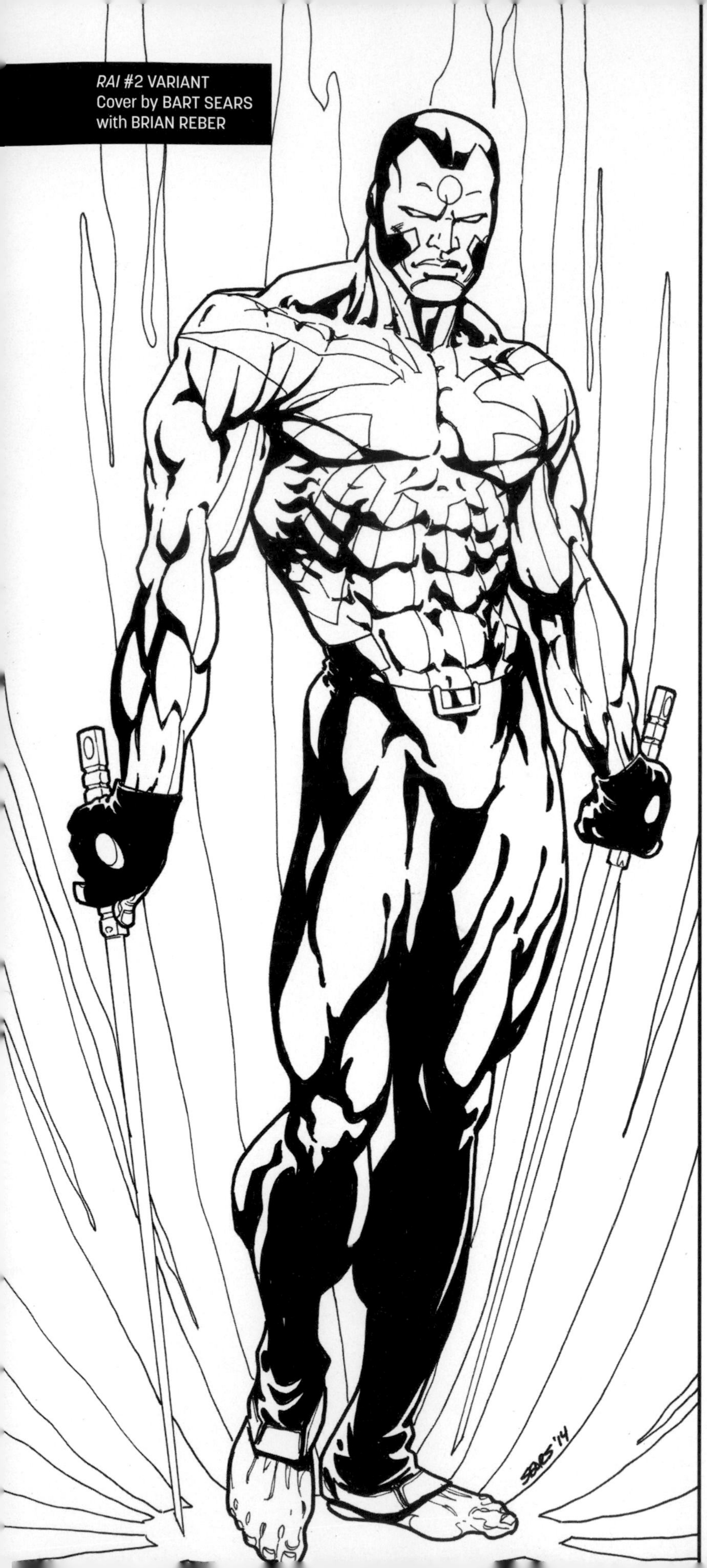

SEARS '14

RAI #2 VARIANT
Cover by BART SEARS
with BRIAN REBER

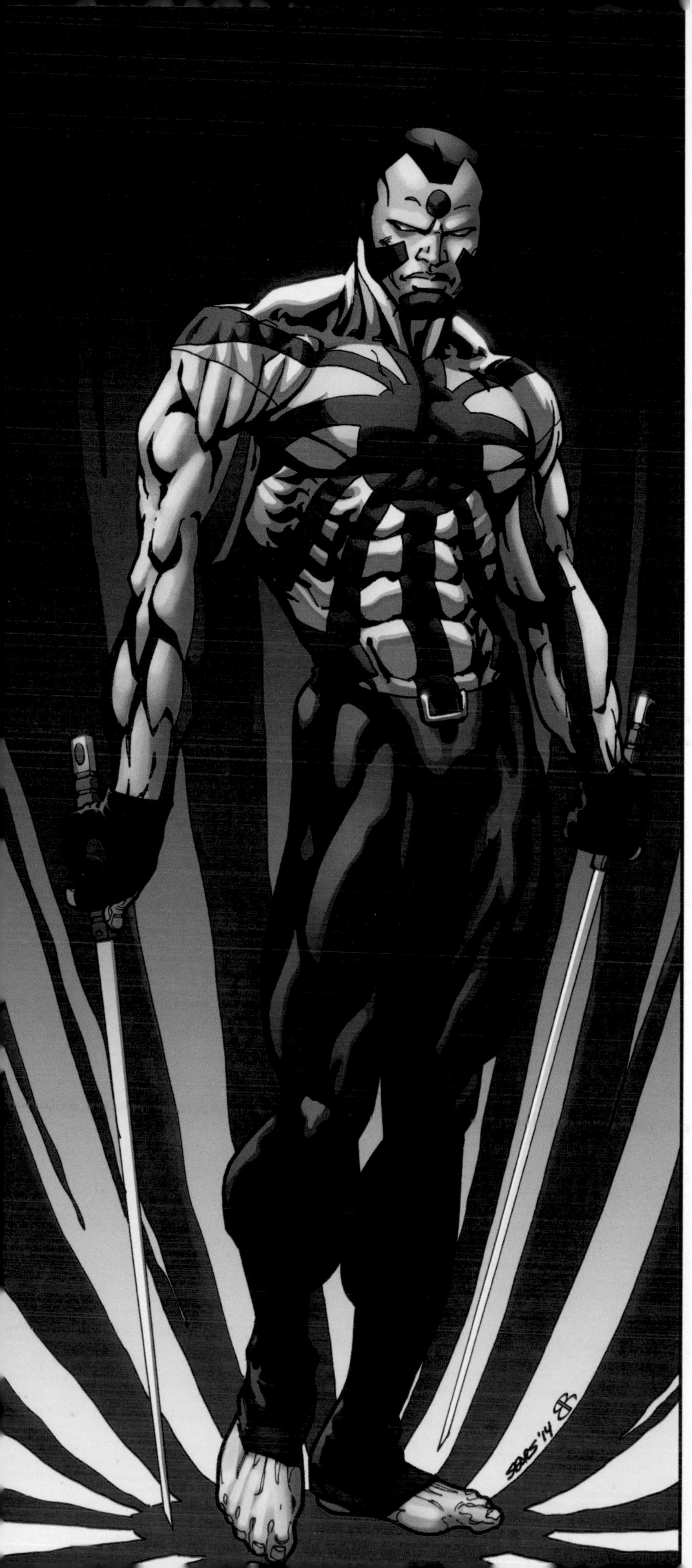
SEARS '14

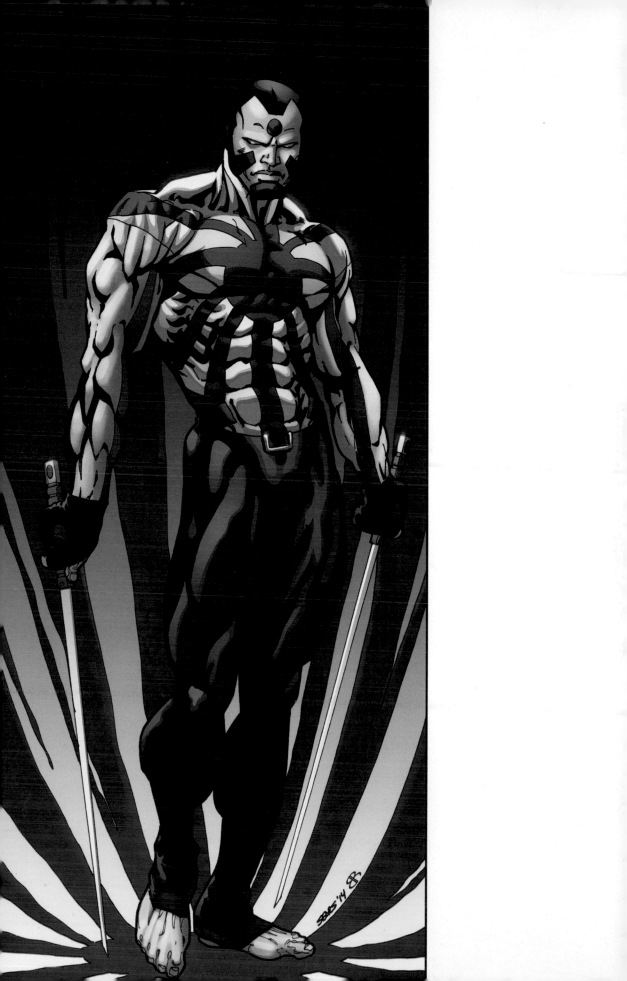

RAI #3 VARIANT
Cover by CAFU

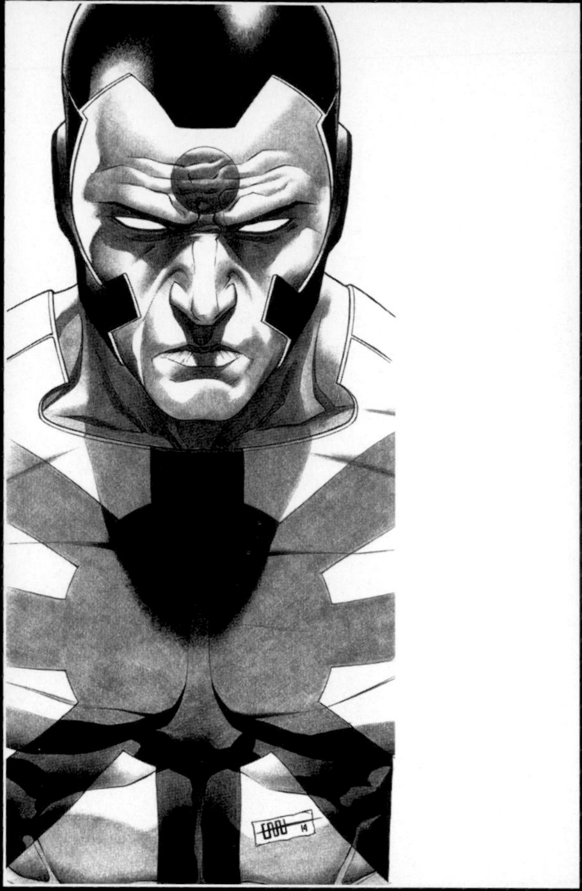

RAI #1 HASTINGS RETAILER VARIANT
Cover by SINA GRACE
with JOHN RAUCH

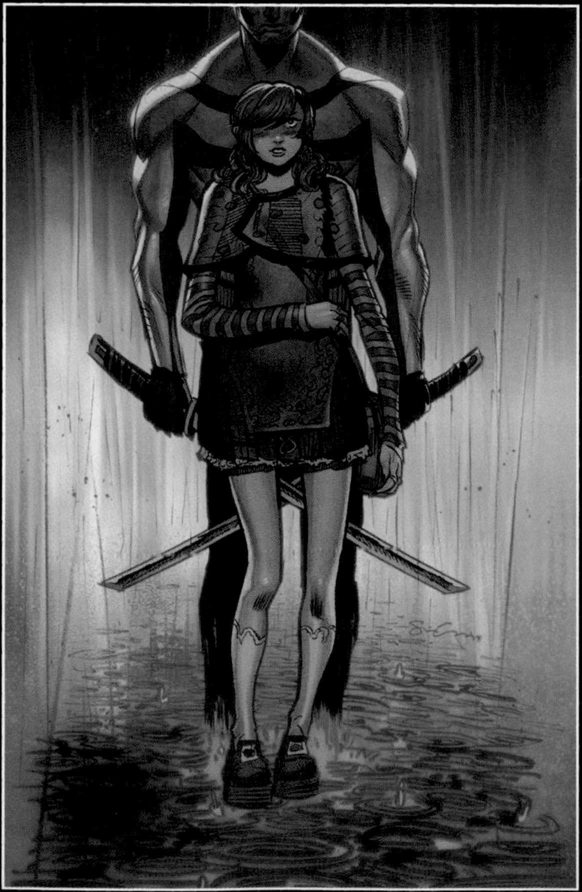

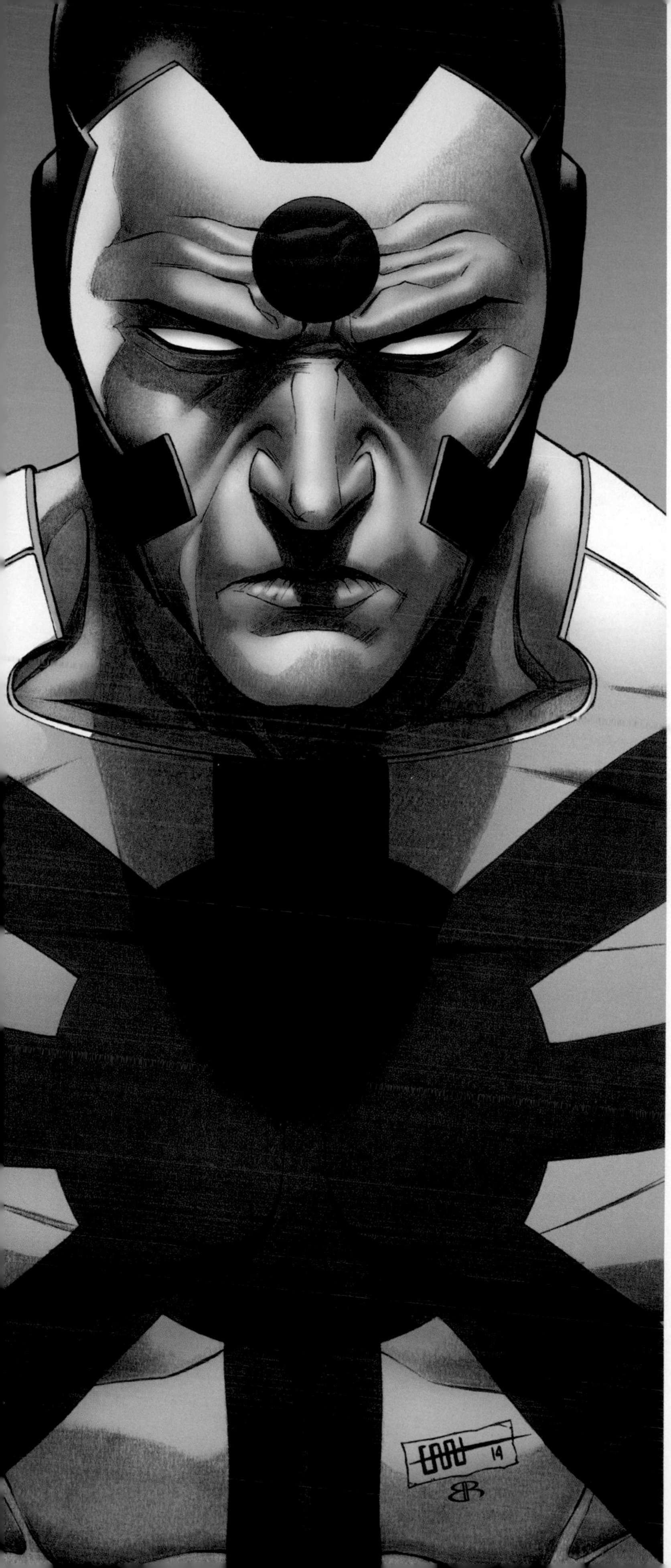

RAI #3 VARIANT
Cover by CAFU with BRIAN REBER

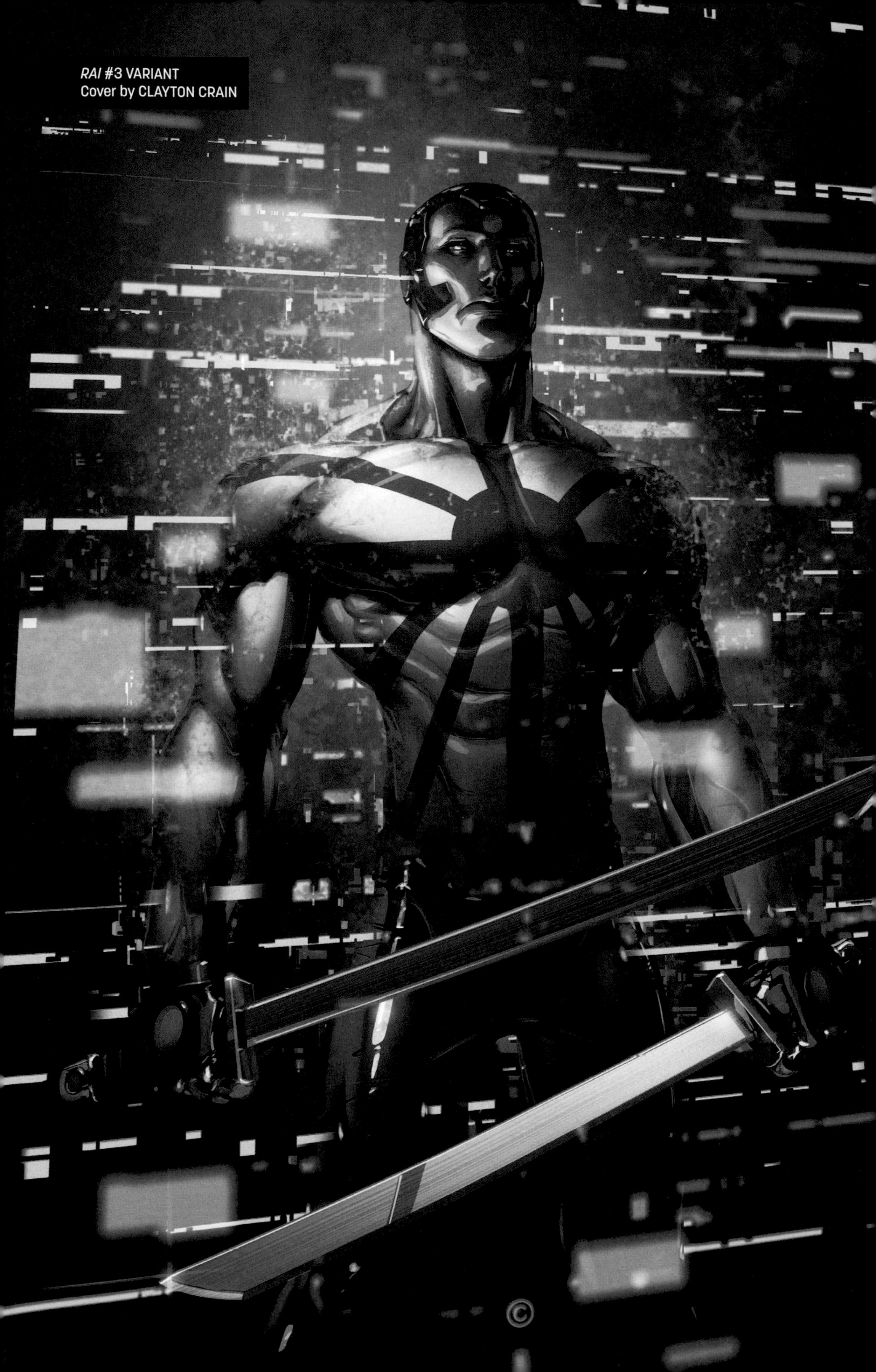

RAI #3 VARIANT
Cover by CLAYTON CRAIN

RAI SKETCHBOOK PAGES

Art, text, and annotations by MATT KINDT

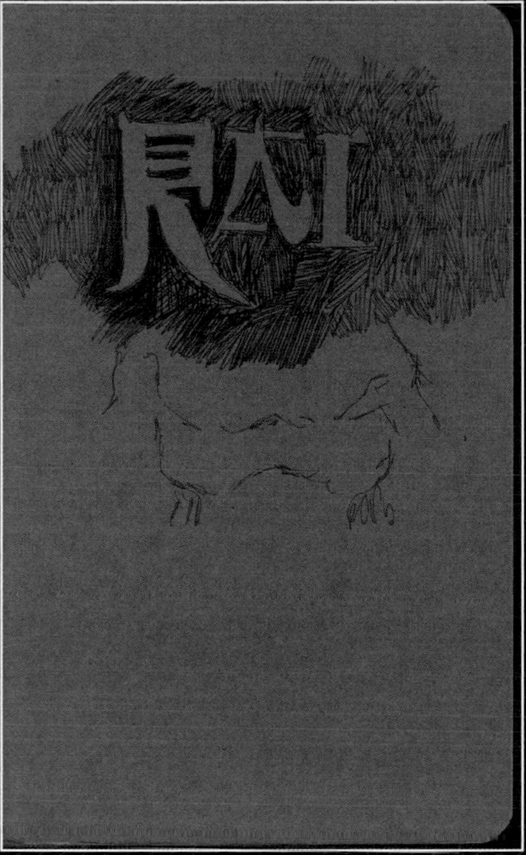
RAI

Cover of the small Moleskine sketchbooks I carry around. A lot of daydreaming happens when developing a new series... the amount of hatching and lines and doodles on a page is usually indicative of how much random daydreaming goes on.

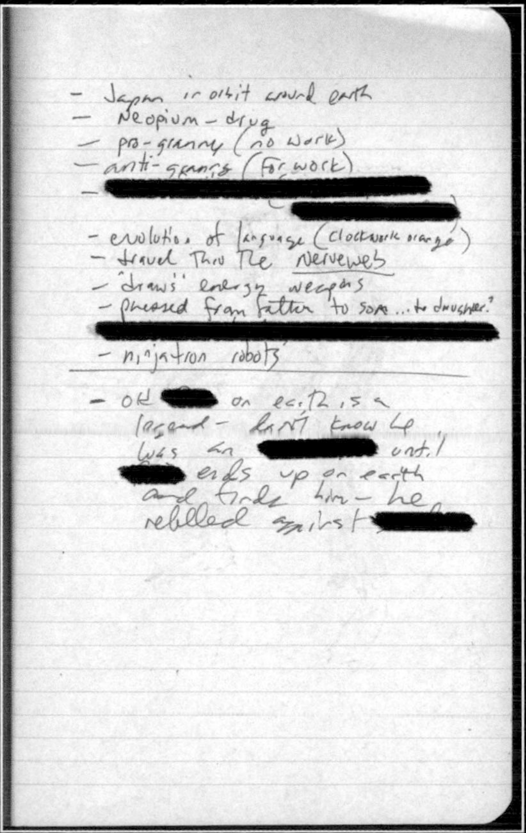
- Japan in orbit around earth
- Neopium - drug
- pro-granny (no work)
- anti-granny (for work)
- [redacted]
- evolution of language (clockwork orange)
- travel thru the Nerveweb
- "draws" energy weapons
- passed from father to son... to daughter?
[redacted]
- ninjatron robots
- old [redacted] on earth is a legend - don't know he was an [redacted] until [redacted] ends up on earth and finds him - he rebelled against [redacted]

I reread every issue of the original RAI series before starting on my own pitch for the series. I would literally have this notebook by me while I read each issue and jot notes and ideas that struck me as interesting. The original RAI series was filthy-rich with great ideas waiting to be mined and retooled and used or have a twist put on them. Reading the series also got my mind going - giving me a lot of new ideas and concepts that I'd eventually be able to fold into the narrative (hence some of the redactions). Note the reference to "Granny" - from the original series - which would eventually change to "Father."

Early stabs at the look of Rai drawn during one of the writer retreats. I don't think I even showed these to anyone. It just helps sometimes to have a mental picture of the character before and during the writing.

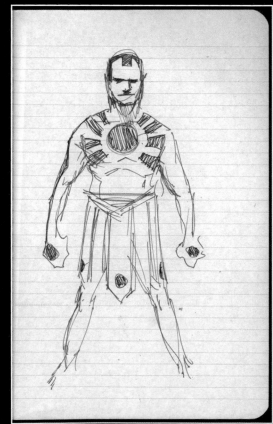

SUN
JAPAN
JAPAN "EXHAUST"
EARTH

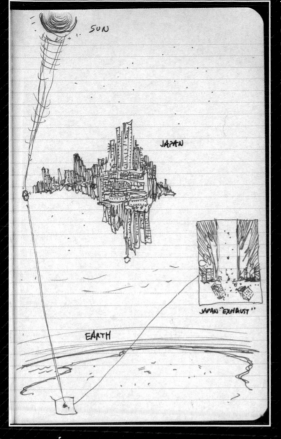

The original idea for how Japan would both be dependent on the sun and Earth and interact with it to catastrophic effect (as shown at the end of issue 4). The idea for the exterior look of Japan was inspired by the original series which literally looked like a dragon. I thought that might be a little too on-the-nose but thought something more subtle, that had the footprint of Earth-bound Japan but had grown up and out to form a sort of dragon-headed shape unintentionally (and subtly) would be a fun update (as seen in the Plus Edition of issue 1). Japan of 4001 is based on old European cities that don't destroy their history but build on and around it - so at the bottom of Japan we'll have a lot of original old architecture and over the course of generations new cultures build new things on top of the old.

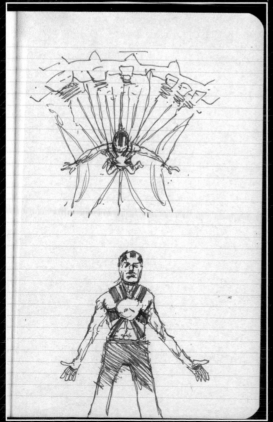

Initial concepts for Rai's look and how he would be created and communicate with "Father." At this point I wasn't sure how Rai would connect with Father or how he would be born. My first thought was that there would be lots of wires but that ended up seeming very outdated for the year 4001. The idea for a sort of mythological Leda/Swan creation came later on in the process after making the decision to switch the "mother" Japan from the original series to a father figure.

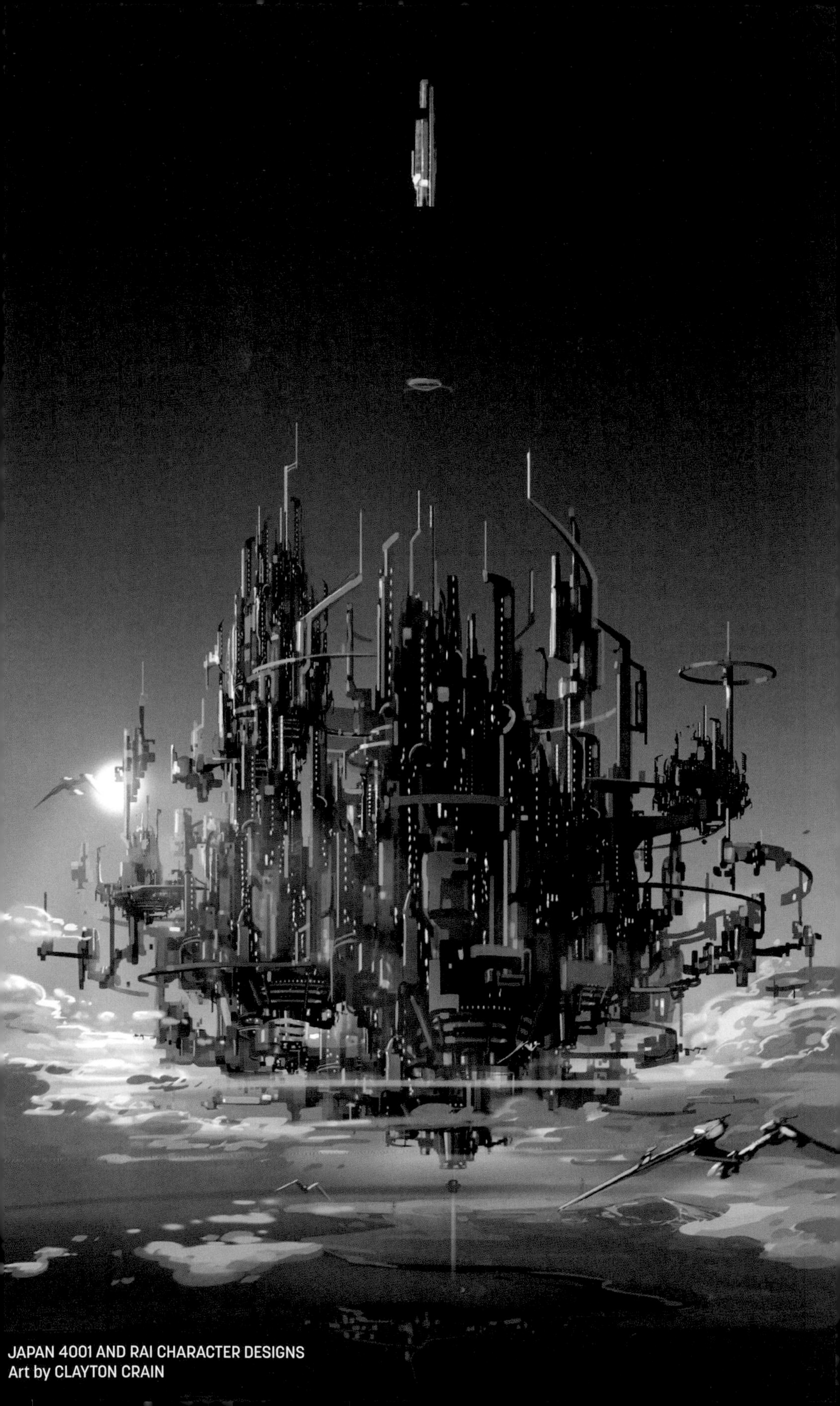

JAPAN 4001 AND RAI CHARACTER DESIGNS
Art by CLAYTON CRAIN

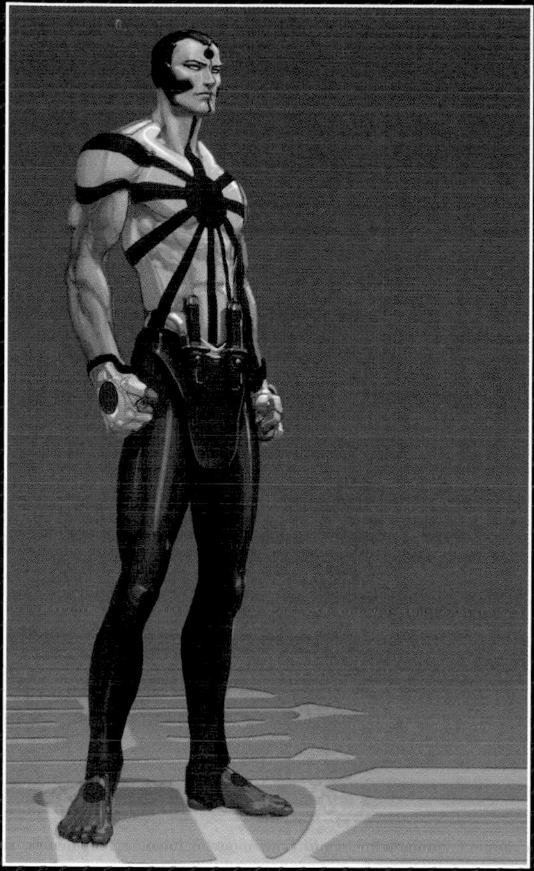
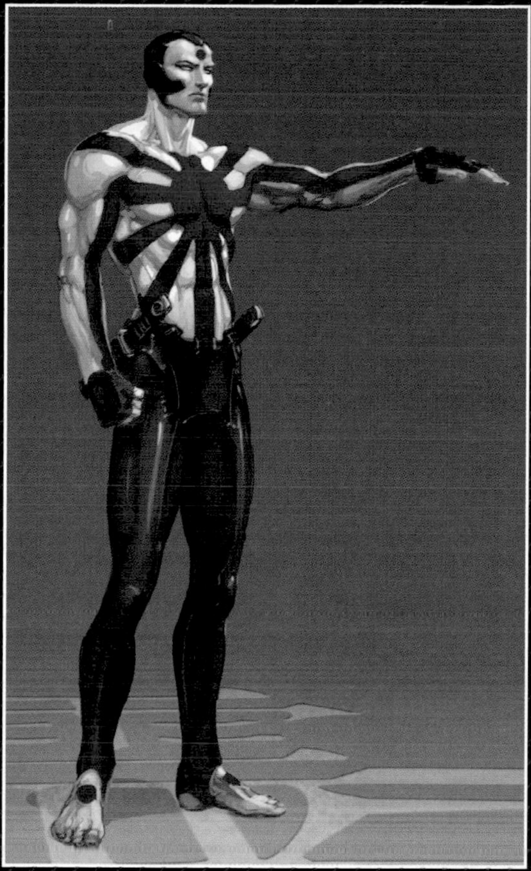
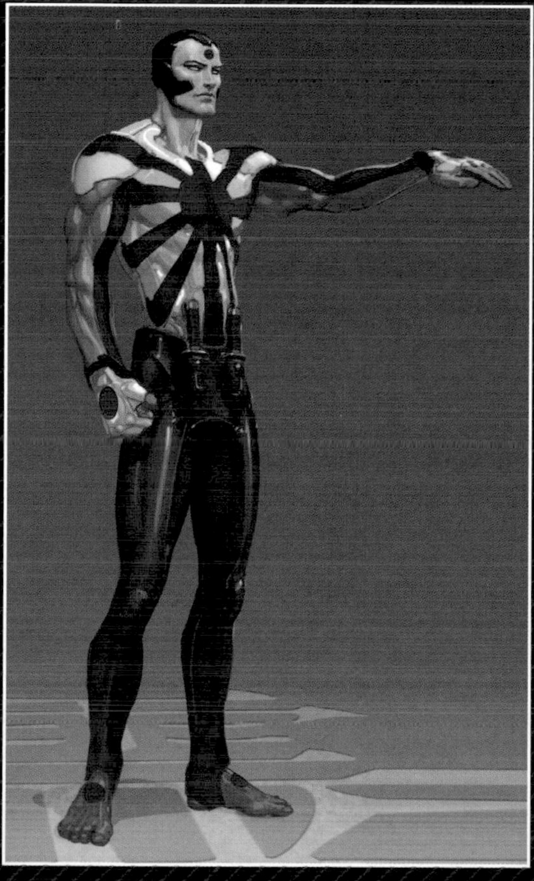

EXPLORE THE VALIANT UNIVERSE

THE MICHELANGELO CODE
ARCHER & ARMSTRONG
VALIANT

SETTING THE WORLD ON FIRE
BLOODSHOT
VALIANT

OMEGA RISING
HARBINGER
VALIANT

BY THE SWORD
X-O MANOWAR
VALIANT

THE WORLD'S WORST SUPERHERO TEAM
QUANTUM AND WOODY!
VALIANT
KLANG.

ARCHER & ARMSTRONG

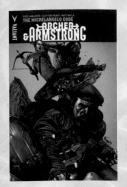

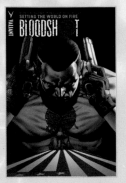

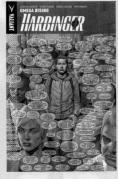

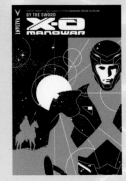

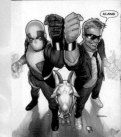

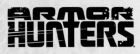

Volume 1: The Michelangelo Code
ISBN: 9780979640988

Volume 2: Wrath of the Eternal Warrior
ISBN: 9781939346049

Volume 3: Far Faraway
ISBN: 9781939346148

Volume 4: Sect Civil War
ISBN: 9781939346254

Volume 5: Mission: Improbable
ISBN: 9781939346353

Volume 6: American Wasteland
ISBN: 9781939346421

ARMOR HUNTERS

Armor Hunters
ISBN: 9781939346452

Armor Hunters: Bloodshot
ISBN: 9781939346469

Armor Hunters: Harbinger
ISBN: 9781939346506

Unity Vol. 3: Armor Hunters
ISBN: 9781939346445

X-O Manowar Vol. 7: Armor Hunters
ISBN: 9781939346476

BLOODSHOT

Volume 1: Setting the World on Fire
ISBN: 9780979640964

Volume 2: The Rise and the Fall
ISBN: 9781939346032

Volume 3: Harbinger Wars
ISBN: 9781939346124

Volume 4: H.A.R.D. Corps
ISBN: 9781939346193

Volume 5: Get Some!
ISBN: 9781939346315

Volume 6: The Glitch and Other Tales
ISBN: 9781939346711

THE DEATH-DEFYING DOCTOR MIRAGE

The Death-Defying Dr. Mirage
ISBN: 9781939346490

THE DELINQUENTS

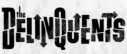

The Delinquents
ISBN: 9781939346513

ETERNAL WARRIOR

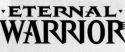

Volume 1: Sword of the Wild
ISBN: 9781939346209

Volume 2: Eternal Emperor
ISBN: 9781939346292

Eternal Warrior: Days of Steel
ISBN: 9781939346742
COMING SOON

HARBINGER

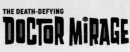

Volume 1: Omega Rising
ISBN: 9780979640957

Volume 2: Renegades
ISBN: 9781939346025

Volume 3: Harbinger Wars
ISBN: 9781939346117

Volume 4: Perfect Day
ISBN: 9781939346155

Volume 5: Death of a Renegade
ISBN: 9781939346339

Volume 6: Omegas
ISBN: 9781939346384

HARBINGER WARS

Harbinger Wars
ISBN: 9781939346094

Bloodshot Vol. 3: Harbinger Wars
ISBN: 9781939346124

Harbinger Vol. 3: Harbinger Wars
ISBN: 9781939346117

QUANTUM AND WOODY!

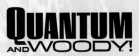

Volume 1: The World's Worst Superhero Team
ISBN: 9781939346186

Volume 2: In Security
ISBN: 9781939346230

Volume 3: Crooked Pasts, Present Tense
ISBN: 9781939346391

Volume 4: Quantum and Woody Must Die!
ISBN: 9781939346629
COMING SOON

EXPLORE THE VALIANT UNIVERSE

VALIANT
KICK ME
QUANTUM AND WOODY
BY PRIEST & BRIGHT
VOL 1: KLANG

VALIANT
BATTLE FOR NEW JAPAN
RAI

VALIANT
THE VALIANT

VALIANT
THE DEATH-DEFYING
DOCTOR MIRAGE

VALIANT
VALIANT ZEROES AND ORIGINS

QUANTUM AND WOODY BY PRIEST & BRIGHT

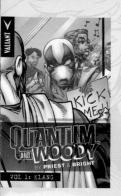

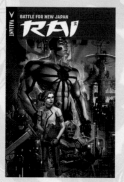

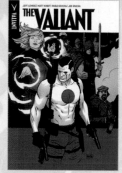

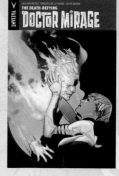

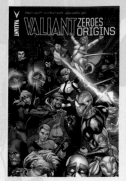

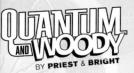

Volume 1: Klang
ISBN: 9781939346780
COMING SOON

RAI

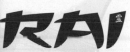

Volume 1: Welcome to New Japan
ISBN: 9781939346414

Volume 2: Battle for New Japan
ISBN: 9781939346612

SHADOWMAN

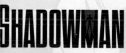

Volume 1: Birth Rites
ISBN: 9781939346001

Volume 2: Darque Reckoning
ISBN: 9781939346056

Volume 3: Deadside Blues
ISBN: 9781939346162

Volume 4: Fear, Blood, And Shadows
ISBN: 9781939346278

Volume 5: End Times
ISBN: 9781939346377

Ivar, Timewalker

Volume 1: Making History
ISBN: 9781939346636
COMING SOON

UNITY

Volume 1: To Kill a King
ISBN: 9781939346261

Volume 2: Trapped by Webnet
ISBN: 9781939346346

Volume 3: Armor Hunters
ISBN: 9781939346445

Volume 4: The United
ISBN: 9781939346544

Volume 5: Homefront
ISBN: 9781939346797

THE VALIANT

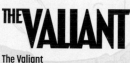

The Valiant
ISBN: 9781939346605

VALIANT ZEROES AND ORIGINS

Valiant: Zeroes and Origins
ISBN: 9781939346582
COMING SOON

X-O MANOWAR

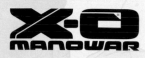

Volume 1: By the Sword
ISBN: 9780979640940

Volume 2: Enter Ninjak
ISBN: 9780979640995

Volume 3: Planet Death
ISBN: 9781939346087

Volume 4: Homecoming
ISBN: 9781939346179

Volume 5: At War With Unity
ISBN: 9781939346247

Volume 6: Prelude to Armor Hunters
ISBN: 9781939346407

Volume 7: Armor Hunters
ISBN: 9781939346476

Volume 8: Enter: Armorines
ISBN: 9781939346551

Volume 9: Dead Hand
ISBN: 9781939346650
COMING SOON

EXPLORE THE VALIANT UNIVERSE

VALIANT
HARBINGER
DELUXE EDITION 2

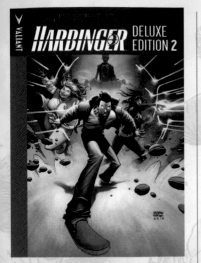

OMNIBUSES

Quantum and Woody: The Complete Classic Omnibus
ISBN: 9781939346360
Collecting QUANTUM AND WOODY (1997) #0, 1-21 and #32, THE GOAT: H.A.E.D.U.S. #1, and X-O MANOWAR (1996) #16

X-O Manowar Classic Omnibus Vol. 1
ISBN: 9781939346308
Collecting X-O MANOWAR (1992) #0-30, ARMORINES #0, X-O DATABASE #1, as well as material from SECRETS OF THE VALIANT UNIVERSE #1

DELUXE EDITIONS

Archer & Armstrong Deluxe Edition Book 1
ISBN: 9781939346223
Collecting ARCHER & ARMSTRONG #0-13

VALIANT
ARMOR HUNTERS
DELUXE EDITION

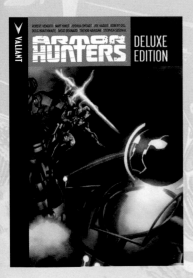

Armor Hunters Deluxe Edition
ISBN: 9781939346728
Collecting ARMOR HUNTERS #1-4, ARMOR HUNTERS: AFTERMATH #1, ARMOR HUNTERS: BLOODSHOT #1-3, ARMOR HUNTERS: HARBINGER #1-3, UNITY #8-11 and X-O MANOWAR #23-29

Bloodshot Deluxe Edition Book 1
ISBN: 9781939346216
Collecting BLOODSHOT #1-13

Harbinger Deluxe Edition Book 1
ISBN: 9781939346131
Collecting HARBINGER #0-14

Harbinger Deluxe Edition Book 2
ISBN: 9781939346773
Collecting HARBINGER #15-25, HARBINGER: OMEGAS #1-3, and HARBINGER: BLEEDING MONK #0

Harbinger Wars Deluxe Edition
ISBN: 9781939346322
Collecting HARBINGER WARS #1-4, HARBINGER #11-14, and BLOODSHOT #10-13

Quantum and Woody Deluxe Edition Book 1
ISBN: 9781939346681
Collecting QUANTUM AND WOODY #1-12 and QUANTUM AND WOODY: THE GOAT #0

Q2: The Return of Quantum and Woody Deluxe Edition
ISBN: 9781939346568
Collecting Q2: THE RETURN OF QUANTUM AND WOODY #1-5

JAMES ASMUS | TOM FOWLER | MING DOYLE
KANO | JORDIE BELLAIRE | DAVE LANPHEAR
VALIANT
QUANTUM AND WOODY!
DELUXE EDITION 1
MEH!

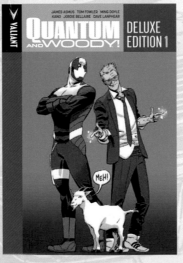

Shadowman Deluxe Edition Book 1
ISBN: 9781939346438
Collecting SHADOWMAN #0-10

X-O Manowar Deluxe Edition Book 1
ISBN: 9781939346100
Collecting X-O MANOWAR #1-14

X-O Manowar Deluxe Edition Book 2
ISBN: 9781939346520
Collecting X-O MANOWAR #15-22, and UNITY #1-4

JIM SHOOTER | DAVID LAPHAM
CHILDREN OF THE EIGHTH DAY
HARBINGER
VALIANT
VALIANT MASTERS

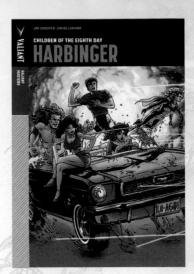

VALIANT MASTERS

Bloodshot Vol. 1 - Blood of the Machine
ISBN: 9780979640933

H.A.R.D. Corps Vol. 1 - Search and Destroy
ISBN: 9781939346285

Harbinger Vol. 1 - Children of the Eighth Day
ISBN: 9781939346483

Ninjak Vol. 1 - Black Water
ISBN: 9780979640971

Rai Vol. 1 - From Honor to Strength
ISBN: 9781939346070

Shadowman Vol. 1 - Spirits Within
ISBN: 9781939346018

KEVIN VANHOOK | DON PERLIN
BLOOD OF THE MACHINE
BLOODSHOT
VALIANT
VALIANT MASTERS

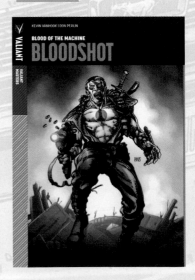

RAI READING ORDER

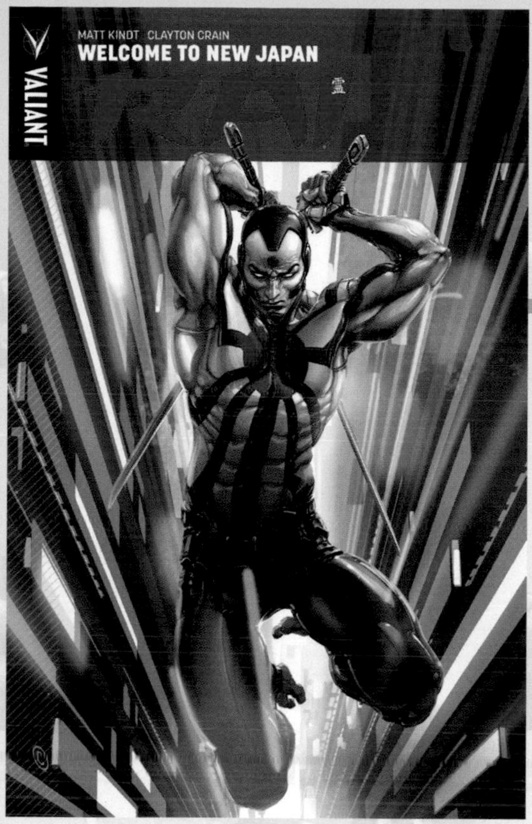
MATT KINDT CLAYTON CRAIN
WELCOME TO NEW JAPAN
VALIANT

Rai Vol. 1: Welcome to New Japan

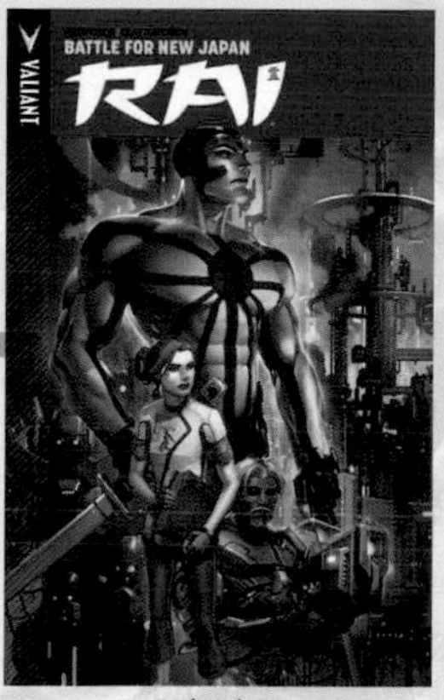
BATTLE FOR NEW JAPAN
RAI
VALIANT

Rai Vol. 2:
Battle for New Japan

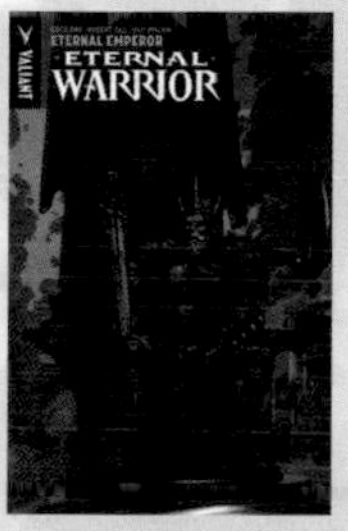
ETERNAL EMPEROR
ETERNAL WARRIOR
VALIANT

Eternal Warrior Vol. 2:
Eternal Emperor
(OPTIONAL)

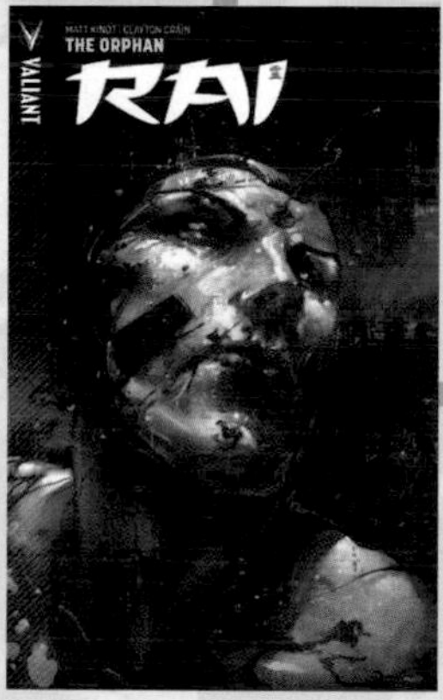
MATT KINDT CLAYTON CRAIN
THE ORPHAN
RAI
VALIANT

Rai Vol. 3: The Orphan

"Nothing less than striking... A brilliant comic." - Wired

"★★★★★... A beautifully visualized, engaging artifact of future noir..." - PopMatters

"★★★★★... Kindt and Crain, easily, are one of the best teams in comics right now." - All-Comic

Experience Japan in the 41st century in this daring new vision of the future!

From New York Times
best-selling writer
MATT KINDT
(*Mind MGMT*, THE VALIANT)

And
superstar artist
CLAYTON CRAIN
(*X-Force*, *Carnage*)

VALIANT

RAI 霊

VOLUME TWO: **BATTLE FOR NEW JAPAN**

THE CRITICALLY ACCLAIMED SERIES CONTINUES AS NEW YORK TIMES BEST-SELLING WRITER MATT KINDT AND SUPERSTAR ARTIST CLAYTON CRAIN RETURN FOR THE SECOND STAGGERING VOLUME OF RAI!

In the aftermath of the devastating battle for 41st-century Japan, Rai must pick up the pieces as he grapples with the startling truth about Father and his purpose. Will Rai remain a champion of the people or will he succumb to the same fate as the men who carried the mantle before him? And why is everyone looking at him so strangely?

Go back to the future with all-star creators Matt Kindt (UNITY, *Mind MGMT*) and Clayton Crain (*X-Force*, *Carnage*) as they crack open a brand-new chapter for Valiant's smash-hit ongoing series! Collecting RAI #5-8.

VALIANT
BATTLE FOR NEW JAPAN
RAI 霊

TRADE PAPERBACK
978-1-939346-61-2

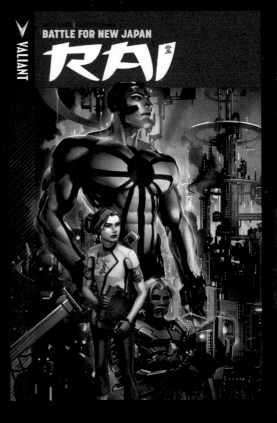